OMIES		
Developing, mainly in Asia, Africa, and Latin America	Consume... White collar workers Management Commercial farmers Factory workers Technologists Stockowners	Commercial farmers Factory workers Manual laborers Landowners Management and stockowners (often foreign)
Revolution in North America		Workers Farmers Capitalist entrepreneurs Inventors
resulting revolution		Merchant capitalists Early industrial craftsmen Peasants Kings Plantation owners Slaves
in Europe		Guildsmen Craftsmen Peasants Church
		Peasants Craftsmen Tradesmen Slaves
minor		Nomadic herdsmen Priesthood
		Peasants Craftsmen Tradesmen Priesthood Slaves

4-5-72

The Evolution
of Economic Society

The Evolution
of Economic Society

AN INTRODUCTION TO ECONOMICS

Martin Gerhard Giesbrecht

Wilmington College, Ohio

W. H. Freeman and Company
San Francisco

Printed in the United States of America

Library of Congress Catalog Card Number: 70-164459

International Standard Book Number: 0-7167-0899-x

1 2 3 4 5 6 7 8 9

To my wife, Pat

Contents

Figures

Tables

Preface

Life on earth, from its very beginnings, was a struggle to exist
and to find nourishment. For many species, it was a struggle
that eventually failed, and there must have been many times in
the long history of humanity when only a hairline's breadth
separated survival from extinction. We may be in such a time
right now. But, over the centuries, mankind has learned to use
the earth and its diverse resources with increasing confidence
and sophistication, and the race has thrived.

This is also the history of economics. The growth of economics
is the story of the organic development of institutions, through
which humanity has carried on its life struggle, and, in recent
centuries, economics has developed into a science that has been
used to understand these institutions better and to sharpen the
effectiveness of human behavior. But by no means is the story of
economics an unqualified success. Although the race is thriving
and growing as never before, inadequate food, shelter, and
clothing are still the main problems of the majority of the
world's population. And for those fortunate enough to live in

affluent economies, industrialization itself creates many problems.

Like so many disciplines, economics can lay claim to being one of the oldest sciences. Yet, in an important sense, the story of economics is just now really beginning. For the first time humanity can see the glimmer of a new day on the economic horizon. The promise of a victorious end to the too often bitter struggle for survival and sustenance is entering the realm of possibility. Ironically, some other sciences, in their own headlong drive for sophistication, have opened a Pandora's box of lethal instruments that can sunder all of mankind's hopes in a crashing catastrophe, and the burgeoning economy itself threatens to destroy the usefulness of our environment. But the way out of this frightening bind is through more intellectual effort and more scientific progress, not less. Certainly, for economists, the most magnificent day of our science may be dawning, if only the world will remain clean enough and at peace long enough to let the dawn break.

All these considerations make up the scope of this book. It is my personal statement about my enthusiasm for economics, and, as such, I hope that it proves contagious. I hope the reader will be infected with a feeling for the brilliance of economic science's intellectual discipline, the broad reach of its relevance to humanity, and its philosophic profundity. Should circumstances or personal preferences prevent the reader from ever touching another book or article on economics, I hope he will have at least gained some understanding of the depth and breadth of this science. But I would be most deeply gratified if this little book tempts the reader into regarding it as the beginning of his study of economics.

Since the book deals both with what actually has gone on economically and with what economists said about what went on, its organization is roughly chronological, to show better how the science and the economies themselves developed. For this reason, it is best to read Chapters 1 through 10 from start to finish, consecutively, rather than to jump around from chapter to chapter. The eleventh chapter, On Further Study, is the exception to this rule. A glance ahead at this chapter will provide a bibliography and study guide that the student may find useful right from the start. If the reader should want to review a particular subject or issue that spans several ages, the index will direct him to the places in the text that deal with it.

I have been blessed with having studied with several truly excellent economics teachers, some of whom were and are nationally recognized economists, others who remain largely unsung except by their pupils, and one who wasn't even an economist. To them go my first indebtedness and my fervent wish that I can do as well as they. I must also acknowledge indebtedness to my many economics students, against whom I've been bouncing off the ideas in this book for many years and who have experienced its long labor of birth. Especially, I must acknowledge my indebtedness to the literate and intelligent noneconomists, my friends, my faculty colleagues, and my wife, who have been the source of an invaluable and not always comfortable feedback while it was being written.

There are, of course, errors in this book. Some have been errors from the day they appeared in the manuscript; they are entirely my own doing. Others will seem to become errors as our knowledge of economics and economies improves with time. I hope this book will have had a hand in that process.

MARTIN GERHARD GIESBRECHT

December 1971

*The Evolution
of Economic Society*

CHAPTER 1

The Beginning
of Economic Life

THE UNIVERSE AND ECONOMICS

There is a theory that when the earth was very young, much less oxygen existed in the air than there is today, perhaps only one-thousandth as much. This wasn't enough for breathing. It wasn't even enough to shield the surface of the earth from the killing blasts of ultraviolet rays coming from the sun. No life, plant or animal, could exist. The world was a shallow sea, a sterile desert-swamp, with no mountain ranges, no oceans, and no weather changes. For several billion years of earth's history, it may have remained that way, constant and void.

But three billion years ago or more, in some quiet waters at a depth of about forty feet—and thus protected from the ultraviolet rays—the first molecular stirrings of life began. The earth would never be the same again! Quickly, in paleontological terms, at least, primitive one-celled plant life covered much of the entire globe with a giant green scum. As it did so, larger amounts of free oxygen, created by the process of photosynthesis, began to appear. The additional oxygen further encouraged life; first, by shielding the earth's surface more effectively from ultraviolet rays and, then, simply by its abundance, the increased oxygen made the respiration of multicellular animal life possible. Soon there was enough oxygen for plants and animals to emerge from the sea and grow on land. Vast forests of ferns came to cover much of the earth, and dinosaurs wallowed, half walking, half swimming, through the endless, leafy marshes.

Vegetation was so rampant that the oxygen level may even have come to exceed that of today. But at the same time that oxygen was created by photosynthesis, carbon dioxide was consumed and locked into the living tissues of the plants themselves. As the large plants died, they fell into the shallow sea-marsh and were covered by water and silt, where they could not ferment and return the carbon dioxide to the atmosphere. Carbon dioxide is an insulator and provides a greenhouse effect that contains the earth's heat. As increasing amounts of it were lost from the atmosphere, the earth began to cool down, and the Ice Ages set in. Many species of plants and animals perished. Mountains, wrinkles of the shriveling earth, appeared. Deep oceans formed, which drained the shallow seas dry. Air currents, which had been able to waft about unhindered, were now stopped up by mountain ranges and propelled forward by the newly created differences between dry land, oceans, and glaciers. Violent storms, with their rain causing erosion and their lightning causing fires, did their work to change the face of the earth. New, hardier, smaller, and more adaptable species of plants and animals made their appearance in this hostile environment. Man was among them.

All this is paleontology and not economics. Why begin an economics book with a theory from another science? The reason is that it enables us to discover some general characteristics about economics at the very start. By analogy, we can see that paleontology has a strong resemblance to economics in several ways. First, paleontology deals with the relationships among a number of diverse factors—ultraviolet rays, oxygen, carbon dioxide, the shape of the earth's surface, the climate, and the evolving plant and animal life. Second, it postulates, implicitly and explicitly, the limits beyond which these relationships and any theories about them do *not* apply, that is, only common "earthly" life, not other-galactic or supernatural life, can be considered. Third, it borrows from other sciences, chemistry, botany, zoology, meteorology, and geology, to define the nature of the possible relationships among the rays, the gasses, the earth, climate, and life forms. And, most important of all, it implies a dynamic force, some kind of life process that takes advantage of opportunity, that rushes in to fill available space, and that explains how the changes actually come about when it is possible for them to do so. In short, paleontology concerns itself with relationships, subject to the restraints of a limited universe, the wisdom from other disciplines, and an immutable life process.

In the same way, economics deals with the relationships among people, between people and their organizations, and between people and their material environment. It also is subject to the restraints imposed by the social, physical, and technical possibilities that exist and is limited to mankind's concerns with material sustenance—earning a living. It also borrows from the other arts and sciences, which are part of our cultural philosophy. And, finally, economics also is driven by a life process: the need for sustenance.

In primitive economies, for example, one relationship among the people is bartering or some other form of crude trade, and a relationship between people and their environment is hunting. In advanced economies, the full force of our entire twentieth century technology in factories and farms spells out the various possibilities for relationships with our material environment. Sophisticated markets, with all the associated commercial and financial complexities, define some of the economic relationships of the people with each other. Whether dealing with primitive or advanced economies, the economist must limit himself to the concerns of human material sustenance, which is often difficult to do because so many other aspects of mankind's entire culture are involved in the effort to earn a living. How much recognition should an economist give to these? Should he also be a sociologist, a political scientist, an engineer? Or does he lose in depth what he gains in breadth when he ventures farther afield than the customary limits of economics? We cannot answer these questions, but it should be understood that economics is a very broad subject and that any particular limit is, of course, arbitrary.

There are two further observations about paleontological theory that may also be applied to economic science. One is that paleontological theory changes with time, as we gain greater experience and sophistication; in fact, what I have described here may be revised by the time you read this. The same can be said of all the theories in economics. A pessimist would say that sooner or later all present economic theories will be proven irrelevant. An optimist would prefer to say that they will be superseded by more accurate theories. But this isn't a problem faced by economics and paleontology alone. All the sciences, indeed, all knowledge—whether it results from reason or is an article of faith—is tenuous and must be tested and retested. It exists only as long as it can prevail against any challenge.

The other observation concerns the dynamic force. From the moment life started in the warm, shallow sea several billion years ago, it extended itself over the world; it prospered and grew. The fossil record is evidence to the paleontologist that the force exists. But he doesn't know why it exists now nor why it existed then. The best he can do is accept it on faith. Likewise, the economist assumes that the basic economic function of people is to earn a living, to obtain material sustenance for themselves. Most people have always wanted adequate and even plentiful material wealth, and they have always wanted to obtain it as efficiently and as painlessly as possible—at least, that is what the evidence demonstrates to the economist. But why? Why does this driving force exist? *That* the economist can't answer. Economics, like paleontology, is essentially one of the life sciences, and its ultimate dynamic force, the source of its libido, its élan vital, is the sweet mystery of life itself.

THE FIRST HUMANS

Now let's turn back to our early humans whom we left groping for an existence during the latter part of the Ice Ages, about fifty thousand years ago, give or take several thousands of years. Although they may have begun to use some form of language and some simple tools, they "earned their living" for the most part like wild animals. They foraged and hunted in the forests and grasslands and left almost no tracks or other evidence of ever having wandered about on the face of the earth. If it weren't for the fossil remains of their bones, we would, in fact, have little inkling of them. Most of their tools must have been unmodified rocks and sticks; their shelters were probably temporary lean-tos made of perishable wood, leaves, bones, and hides; and of their clothes, we barely have any trace.

But the dynamic force of economics was already at work. Slowly, over centuries, accidentally or not, it must have become evident to these early humans that such primitive means of obtaining material sustenance were not the best of all possible alternatives. A little time and effort invested in changing a crude rock into a hand ax or a simple stick into a sharpened spear would pay off many times over in increased efficiency. A little forethought and preparation in building a trap would mean a bigger dinner in the end. And at this moment, economic man was born. This economic man made plans and preparations and invested time and effort to obtain the material needs of his life in the most efficient, most productive, and least costly way known to him. Evidence of his existence became not merely fossil bones but also the remains of his tools and his camps. A well-sharpened spear point lodged in the vertebra of a mammoth fossil tells a dramatic story of a rather sophisticated hunter, enjoying quite a large kill, followed by what must have been a gigantic feast.

Other important developments were also taking place at this time—let's say about forty thousand years ago. Language was improving; sewn clothes and ornaments were being worn; fire was used for cooking; and art and religion were practiced. Like the economic developments, these social and cultural developments proceeded very slowly, slow enough, in fact, that no differences could have existed among any sector of the human race. Archeological evidence indicates that culturally and racially, humans were homogeneous. People looked the same and lived pretty much the same, whether they were in what is today England, South Africa, or India.

For a few groups, this stage of development became permanent. These "high-hunting societies" hunted and foraged, moved with the seasons if necessary, and never changed their way of life. Aborigines found in the modern world may be the last survivors of these people. For most groups of humans, however, change had a snowballing effect. Success only whet the appetite, and the desire for a still better and more dependable standard of living grew. Hunters became farmers. Redesigning their tomahawks into stoneheaded hoes, they dug in the light and fertile, wind-blown loess soil that was left by the receding glaciers and planted grain. As the soil in one plot wore out in a few seasons, they would move on to a new one, and thus they pushed northward in the warming post-glacial age, spreading humanity wider than ever over the globe. Change came more and more rapidly as the different groups adjusted to their various and new environments. In the process, the cultural and racial homogeneity of the human species was lost forever.

Not only did humans change, but they changed nature too. Until this time, man's economic drive to better himself materially had always been in terms of better adjusting himself to his natural surrounding. But the advent of farming turned the process around. Man adjusted nature to suit his needs. He created a supply of food that nature itself could not have offered. And because agriculture also drives out the wild flora and fauna that had been the natural food supply, man became quite dependent on his artificial food supply. This alone is an economic turning point. But even more important, through farming, man was making the first changes in his environment. For example, simply by harvesting successfully only those ripened grains that had not fallen from their stalks and using a portion of the harvest for the next year's seed, he was selectively breeding strains of plants that had the characteristic of not dropping their ripened grains. This works out very nicely for the farmer, but it is a suicidal characteristic for a species of grain trying to survive in the natural state. This first intervention in the order of things was the beginning of man's headlong rush through the ages to subordinate nature to his own designs in the quest for economic enrichment, and it was not the last time that unknowingly or unheedingly the delicate natural balance of a living species was upset.

RIVER VALLEY CIVILIZATIONS

Some fortunate groups of farmers did not have to move on repeatedly to new ground as their old soil wore out. Those living along rivers that flooded annually had instead the new soil brought to them. The angle of flow and the seasonal volume of water carried by the Tigris and Euphrates rivers, in what was to become ancient Mesopotamia, and by the Nile River, in what was to become Egypt, were such that, at a regular season each year, the broad, flat river valleys would flood, and a layer of rich silt would be deposited. When the water receded, the new soil was left behind, along with an ample supply of ground water. The soil was so rich and the crops so dependable that, not only could the people stay in that one place year after year, generation after generation, but they could increase in number without exceeding the limits of the food supply obtainable from the land. Just before any of the river valley civilizations developed, the entire human population over the whole globe may have been six or eight million people. Around 8000 B.C., when these river civilizations had begun, the world population is estimated to have been about ten million. By the time the population had grown in the river valleys, about six thousand years later (2000 B.C.), cities were numerous, and some had populations larger than a quarter or even a third of a million. At the time of Christ, the world population was around 250,000,000.

Cities mean civilization. (Both words have the same Latin root.) Archeologists keep uncovering evidences of earlier and earlier cities, but it's safe to say that substantial urbanization was progressing by 5000 B.C. along the Tigris and Euphrates rivers and along the Nile River. And the level of economic development and cultural sophistication achieved at the height of this first age of civilization can hardly be overestimated. First of all, cities take us out of the Stone Age and into the Bronze Age. In every aspect of earning his material sustenance, civilized man showed increased efficiency. Not only had he learned how to make metals with heat and ore, he also developed advanced technologies in practically every area of human endeavor, from agriculture to zoology. The cities had paved streets laid out in rectangular blocks; the houses were often two stories high and made of stone or mud brick and typically had a courtyard in the middle. There was sewage and running water. The people wore sewn garments made of woolen cloth in Mesopotamia and of linen in Egypt. Mathematics, engineering, medicine—even surgery—the arts, and religion flourished. Much of the science and technology that we use today is either directly taken from or derived from the knowledge of that first flowering of civilization. Or it was lost in some intervening period and was rediscovered anew. But the most important cultural advance of civilization was the development of a written language.

For man, who, because he is not particularly swift or fierce or tough, must rely on his knowledge to survive and thrive in the world, writing was the most important technological breakthrough. Only by keeping records could knowledge be protected from the decay and loss it suffered when it was stored only in the minds of men. It could be safely accumulated over generations, kept in its original form in libraries of papyrus scrolls, clay tablets, or inscribed bones, and eventually in books, microfilm, and computer tapes. But writing did more than help man preserve knowledge and keep it fresh. It helped keep his relations with other people orderly, by facilitating communication over distances and, again, by keeping records. Some of the earliest clay tablets found in the archeological digs of ancient Mesopotamia are IOU's between people, purchase receipts, and bookkeeping accounts.

In order to make full use of this abundance of knowledge, the human animal has to have time in his life span to learn. He must not only have a fully developed mind, but he must be relieved sometime of the pressing duties of mating, reproducing, and providing sustenance and protection for his family. And if some are to learn, others must have the time to teach, and so time must also be provided for that. Fortunately, man's life span is equipped with two pauses that provided the original opportunities to learn and teach. Unlike any other animal, man has a few years between the time when his mind is fully developed for learning, let's say about five years of age, and the time when he begins assuming the responsibilities of maturity, traditionally at the age of puberty. During this pause, he is taught by people who have grown old and wise, according to the basic anthropological pattern. And according to this pattern, these teachers were still alive because they had successfully survived their reproductive years and were now relieved of most of life's productive and reproductive responsibilities and travails. Of course, today the normal age range for students and teachers is much broader than that provided by these two biological pauses, but that should not blur the fact that if these pauses called childhood and old age were eliminated, the basic foundation for our cultural continuity would be undermined, and the existence of civilization would be threatened.

Girded with these human attributes, civilization wrought a whole new way of life. The increased knowledge brought on increased production and improvement in the standard of living. For the first time in history, a surplus of goods above subsistence needs was regularly produced. This encouraged the development of trade centers, which eventually grew into cities. At first, these cities were entirely parasitic on the countryside, depending on the rural areas to produce all the commodities. But soon the production of commodities began in the cities too, and they grew from mere terminal points on trade routes to manufacturing centers with a population of craftsmen, workers and slaves, professional doctors and barbers, as well as shopkeepers, riverboatmen, traders, and agents of the government.

Of course, city people have to eat too. Probably many families kept a little kitchen garden, or even a pig or goat, somewhere behind the house, but they were not the self-sufficient farming families of pre-civilization. They got their food from the farmers in the countryside up and down the rivers. To accommodate the demand for food in the cities, these farmers became commercial, earning, in return, the right to many of the city's products. Civilization, then, meant a big change for all of society, for those living out of the city as well as for those living in it.

Specialization of labor naturally evokes trade. The products of the city and the country must be exchanged if either place is to maintain its standard of living, and this exchange necessitates a whole new battery of social institutions, such as markets, transportation routes, warehouses, traders, some kind of applicable code of ethics or law to govern these new relationships among men, and it necessitates money. To use credit, that is, IOU's, instead of relying only on specie money—gold, silver, and coins— seems to have been a practice of even the earliest civilizations, as evidenced by the archeological findings of the clay tablet records of the credit transactions. But specie money, then as now, was the basis of measuring value, and currency units such as talents and shekels were defined in terms of gold.

All relationships between humans must be subject to some code of morality, and economic relationships are no exception. The particular code of ethics applied in business is usually a direct outgrowth of the society's general morality. Such characteristics as honesty, accountability, a generally tactful and courteous attitude are considered the building blocks of social morality and also the best basic tenets of good business administration. But everyday business can run into snags that can only be unraveled by specific interpretations of the general morality. The Code of Hammurabi, that great body of Mesopotamian law created around 1700 B.C., among many other things, spelled out the rights and duties of employees in their relationships with employers, the legal relationships between businessmen and customers—including the responsibilities of doctors to their patients. It specified the allowable interest charges for different kinds of loans (a range of 20 to 33⅓ percent per annum) and the fines levied for various forms of misbehavior, fining the upper classes more stringently and holding them more acutely responsible for their behavior than the lower classes.

Civilization also ushered in international trade. Earliest aboriginal man could carry pieces of pottery, trading from hand to hand, all the way from France to India or Africa, but regularized international trade had to wait for the improved technology of production and transportation that came with civilization. The main reason for international trade, then as now, was that different areas and different countries specialized in different products. Just as the city and countryside traded their products with one another, so Egypt, which was mostly agricultural, traded its products with the Mesopotamian cities, which had developed manufacturing. In turn, manufacturing centers traded their products for metals and raw materials produced in areas that had developed these industries. Facilitated by good travel routes, international trade prospered. Overland routes were always difficult and costly, but the navigable parts of the rivers—the Tigris, Euphrates, and especially the Nile—and the easy access to several seas—the Mediterranean, the Red, and the Arabian through the Persian Gulf—helped establish the trading network. Cities strategically located on the network, such as Byblos and Tyre in Phoenicia, specialized in international transportation and trade.

The nations differed not only in what they produced but also in their total socioeconomic and political organization. Nations of the greater Mesopotamian area, such as Sumeria, Babylon, and Assyria, were kingdoms based usually in one major capital, which was theoretically ruled by the city's own god, but which was, in fact, ruled by the god's chief agent, the king, and administered by a priesthood. Several social classes, from peasants to professional craftsmen to priests, were defined and maintained by law, and there was no hint of democracy or popular government. Yet, the areas of life that remained open to individual free choice were large. The Mesopotamian nations did not develop an extreme sense of national grandeur; nor were they politically totalitarian, perhaps because the kingdoms themselves were relatively small, making escape a possibility, perhaps because city life itself tends to be urbane and sophisticated. Individualism and the profit motive could thrive.

In contrast, Egypt, in its prime, was a single, large, totalitarian state. Although Egypt looks ungainly on the map, the Nile River made the area uniquely suited to centralized administration. Most of the year, the wind blows upstream. The current, of course, flows downstream. Thus, travel up and down the entire nation was easy: just sail up, and then float down. The very rich agriculture made most other activities seem unworthwhile, and since shipping on the Nile was available to practically every part of the nation, centers for manufacturing or trading weren't needed and didn't develop. Furthermore, Egypt was ruled by a pharaoh, who was not considered god's agent but a god himself and who laid claim to the entire country as a personal possession and all the people therein as personal servants. This totalitarian point of view had as its redeeming quality the fact that everyone was cast into servitude with equality. Eventually the pharaoh's agents, the priests, began to separate out as the cream on top of the otherwise still homogeneous peasant mass. But social mobility, the profit motive, and individualism were not much tolerated. Craftsmen who excelled in specific arts often had to be imported from the "free world," such as it was, of the Mesopotamian countries because the undifferentiated Egyptian masses couldn't produce men skilled in special ways.

By the end of the Old Kingdom in Egypt, about 2700 B.C., the civilizations in both greater Mesopotamia (including those nations on the eastern shores of the Mediterranean) and Egypt had reached their zeniths. Most of the great discoveries in science and technology and all the innovations in the culture, the society, and the economy had been made. From this time on, a decline set in, but, of course, the peak continued for many centuries. Some nations even indulged in imperialist expansions, but the direction of civilization's development had changed from growth to deterioration.

Historians have offered many explanations for this decline. The postglacial desiccation, which made the land inhabitable in the first place, probably continued, passing through the optimum degree of moisture and tending toward semi-aridity at that time. Overcropping, overgrazing, and soil salinization caused by continuous irrigation may have aggravated this process and also caused severe weather disturbances, perhaps including the floods of mythical and Biblical fame. And of course, there were wars and attacks from nomadic tribes in both Mesopotamia and Egypt that might be used to explain the decline. But there were also extended periods of peace and a high standard of living. Perhaps it was the imbalance caused by the very rapid technological progress of this Bronze Age, which was unaccompanied by any comparable growth of philosophic thought. This could lead to a crude materialism, and, indeed, Mesopotamian society, especially, was very materialistic. The progress possible under the motivation of materialism has its own built-in "off" button as soon as adequate material wealth and well-being is achieved. When a given work routine yields a comfortable living, why expend extra energy on new research and development?

Yet, even at the height of this "golden age," there must have been some dissatisfaction with the level of achievement that might have inspired further progress. But by this time technology seems to have become frozen. No further advance was made. Perhaps it was because, in spite of civilization's advance, the world had not yet seen an age of reason. Man's world was a theocracy. Every city and every nation was ruled by a deity, and so was every trade and every science. Young blacksmith apprentices, for example, weren't taught the physical and chemical facts of smelting, alloying, and annealing metals. They were taught the "mysteries" of the art and were initiated into the magic cult of blacksmithing. Naturally, this wouldn't lead to the growth and spread of established technologies but to the keeping of secrets and to the eventual rigor mortis of technology.

Whatever the reason, the golden age is generally considered to have ended by about 1200 B.C. How much was lost? We can never be sure because we don't know about those things that were never found. But certainly some arts were lost. Certainly some of the old established cities declined in population and importance and eventually simply disappeared. The grander aspects of the culture, such as the fine temple architecture, the irrigation systems, the sculpture and other visual arts, were left to slow ruin. The property owners, tradesmen, craftsmen—in other words, the middle class—disappeared. Writing and technology, to the degree that it survived into later ages, was kept alive by small groups of craftsmen living as islands of culture in the more primitive society that followed. All the various aspects of the decline added up to the destruction of the social organization and the economic system that had been the bases of this civilization. What was left was largely a return to village and pastoral nomadic clans that earned a subsistence standard of living under a succession of frequently warring kingdoms.

And how much was saved? In the main productive activity, agriculture, quite a bit. By 1200 B.C., the selection of the crops most practical for agriculture was complete, and the pattern continues pretty much unchanged even into our own times. Practically all the important grain, vegetable, and fiber crops used today were known and used then. The roster of domesticated animals, as well, was set. In the very beginning of animal domestication, during the early farming period of pre-civilization, animals had been selected for their manageableness, which meant that they had to be small. But by about 3000 B.C., the wooden plow, drawn by oxen and cattle, was used, and these animals were bred for size and strength, as well as for the latter's milk and meat, as they have been since. The development of the plow was of the greatest importance to all future civilizations because it emancipated mankind from the necessity of being in a rich river valley. The plow allowed the development of extensive, rather than intensive, agriculture—concurrently resulting in the invention of the sickle and scythe to harvest crops. Our modern multiple gang plows and giant harvesting machines may be seen figuratively as just another step in civilization's efforts to get up out of the confines of the river valley.

Perhaps more important than how much of the greatness of Mesopotamian and Egyptian civilization was saved in these countries—and we must remember that it declined very slowly—is how much was transplanted into new ground on the periphery of the old civilizations, where it could bloom again in the spring of another great age. The Minoan civilization on the island of

Crete played an especially important transitional role. It reached a minor golden age around 1700 to 1400 B.C. and was the first significant civilization not based in an alluvial river valley. It was largely derived from the powerful influence of Egyptian culture, but it was also influenced by such factors as Babylonian cuneiform writing on clay tablets and the mother-goddess religions of Asia Minor. By emphasizing olive oil, wine, and fish as supplements to wheat, the Minoans did not exhaust the soil, a pattern followed henceforth by all future nonalluvial civilizations in the Mediterranean. Minoan civilization seems to have been reaching heights never before reached by man when it was cataclysmically destroyed by a spectacular volcanic eruption in nearby Santorini Island, which dumped enough ash on Crete to suffocate all agricultural and economic activity.

The Minoan refugees that fled to the Greek peninsula must have been a powerful influence on the developing Mycenaean civilization. Also influential were the Phoenicians, who, by the way, traded over the entire area and introduced the Greeks to civilization's products, including the alphabet, which the Greeks eventually changed to meet their own needs.

The most important legacy of the first golden age for all future golden ages was the very fact that it existed at all. It served (and still serves) as an example against which all future ages could be compared. Although this book cannot chronicle all the branches of human history and will have to ignore those branches that aren't on the main stem from which the present twentieth century grows, suffice it to say that civilization became one of mankind's habits. Time and time again, on almost all the continents of the world, mankind would turn to building cities, developing technologies, establishing industries and trade, instituting the division of labor and the use of money, in order to increase the level of material sustenance above bare subsistence. In those instances where mankind tried other paths to greatness, it usually hit a dead end before the goal was reached. The high cultures of the Huang Ho River and the Indus River and the advanced hoe-using cultures of what are now Mexico, Guatemala, Nicaragua, Peru, and Bolivia all peaked out before reaching anything like the momentum of greatness of the golden age of Egypt and Mesopotamia. The former cultures reached their zeniths coincidentally from about 1600 to 1000 B.C., even though they were scattered far and wide over the globe and must have been completely unknown to one another at the time. Neither their technology nor their trade developed enough, nor did the static feudal kind of social organization that existed, especially along the Huang Ho, nurture a sufficiently dynamic force for progress. It seems that if other paths to greatness existed, they had not been tried yet.

Now what about economics at this time? As far as the science of economics goes, there wasn't any. There was no one body of knowledge that pertained to economics exclusively, and there wasn't to be any until many centuries later. All knowledge, indeed all the aspects of the culture, tended to be integrated into one organic whole. For example, the Code of Hammurabi dealt with political, economic, social, and religious ethics as though they were one. Even the economic activities themselves, the planting of the fields, the making of brass, were also social and religious, even magical, events. Such integration of the total world of human experience has been "standard operating procedure" for most societies most of the time. Only during the past few centuries in our Western civilization has society been disaggregated into the fragments of functions and experience that our advanced technology seems to require.

However, as we look back at the first golden age from our present vantage point, we can see the theoretical framework that operated in the economy. The people wanted to earn a living. Most of them wanted only to live comfortably; some wanted to get rich. This desire was the dynamic force that informed the economic system. We have seen how they developed some rather advanced productive and commercial practices. These were the relationships with their environment and with each other that defined how productive the economy could become. And the universe within which the economy functioned was the extent of the known world at that time. This theoretical framework has remained through the ages. Only the details which flesh it out have changed.

CLASSICAL MEDITERRANEAN CIVILIZATION

The next golden ages of civilization, classical Greece and Rome (taken together as an age), have interested historians immensely for centuries, especially since the beginning of the Renaissance. The general economist, however, will not find very many new directions or new patterns to prick his curiosity here. The technology of agriculture that this age inherited from previous civilizations (including the plow and the Minoan practice of olive and wine production and fishing as supplements to grain cultivation and animal pasturage) was well suited to the more extensive farming required in this Mediterranean area, which does not have the rich river basins that Egypt or Mesopotamia had. For those farmers who had slaves to help with the labor, it was even possible to produce in excess of the subsistence needs of their families. As happened once before in ancient Mesopotamia and Egypt around 4500 B.C., and as was to happen once again in medieval Europe around 1000 A.D., this surplus of productive power was turned to the manufacture of luxury goods, which resulted in the development of some trade in these goods. The trade, in turn, caused the development of towns as trading centers, and the towns eventually became manufacturing centers as well, resulting in the development of trade in staple food products between towns and the countryside. With the attendant increase in population and knowledge, around 900 B.C. a new civilization was born.

The main developments of this Greco-Roman civilization, especially of the Greeks, were philosophy, cultural refinements, and the idea of a way of life. This is why historians, philosophers, and artists are so interested in this age. The Greeks were an aristocratic, genteel, honor-oriented society. They were also class-conscious and disdained the dirty work of the farmer and manufacturer, which was better left to slaves—or at least to peasants. Although the Greco-Roman empires became extremely wealthy, business and trade were always regarded as inferior occupations. Both Homer's *Iliad* and *Odyssey* concern themselves at length with gift-giving and receiving as a means of exchange—

a much more noble means than profit-motivated trade and commerce. The Greek god Hermes was a messenger to mortals and the protector of flocks, cattle, thieves, mischief-makers, and wayfarers. On the day he was born, this "con artist" stole Apollo's cattle and, when he was caught, talked his way out of it by claiming he was too young to steal. Pointedly, he was the god of orators, writers, commerce, and the marketplace. The Romans, with their much greater wealth and their love of luxury and exotic imports, were even more emphatic. Their god of merchants, Mercury, became the god of cheats and sharpers, which was what business was all about, according to the Romans.

Undeniably, the Greek lack of commercial concern and of materialism contributed to the soaring spirit of the Greek age, the magnificence of the architecture, and the agelessness of much of its literature and philosophy. Superstitions and myths of the past had no place in the enlightened, secular culture of the Greeks, where even the gods were as fallible as humans, and where logic could solve all problems and the Socratic method could discover all truths. Their ideals of democracy, temperance, and moderation as a way of life, the glory of pure reason, these still serve as models for comparison with present societies. That these ideals were short-lived in the Greco-Roman age, that they were enjoyed only by an elite few, or that they often existed only in the minds of philosophers, does not deny their validity.

The Greeks did some thinking about economics also. Plato recognized the necessity of specialization and the division of labor in society and claimed that it arose from the differences in abilities among men. In the ideal utopian state that he describes in his *Republic*, the most able men were not expected to do any work at all, but were to occupy themselves only with the job of ruling society. Material wealth and production were considered inferior functions of mankind. Xenophon recognized that the more division of labor there was, the greater production was likely to be, and he was in favor of increasing production. When he encouraged the development of commerce and industry, however, he was not being more materialistic than Plato. It was merely a convenient way of assuring a high enough productivity so that the ruling classes would be entirely free from any demeaning labor.

Aristotle also believed that production (shall we call it work?) was an inferior occupation. But he contributed an important idea to economic science. He distinguished between the use value of a commodity and the value it would bring in exchange, that is, its price. He considered the expenditure of time and effort in production for utilitarian purposes a virtuous enterprise. However, efforts to derive profits from trade, from exchange, and, worst of all, from speculation and the charging of interest on money were seriously suspect. He thought that men could only be corrupted by these practices.

Perhaps the most important contribution of the Greeks was that they recognized the existence of an economy. As we saw, any previous economic thought, such as the Code of Hammurabi, was completely integrated with the total body of socioreligious thought. Only interpretations by today's economic historians can separate the economic part from the whole. But the Greeks could abstract the political and economic subsystems from society. The word "economy" comes from the Greek *oikos*, meaning "house," and *nomos*, meaning "manager." The early Greek economist, then, was the manager of the household of the farm or city-state. We can also note that the economist was the steward who directed the production of use values and not a speculator, merchant, or commercial entrepreneur.

The Romans followed in the path set by the Greeks. They too did not esteem the profit-motivated businessman. (It seems that after enjoying good social standing in ancient Mesopotamia, the businessman fell from grace during all the ensuing millenia until the end of feudal times, when he was grudgingly granted some status again.) But many Romans grew rich by developing the Greek pattern of a slave-and-plantation economy much further than the Greeks ever did. What had been peasant family farms became large plantation estates, called *latifundia*, and what were once loyal citizen soldiers became mercenary soldiers. The Roman ideal became the aristocratic land-owning life, with slaves to do all the work and abusing them a commonplace. When the small peasants were forced off the land to make room for these estates, they flocked to Rome, where most of them wasted away as a large, restless, and parasitic mass of unemployed. Meanwhile, the legions of mercenary soldiers had to range farther and farther afield to capture the slaves needed to replenish the labor supply, a supply which could not replenish itself and which was extremely inefficient.

Wealth encourages trade, and trade with the far corners of the then known world flourished. Muslin from India and silk from China were imported in exchange for manufactured articles and gold. Household manufacture may have been typical, but large factories for the production of iron and even steel (by about 150 A.D.), furniture, pottery, textiles, glass, and cosmetics also existed. The production of salt and precious metals and the minting of coinage were state monopolies; later, other products came under the sway of the state monopolies. The large worker population was housed in slums or in tenement houses constructed of brick and mortar, some of which were five or six stories high. The upper classes continued to live in the atrium house, which was the dwelling of the rich for millenia. Mechanization—water and windmills and even a screw-type wine press—was not unknown.

Trade routes to distant lands usually combined overland and sea travel, the latter being more treacherous because of the brazen piracy tolerated by the Roman administrators (an indication of the low status of traders). Money was borrowed for overland trade ventures at the general rate of interest, 12 percent, but overseas ventures required 30 percent. Eventually, the drain of gold from Rome to the East necessitated debasement of the currency (reminting the coins with more cheap alloy in the gold and silver). This did not destroy trade within regions, but it did ultimately lead to the end of the East-West trade. With less trade and a scarcity of slaves, the latifundia were more and more subdivided into small tenant family farms, with a "pater familias" at the head, assisted by several slaves and a few hired hands at the peak seasons. This created greater self-sufficiency of the latifundia and decreased their trade and cultural contact with the cities, but, with the encourangement of Christianity, they also became the way to rid the culture of the institution of slavery, which almost disappeared in the Roman Empire during the first several centuries after the birth of Christ.

Compounding these developments with a graft-ridden and irrational central government, costly wars fought by Roman infantries that were increasingly outclassed by the opposing cavalries, ruthless and arbitrary tax collection, and perhaps a systematic genocide of the ruling classes through lead poisoning caused by consuming food and wine prepared in leaden vessels, it is a wonder that the empire's decline took as long as it did. But, eventually, the magnificent civilization developed by the Greeks and extended far beyond the Mediterranean world by the Romans had played itself out. No one believed in the classical ideals any more. Crass materialism and opportunism brutalized the relationships among men. By about 400 A.D., over a thousand years after it had begun, the Greco-Roman golden age had crumbled.

The eastern half of the great empire, Byzantium, lasted another thousand years. Industry and trade continued to flourish there long after they had died in Rome, probably mainly because the Eastern Empire never seemed to alienate its citizenry the way Rome did. Perhaps they were more accustomed to submitting to an imperial regime. Certainly, there was less friction in matters of tax collection and the acceptance of Christianity.

Except for Byzantium, then, the stage was set for the transition to feudalism. The large Roman estates were more and more self-sufficient. They wanted to have as little to do with Rome or any other city as possible because cities meant armies, tax collectors, and all the other ills of empire. There was a marked tendency toward building protective walls and castles. Trade was not worth much anyway, with money being debased and each estate being self-sufficient. There was also a geographic drawing away from the sea. The Mediterranean Sea, the *mare nostrum*—"our sea" to the Romans—had not only provided merchants with trade routes but also provided legionnaires with easy access to many Roman lands. It had been the base for the empire, and, as such, was to be avoided. Thus, feudal society was an inland civilization located more deeply in the European subcontinent.

With this increased isolation came a decrease in communication and literacy. Business records no longer needed to be kept; messages no longer needed to be sent. Such writing and reading as was being done was the province of the clergy. As happened before when golden ages declined, a great deal of knowledge disappeared. Industrial technologies were lost. The sophistication of Greco-Roman thought was barely preserved in unused libraries. Not only were civilization, knowledge, technology, wealth, and trade lost, but, because these losses meant a lowered efficiency and productivity of the economy, the land that had once been the empire was no longer able to sustain the population, which declined by perhaps as much as one-half.

Both as contributors to the decline and as exploiters of a decline already in progress were the invading barbarians. Had they done nothing to maintain the greatness of the culture or the wealth of the economy, they would still have left it better off than they did by their wholesale plundering and destruction, which was their customary behavior. They seemed totally unaware that peaceful production and trade were the only ways to accumulate wealth in the long run. For centuries they had subsisted on the most meager of pastoral and foraging economies in the forests of Northern Europe and the plains of Asia, occasionally finding temporary enrichment through the rapine and plunder of other tribes. When they invaded the richest plum of all, the Roman Empire, they completely failed to understand the nature of the wealth they encountered. We can only speculate today whether or not they were surprised that the great civilization they conquered seemed to trickle away through their grasping fingers.

CHAPTER 2

Archetypal Pre-Industrial Economies

THE PEASANT ECONOMY

The Case in Europe

As happened after the decline of previous civilizations, a peasant subsistence economy set in after the decline of Rome. Almost the entire population, with the exception of only a few tribal or feudal chiefs, spent its energies on feeding, clothing, and sheltering itself in the crudest manner. Many of the peasants had begun cultivating the land on a three-year rotation pattern: two years of crops and one of fallow. This change did represent an increase in the intensity of land use over the two-year rotation pattern, which alternated crops with fallow and was widely used in the times of the Greco-Roman golden age. The heavier rainfall in the non-Mediterranean sections of Europe made this three-year pattern possible, but working against it was the fact that the soil was more rapidly exhausted because animal manure could not be obtained from the animals, which were grazed on open land and in the woods and not fenced in. The grazing of livestock was the most widespread agricultural activity, and smaller animals were preferred. Pigs, goats, and sheep made up the vast majority of animals raised for their meat, milk, wool, and skins, with bees for honey, the only sweetening available to these isolated peasants, and horses and bulls raised mainly for the sport of those few chiefs and nobles who were rich enough to afford them. A substantial proportion of the subsistence of the European peasant at this time still came from sources that did not involve the regular application of productive labor. Like the barbarians, they hunted, foraged, and fished in the vast, unbroken forests that covered most of Europe then.

Mud and straw, rock rubble, and timbers, those primitive building materials used since time immemorial, determined the architecture. Even for the chiefs and feudal nobility, an earthen floor with a fire pit in the middle, a thatched roof with a hole in it to let the smoke out, and mud and rock walls with only one opening—a door—had to suffice. One room made the entire hovel; a second room would be added by the rich as a stable. The furniture was roughhewn, and the clothes were coarse linen or wool or even animal skins and furs. The complete absence of trade or money meant that everything was homemade. In some areas, especially the Germanic lands that had never been part of the Roman Empire, the peasants grouped into villages. In former empire lands, they tended to cluster around the fortified castles (larger hovels) of the nobility.

This peasant economy was static at the very lowest level of subsistence. No surplus production was possible. The least failure in the harvest meant famine. The habits of the peasants were little better than those of the barbarian marauders who contributed to the fall of Rome and subjected the population to its primitive condition. They had little love of labor or respect for its fruits. Brawls, murders, theft, and immorality were the way of life. The nobility ruthlessly exploited the peasants, confiscating whatever they may have produced that was in excess of

the minimum needed to keep body and soul together and harass-
ing them in a multiplicity of ways that seem designed to keep
their productivity low. The land the peasant farmed was owned
by the lord, and the peasants wasted little energy in making
special efforts to take care of it.

In response to these frustrations, the peasants periodically
boiled over in a rampage of pillage, arson, torture, and massacre
directed against their seignorial oppressors, rampages that could
only be ended by still greater oppression. The only amelioration
of this brutal situation came from the Christian church, which,
while having little to say pro or con about the structure of this
primitive peasant economy, did continue to inveigh against the
excesses of oppression, slavery, intimidation, and exploitation.
Ultimately, the church was to play a major role in turning the
economy on to a new and more hopeful path.

In the meantime, this period, the sixth and seventh centuries
A.D., shows us a good example of a most primitive peasant economy. It was unable to sustain a large population, self-sufficient
only by virtue of consuming the crudest and simplest homemade
products, disdainful of the kind of labor that was, ironically, its
only source of productive energy—the manual work of the peasants—and unmindful of even the most basic practices that would
contribute to greater production efficiency and economic health.
Yet, again and again through history, before civilizations are
established or after they have passed, this form of economy seems
to be the one to which humans naturally turn. We might think
that this happens because it is impossible to sink any lower, but
we must remember that for nomadic tribes, a peasant economy
may be a step upward. It involves a more intensive use of land
and human labor and bigger accumulations of wealth, however
unfairly and unequally it is distributed, than the nomadic way
of life.

The Case in Monsoon Asia

Not all peasant economies need to be so minimal. For example,
in the monsoon lands of Asia, a fortunate set of circumstances
made the peasant economy so productive that it has persisted

as the preferred form of economic organization through dozens of centuries to the present day, even though opportunities to take off in the direction of urbanization have abounded. The monsoon winds bring rainy seasons that are almost as regular and dependable as the flood waters of the Nile. The summer monsoon winds are caused by the hot air rising from the Asian land mass, drawing in moist air from the ocean. As this moist air blows on to the higher elevation of the land, it is forced to drop its water content. The winter monsoon, essentially a dry wind, is the reverse of this process, blowing from the land onto the ocean. However, in some areas, even the winter monsoons can bring rain. The air may pass over intermediate bodies of water on its way to the ocean, or it may also flow inland and bring rain because the rapidly cooling land contracts the air above it, pulling in moist ocean air. Whatever the particular characteristics of the monsoons in a given area, they bring generally predictable and regular rains because they are caused by the movement of the sun's noonday position from being vertical above the Tropic of Cancer in the summer to being vertical above the Tropic of Capricorn in the winter. The climate is warm and temperate, and the land is fertile enough to allow intensive farming and several harvests of several crops each year. Add to this the high nutritive value of rice, the main crop in these lands, and we have an explanation for the very large populations that are able to sustain themselves in these areas.

Every aspect of this peasant economy has been carefully worked out so that the land can be used as intensively as possible and so that there will be no exhaustion of the soil. A remarkable ecological balance is created. An example of this ideal balance is illustrated in Figure 1. (1) The population eats the rice and vegetables grown in an irrigated paddy; (2) kitchen refuse is eaten by a pig and some chickens, which also supply (4) food— eggs, pork, fowl—to the people; (3) all the excrement from the animals and humans is thrown into a pond, which is stocked with carp (to keep it clean), water chestnuts, and a few ducks, all of which (4) are another source of food; (5) the fertile pond water is used to irrigate and fertilize the rice and vegetable plot (1), which may yield several crops each year. Ideally, each

Monsoon rains

Fruits, nuts, mushrooms, building materials, fuel

6.

2. Kitchen refuse

Excrement

3.

4.

Fish, fowl, water chestnuts, pork, eggs

5.

Fertile pond water

1. Rice and vegetables

Figure 1. Monsoon peasant ecologic cycle.

peasant family also has access to (6): some hillside wooded land as a source of building materials, additional rooting ground for the pig, and occasional nuts, berries, and mushrooms. This wooded plot also serves as the source of fuel, but, fortunately, since forests are rather few and far between in this highly populated area, little fuel is needed; the climate is warm; and rice, the main staple, requires only boiling, not the high oven temperatures of bread. Not all Asian peasant units have all these characteristics, but they come as close to the ideal type as their wealth and natural resources allow.

The monsoon peasant economic system has proved to be very stable even today. Energetic labor and careful farming practices are encouraged not just for their economic necessity but also because the social values are such that they are considered honorable and dignified traits. The success of this system has been clearly visible. The surplus productivity has allowed for the more intensive utilization of the basic resource, land, and populations have grown very large. Today, two-thirds of the peasants in Japan have less than $2\frac{1}{2}$ acres of land per family; in Taiwan, the average peasant has barely more than one acre. Yet, in these two countries peasants have enough to eat, and even agricultural exports are possible. Even though cities have developed in Asia and trade does exist, the unique character-istic of the peasant economic system is that it is not dependent on these cities or the trade. The sophisticated culture of these Asian peoples seems to be less a creation of *civi*lization and more the creation of their special way of life.

Still, a peasant economy, even a successful one, faces many problems. Superstition reigns in place of reason. Habit and cus-tom preclude any innovations. The stability of some peasant economies is a virtue in that it usually implies greater security for the population, but it can also be a disadvantage in that it results in rigidities of social and economic behavior that leave little room for adjustment to new conditions. Subsistence-level living means that any innovations that are undertaken but fail may shift the economic balance downward and may result in famine or even the extinction of the society. Obviously, then, there is great resistance to change and new influences in peasant economies. Individual expression or enterprise are patently discouraged. Such a static society can hardly be expected to take advantage of many of the advances of the twentieth century. In order to introduce modern hygiene, medicine, and technology, new economic, social, and political customs would have to be introduced to replace many of those of the peasant society.

The Case in Some Underdeveloped Countries Today

Thus, the picture of even highly sophisticated monsoon peasant economies is not completely rosy. Unfortunately, in most parts of the world blessed neither by fertile river valleys, monsoon rains, temperately warm climate, or fertile soil, the picture of the peasant economy is much bleaker. The peasant farming villages and tribes of the undeveloped parts of Africa, Asia, Oceania, and South America cannot sustain a very large population even on the barest subsistence level.

Their farming practices are of the most rudimentary nature. Often the land is so rapidly exhausted that new forests must be burned and the agriculture shifted to these new lands every several years. Sometimes, especially in parts of Asia where land is not abundant enough for shifts to be made onto virgin land, the shifts are made in a regular cycle, in which the peasant community returns to the same land every ten or fifteen years. If all the available soil is exhausted too soon, the peasants will have to return to their starting plot before it has fully recovered its fertility. Where land seems practically limitless to the peasants, as in the great forest areas of Brazil, the shifts tend to be made onto virgin land. In addition to gaining access to fresh fertile soil, the shift is also an escape from crop diseases and pests that will have begun to concentrate in the area of cultivation after a few years. Yet the limitless land does not mean that large acreages are brought under cultivation. Clearing out virgin forests is so difficult that typically only an acre or less per family is actually available for planting.

The sustenance derived from this agriculture is irregular, monotonous, and low in proteins. Depending on the climate and soil conditions, such crops as manioc, yams, and taro roots, peanuts and many different kinds of beans and peas, cucumbers, tomatoes, pimentos, bananas, and sugar cane are grown. The main grains are maize corn in the Americas, sorghum and millet in Africa, and rice in all the Asian lands. These crops may be superimposed on one another on the same land, with root crops growing directly under the grain, and something higher, like bananas, branching out above. With soil fertility low to begin with, this practice leads to poor crops for all of the different plants. The seeds for these crops are unimproved strains that are neither resistant to disease nor specially developed for the local agricultural conditions. The farm implements are primitive sharpened sticks, machetes, picks, hoes, and spades made of simple materials. Nor do the animals contribute much to the peasant's productivity. They are typically those that can feed themselves in a semiwild way, such as ducks, chickens, and goats. Their manure cannot be collected and used to fertilize the tilled soil. In the highlands above the timberline, or in areas where all the forests have been burned off, the dung that can be collected is often used for fuel instead of fertilizer.

Through the ages, the nonfarming activities of hunting and foraging, as well as the pastoral activity of herding animals, have been a supplement to peasant farming production. Large land and forest areas to which the peasants have free access are necessary for this form of production activity to take place, and the medieval European peasant had his commons, the African his open veldt, and the peasant in the tropics his jungle. But in most of the world's areas where agriculture is a rewarding activity, there has been an inexorable tendency to enclose these open lands for private farming, more often than not by rich landowners. Thus, the medieval European commons gradually disappeared and became the private lands of the large feudal estates; a few centuries later the hunting grounds of both the African natives and the American Indians came under the control of the farming white settlers; and thousands of years ago the open lands of monsoon Asia were sectioned off into peasant units (though often owned by rich landlords) when that efficient form of peasant economy developed.

Hunting, foraging, and animal herding on open land, then, remain today as the main productive activities only in those places where it is too cold, too dry, or too hot to farm. The only notable subpeasant economies that exist today are those of the Eskimos of the Arctic, who are magnificent hunters, the few groups of animal herding nomads in the desert regions in the centers of the Asian, African, and Australian continents, and the foraging and hunting tribes of the tropical rain forest areas near the Equator. For the rest of humanity that lives in more temperate climates and in more arable regions, land ownership or security of land use is the most important factor in determining the well-being of the individual peasant and his family.

Today, land tenure, that is, land use and ownership, has come under very close scrutiny by both social historians dealing with past societies and economists dealing with present societies. Land reform is a major plank in the platform of the reform parties in any developing nation; it is the war cry of the revolutionaries. Obviously, if a minority of rich landowners or overlords can maneuver themselves into a position where they can exploit the mass of peasants through heavy taxes and duties or even deny them land tenure and merely employ them as serfs or slaves, the resulting frustrations and tensions can lead to change—sometimes explosively.

THE HIGH MIDDLE AGES

Although the medieval period between the Greco-Roman and modern-day civilizations is often treated as a wasteland of history, a monotonous time of nothing more than primitive peasant life, knights in armor, and an occasional Meistersinger, it was in Byzantium and in the Arab world another golden age.[1] Even in Europe, it was a period that saw many important changes in the way of life, and the years from about 1000 to 1300 showed enough progress to earn the title High Middle Ages from historians. These changes served as the foundation on which our

---

[1] These civilizations make rich soil for the diggings of all kinds of students, including economists and economic historians. But since they do not form the main stem of history from which our twentieth century has grown, we must reluctantly ignore them here.

present phenomenal period of growth and affluence in Western society is based. Probably in no other part of the world was there as much transition as in medieval Europe, which may be one of the main reasons why the twentieth century today is primarily a phenomenon of Western civilization.

That transition was possible, in most part, because of the survival of the agricultural economy. At the same time that the peasant economy was both primitive and static, it was also very stable. And so although up to about 700 A.D. there had been a steady decline in practically every aspect of human culture—technology, the arts, literacy, trade and commerce, total productivity, and even the number of human beings—there were two areas which provided the potential for an improved agriculture: they were the three-year rotation of crops and the eventual disappearance of slavery.

Christianity can take most of the credit for ridding society of the institution of slavery. It pursued this social reform tenaciously and persistently. Even so, slavery did not completely disappear for all time or in all corners of the Christian world. It appeared again and again in various places and at different times under a variety of rationalizations. Furthermore, the serfdom that replaced the institution of slavery was, in many instances, not much of an improvement. But the end of outright slavery saw the beginning of more energetic and more responsible labor, and this was very important to economic progress.

The three-year rotation of crops, as mentioned before, was possible because of the greater rainfall that the European peasant had as compared with what existed for the Mediterranean farmer during Roman times, when the two-year pattern was the practice. (Centuries before this time, Tacitus, the historian who accompanied the Roman legion into Europe, complained about the clammy weather there; today, centuries later, the American tourist in Europe has the same complaint.) Furthermore, in those uncivilized times, land use had to be intensive because extensively cultivated lands could not have been protected from marauders and thieves. Nor did the medieval serf have the armies of slaves—or any other kind of labor—to turn the soil on large tracts of land. However, with the gradual increase in the use of beasts of burden for plowing, mainly oxen, as well as the gradual rebuilding of the size of the population, more and more land was put into cultivation.

Other agricultural improvements were also introduced to the peasant over the next centuries. Often they were not readily adopted, and many areas of Europe remained more backward than others. The three-year crop rotation system itself was probably not used by more than half the feudal landowners even as late as the thirteenth century, the old two-year rotation hanging on because of social rigidities, fear of experimentation, and lack of interest in improvement. But progress was made. New crops were introduced, and the old ones were redistributed so that they would better suit the land on which they were grown and the needs of the people. There was an increase in the cultivation of wheat, one of the more productive grains. Root crops, such as rutabagas, beets, and turnips, were worked into the three-year rotation in place of one of the grain crops or, in very fertile soil, in place of the fallow year. Because these root crops were planted in rows, the field could still be cultivated and kept free of weeds for a season, thus preparing it for the broadcast seeding of grain the next year.

One of the more important reasons for the economic progress that was made in medieval Europe was the special leadership in agriculture displayed by the monasteries, especially those of the Cistercian and Cluniac orders in France. On their abbey lands these monks set up model farms that showed the way of progress to the feudal landowners and their peasants. They were the first to introduce new crops and experiment with new methods. They built water and windmill wheels that supplied mechanical power not only for milling flour but also for textile fulling and leather working, and, in doing so, were the only ones that preserved the limited advances in mechanical power made in the last years of Rome's golden age. They developed the brewing, fermenting, and distilling processes that make a gastronomic tour of French and German monasteries a "spirituous" experience to this day.

Above all, the church abbeys brought a new spirit to peasant life. They inveighed against the brutalities of feudalism, the exploitation of the weak by the strong, and the irrational destruction of property and productive capacity that went along with feudal quarreling. By encouraging chivalrous behavior, the monks tried to civilize the relationships between individual men and women. They also tried to soften and rationalize the relationships between the feudal lords and their serfs. The medieval popes, from Gregory VII to Innocent III (1073 to 1216), supported their reformist monks, and the Lateran Council of 1179 condemned the imposition of arbitrary and exploitive taxes by the lords on their serfs. The Franciscan monks even went so far as to encourage the freeing of serfs and the refusal to pay the seignorial dues to the feudal lords. But, generally, the churchmen worked for reform within the framework of the existing social order.

The most important contribution of the monks from the point of view of economics was to elevate the status of hard work. More often than not, honest, hard work had been in disfavor. Except, perhaps, in the monsoon lands of Southeast Asia, peasant life means much idleness and underemployment as well as drudgery. The churchmen recognized that after centuries of lack of opportunity, underemployment tends to become a way of life, and even if new opportunities appear to beckon the enterprising spirit, no one recognizes them, and life goes on unchanged. Supported by a tradition of disdain for labor that came from antiquity, such lack of enterprise and acceptance of a life that was frequently idle was the lot of the medieval peasant. The churchmen set about to change this situation. They praised labor and taught that good work was a means of salvation, and, most important, they worked hard themselves. The orchards, gardens, and fields of the monasteries hung heavy with fruit. Their productive and efficient methods inspired peasants and landlords alike. By giving each member of the monastery a reasonable and regular workload and by letting each have a fair share of the product, they showed how labor could bring the satisfaction of a job well done. And the monks did not stop work when they had produced enough for themselves. They were builders. They showed that surplus production was possible, even in the European peasant economy, and that the surplus could be used to build better homes, better roads, mills, breweries—in short, a better world in which to live. **1661466**

Many other changes were taking place in medieval society by the year 1000. Christianity was spreading to the far reaches of the European subcontinent, and a new confrontation with the East was imminent. The Byzantine Empire, centered in Constantinople, had retained the glory and wealth of the ancient Roman Empire, and Western Europe was immensely impressed by this great civilization. Once again, as had happened several times before, the growing surplus production led to the development of trade, first in luxury goods, then in more common staple goods. Much of this trade from feudal Europe went eastward, and the tales brought home by the traveling merchant planted dreams of a magnificent world into feudal heads. At the same time, the Crusades to recover the Holy Land were beginning, and returning crusaders told how, instead of finding the simplest pagans in the non-Christian land of the Near and Middle East through which they traveled, they had found the wonders of Baghdad and other large cities. They found beautiful buildings, marketplaces bustling with marvelous things to eat, to wear, and to use, and even civilized people. Light from the rest of the world was creeping into the Dark Ages in Europe, and Europe would never be the same again.

Medieval Towns

Stimulated by the surplus production over bare subsistence and by new influences that were being introduced into feudal society by the renewed contacts with the East, trade grew. And to service this developing trade, towns began to reappear. A variety of different reasons determined where the new towns cropped up, but the central motive was that trade was possible there. A junction of trade routes (a "wick," hence, such names as Brunswick, Greenwich, etc.) or a marketplace set up just outside the gates of a walled castle, at the mouth of a river, or at the site of an annual fair—all were likely places. In these still rugged times, the townsmen were as liable to attack from marauders as were the feudal estates. Thus, if they weren't already conveniently near a walled fortification to which they could scurry for protection, they built walls around the new towns just as there had been around the castles. The walled towns, called "bourg" in French, "burg" in German, and "borough" in English (hence, Strasbourg, Hamburg, Peterborough, etc.), gave their name to the people who lived in them, who were called burghers or the bourgeoisie.

By the year 1000, many new towns were developing, trade was growing, and the High Middle Ages were coming into full bloom. Technical skills long since forgotten were rediscovered. Literacy, an important skill in running a business, began to increase as education began to increase. Soon the special advantages of the natural resources, agriculture, and the crafts in certain regions began to be recognized, and surplus production for export of these specialized commodities was encouraged by the burghers who were interested in working up a profitable commercial venture. French and Rhine wines were shipped to England, The Netherlands, and the Scandinavian countries. Furs from Scandinavia and Russia were sent to Europe. Utilizing the excellent river and sea routes available throughout Europe, the burghers soon traded more substantial commodities in addition to these luxury goods. Fish came from the northern waters, salt from the Bay of Biscay and the springs of Lüneburg, copper and iron from Sweden, wool and leather from Spain, cotton from Syria, textiles from Flanders, sulphur from Sicily, and, of course, the spice trade from the Orient, the fattest plum of all. To facilitate all this growth in trading, bigger and safer boats were built, and money became more and more the means of exchange.

But trade was still a very hazardous undertaking. Everywhere they went, traders were considered outsiders, adventurers, suspicious characters who made their living by wheeling and dealing rather than by the honest toil of the peasant or the honorably gained spoils of the knight's battles. They were fair game for big and smalltime thieves. Up and down the Rhine and Mosel rivers, robber barons would descend on the merchant vessels from their castles on the high banks and extract exorbitant fees for "protection"; everywhere in the country, highway robbers ambushed caravans; and on the high seas piracy was taken for granted, as it had always been. The merchants found safety from some of these hazards in the large trade fairs that developed at this time. These fairs were well organized by the merchants, with provisions for currency exchange, mercantile jurisprudence, and police protection—usually supplied by a powerful king or noble. The most famous fairs were in Champagne, in the southeast of Paris, and they were at the height of their importance for about two centuries from 1100 to 1300. Smaller fairs by the hundreds were scattered all over medieval Europe. And the towns themselves, especially those in northern Europe that had joined together into a kind of chamber of commerce called the Hanseatic League, worked hard to keep themselves safe for business.

The populations of the new towns were members of a new class, with a new way of life. They were free men who were neither beholden to a lord, like a serf, nor possessed of aristocratic birth rights, like a lord. Furthermore, their source of wealth was neither simple manual labor in the fields nor ownership of land. They made their money by trade, and some of them, like the family of traders and bankers named Fugger of Augsburg and the Medici family of Florence, made a lot of it. At first, the merchants would travel with their ships and caravans to the distant towns and fairs that were their markets. As they became wealthier, they would leave the traveling to agents and manage the business from a home office. Eventually, the lending of money, not only for investments in all kinds of commercial ventures but also as loans to kings and the nobility, became the most important function of these merchants.

The skills of these merchants formed a solid foundation for economic expansion. In spite of tremendous social pressures against credit, they learned two techniques for making it flow: lending money at interest, and banking. They also invented two incredibly useful devices for a mercantile civilization: double-entry bookkeeping and the joint stock company. The former of these two inventions is as important to the accountant as the law of conservation of energy is to the physicist. The joint stock company, especially in its modern form, the corporation, was the first new social unit for the control of production since the family.

Not formally recognized in theory until the monk Fra Luca Pacioli included it in his magnum opus *Everything About Arithmetic, Geometry, Proportion, and Proportionality* in 1494, double-entry bookkeeping put the concept of ownership and indebtedness into a new perspective. Double-entry bookkeeping views ownership and indebtedness from the standpoint of the business rather than from that of the individual. Thus, a company's total value, its *assets*, is divided up between those to whom it owes money, its creditors, and those who own the business. What the company owes its creditors is called *liabilities*; what the owners get is called the *net worth* (usually in the form of stocks today). As the assets grow in a successful business, so does the "indebtedness" to the creditors *and* the owners. Thus, assets always equal liabilities plus net worth, and a balance is struck. Table 1 is an example of a balance sheet that is typical for thousands of small manufacturing firms operating everywhere today.

Table 1. The balance sheet

ASSETS		LIABILITIES	
Current assets		**Current liabilities**	
Cash	$ 25,000	Accounts payable	$ 25,000
Inventory	75,000	Notes payable	25,000
Fixed assets		**Long-term liabilities**	
Machines	150,000	Bonds payable	100,000
Buildings and land	100,000	NET WORTH	
		Stock	200,000
		Total liabilities and	
Total assets	$350,000	**net worth**	$350,000

With the firm viewed as an autonomous entity for bookkeeping purposes, it is possible for several individuals to have a hand in it, and that is the idea behind the joint stock company. In the first joint stock companies, several merchants would pool their money for a trading trip to the East or to a neighboring region. When the trip was completed, they would split the profits or losses by each taking their proportional share of the net worth (assets minus liabilities) of the venture. They could retire from business and go to live on a landed estate purchased with their earnings (it is surprising how, even to this day, this is often an irresistible urge for many businessmen), or they could reinvest in a new venture. Soon the trading ventures became continuous, with established agents in the major market centers, and the joint stock company became an institution with a permanent life, independent of and outlasting the lives of its owners. And just as trade led to manufacturing, so the joint stock company led to the industrial corporation.

Medieval morality and theology were firmly opposed to many of these new business developments. Merchants' prices and the necessity of charging interest on business loans—the latter called usury—were highly suspect. St. Thomas Aquinas, writing around 1260, argued that all usury was the unfair exploitation of a fellow man at a time of his greatest need and distress. He painted a picture of needy peasants and widows being denied financial help unless a vicious interest rate was paid to the greedy moneylenders. He also saw rich nobles borrowing money to squander on wars and destruction while the moneylenders grew rich. Writing in the early 1300s, Dante, in his *Divine Comedy*, considered usurers bestial and put them in a low level of hell with blasphemers and perverts. In *The Merchant of Venice*, written around 1600, Shakespeare also had little good to say about them. Less than a century earlier, Martin Luther had vented his medieval wrath against usury, fraud, trickery, avarice, and all the other unscrupulous schemes of traders and merchants. What was and what wasn't a "just price" for goods sold was heatedly argued by theologians, who regarded most businessmen as nonproductive and parasitic types and who thought little of the service rendered by the merchant or the cost of this service.

Certainly, in a primitive peasant economy, where there was little opportunity for investment in new businesses, moneylending at interest may very well have been usurous exploitation of a fellow man's misfortune. And, knowing human nature, we can be just as certain that in these early times there were many gullible peasants and war-hungry nobles and no shortage of con artists to take advantage of them with unjust prices and fraudulent practices. But with the growth of trade, new towns, new industry, and new business opportunities, lending money for commercial ventures could hardly be called usury. Because risks and uncertainty in these times were great, the interest rates had to be high. In principle, at least, the lending of money was a business and not exploitation, and most borrowers were other merchants, kings, and producers, not poor peasants or petty nobles.

Guilds and the Honor of Business

Leadership of the new bourgeois class was supplied by the Merchants' Guild, the trade organization of the leading merchants in each town. These guilds were also the towns' councils, and from their memberships came also the judges of the courts, and from their treasuries came the money to pay the towns' gendarmeries. The guilds developed a body of rules according to which trade was regulated. Honesty in contracts, fair pricing of commodities, responsibility toward one's fellow merchants, religious piety, charity, and a generally virtuous attitude were the prescribed behavior. Any guild member who broke these rules could be expelled, which would mean the end of his livelihood and a complete loss of social position in his town. Clearly, with so much power, the guilds raised the status of business and commerce to a new level. What the monks did for the dignity of labor, the town guilds did for the dignity of trade. For the first time in history, businessmen ennobled their profession with a code of ethics and, thus, began to destroy the suspicion and mistrust of the rest of the community that had always been the onus of the enterprising trader.

The spirit of these business leaders was substantially more democratic than that of the two feudal classes, the serfs and the lords. They replaced the autocratic rule by individual nobles, which had been limited only minimally by social custom or the church, with a government consisting of committees acting according to a body of laws. Reasonableness and rationality in civic government were substantially enhanced by the adoption of rule by these bureaucratic bodies. However pejorative that word sounds to us today or however much the proliferation of committees has come to plague our modern life, we must recognize that those committees were the first flowering of parliamentary government, and even today they are our only hope that the ulterior motives of individuals and their whimsical and illogical irrationalities will be eliminated in favor of reason and legality.

So it came to be said that "town air is free air." Enterprising young serfs could buy their freedom from their lords—or run away for one year and a day after which time they would be declared free—and move into the towns. And so the populations of the towns grew. Technology, science, and literacy thrived there and stimulated the development of new craft industries. The new craftsmen also formed guilds, which attempted to raise the prestige of their crafts by insuring quality products and responsible business practices. They instituted the training of workers through long periods of apprenticeship, usually seven years, and granted a master craftsman degree on the completion of the apprenticeship period and the production of a "masterpiece" as evidence of skill.

As the armorers, stonemasons, weavers, shoemakers, ironmongers, goldsmiths, etc., improved their crafts, increased their efficiency, and produced larger quantities of goods, the standard of living rose. In order to purchase these goods, it was, of course, necessary to have more money, and the feudal lords became eager to "monetize" their relationships with their serfs. Whereas before they had been collecting their share of the product of the feudal estate in kind—so many bushels of grain, so many pigs, so many days of labor per year from each serf—the lords now preferred simply to collect rents and taxes from their serfs in the form of money. This put a greater distance between the lords and serfs in what had been a rather personal (if not always personable) relationship and contributed to the development of markets for agricultural products where barter exchange had existed before. More gold and silver—mostly silver—were mined, and they did not burn a hole in people's pockets for long but were eagerly spent on the new and plentiful commodities.

With more money around and with the money being spent and respent more rapidly in the growing markets, the proportion of money offered in exchange for goods increased. Whenever money offered to buy goods increases faster than the goods offered for sale, prices, which are the visible manifestation of this ratio, tend to rise, and the familiar condition we call inflation prevails. From the years 1000 to 1300, prices went up by about three times—not a very rapid inflation by twentieth century standards where prices can triple in decades or less, but quite rapid for this period of relatively slower social change. At first, this inflation must have had a rather stimulating effect on industry and trade because increasing prices tend to make businesses seem successful, for no other reason than that the money value of existing property owned by businesses—the buildings, tools, raw materials, and land—tends to increase. But soon those groups with a fixed money income began to suffer a decline in their purchasing power, that is, their unchanging income could be exchanged for fewer and fewer goods as the prices of these goods increased. One such group was the nobility that had just fixed and monetized its relationship with the serfs before the long inflation began. By 1300 many nobles were substantially impoverished. Not having learned any bourgeois skills, not even reading and writing, and being forbidden (everywhere except in England) by the feudal code to go into business or marry out of the nobility, there was nothing they could do except go to war. Conveniently, perhaps, in the period 1300 to 1500 there were more than the usual number of wars, including the Hundred Years' War, in which the nobles fought as mercenaries.

During this time, the turn of events was less than fortunate for others as well. The mines that had supplied the new gold and silver for the increased trade and commerce were beginning to become depleted. They had to be dug deeper and deeper, and the primitive suction pumps used in those days couldn't keep the water out. Without a sufficient supply of these precious metals, the medieval economy suffered what we would call today a *liquidity crisis,* that is, a crisis caused by not enough money (gold and silver, in this case) to meet the demands of business. Of course, when the supply of money relative to the supply of goods decreases, prices tend to go down in exactly the reverse of the inflationary process, in which the supply of money increases relative to the supply of goods. And because business property also declines in money value in exactly the reverse process, this "deflation" was not regarded happily by businessmen, who tried desperately to get their money out of their investments before it was too late. Everywhere, declining business, foreclosures, and bankruptcies were the result. This sorry state of affairs, on top of the decline in the purchasing power of the nobility, caused a serious decline in the aggregate demand for almost all commodities.

But these were only some of the troubles. By 1300, at the end of the High Middle Ages, the monasteries, which had put so much steam into the agricultural sector of the economy, had grown rich and fat from the prosperity of their surplus production. No longer did they set a shining example of hard work and simple living. In fact, the not-completely Christian behavior of the universal Catholic Church was dismaying many people. A further demoralizing influence came from the Black Death, which was making several rampages through Europe at this time, the first and worst epidemic being from 1346 to 1350. This bubonic plague, a new disease in Europe, came, literally, on the back of a rat, the black rat of Asia, which had originally been an undomesticated desert rat carrying the flea that harbored the disease. The dry summer heat in the rat's native Asian desert habitat killed the flea every year, fortunately for the rat. As a human disease, it had flickered on and off in tropical Asia probably for centuries. But when the rats landed in Europe in the early 1300s, most likely from the hold of a merchant ship, they spread like a prairie fire in this virgin terrain. Soon rat killing became one of the noble arts, and every self-respecting town had its official rat killer, its Pied Piper. But with the total ignorance of sanitation in that day, the rats, the lice, and the plague won the battle. Furthermore, the plague did not fight single-handedly. Extraordinarily bad weather ruined crops and brought serious famines in some parts of Europe. Smallpox, dysentery, cholera, diphtheria, scarlet fever, all were ready to strike a weakened population in epidemic proportions, given the opportunity. Altogether, the plagues concentrated their severest effects on the more crowded population centers, the cities, seaports, and monasteries, thus destroying precisely those places that had developed as a result of the increased trade and economic activity and that were the most important to the economy. Had the urban concentrations and the trade not developed, it is very likely that the plague would have remained bottled up in the East. By 1400, about a third of the European population had died, leaving only about forty-five million people, the same population size as in 1000. Aggregate total production declined even more than aggregate demand, and the labor shortage in the towns caused by people fleeing to the countryside pushed wage rates up.

With sales declining, money and credit unavailable, wage rates going up, social conditions in utter confusion because of plague epidemics, demoralization, and wars, the business outlook was downright dismal. And in an attempt to cope with this situation, businessmen made what we can recognize today as the typical defeatist mistake—they tried to protect their own interests by shutting off competition. Led by the guilds, they tried to monopolize the business in their own regions and towns by excluding all imports from outside. They established regulations that prohibited the sale of any new or improved commodities. New production methods, new materials, new tools, even new locations of workshops were forbidden. Instead of seeking new opportunities as a way out of their misfortune, instead of trying to restimulate commerce, the businessmen sought to protect what they still had left by pulling their necks into the safety of their own town walls. Thus, they shut out the very sources that might have saved their businesses. Even though the guilds had been able to raise the status and prestige of business to an all-time high, businessmen had still not learned the lesson of free enterprise.

By the end of the 1300s, the Middle Ages looked more like the Dark Ages once again. Superstition, immorality, social disorder, and the general brutalization of human relationships increased. Slavery cropped up again. The people had always taken witches seriously but had not feared them too much because they felt protected by their firm faith in Christianity. Now, with disaster all around them, even some of the so-called witches themselves began to think that they may have sold themselves to the devil. Cruelty, torture, and burnings at the stake increased. Bands of robbers, often impoverished nobles, pillaged the countryside. Some unfortunates gave up all hope for the future and indulged themselves in wild orgies. Others joined orders of flagellants and tried to expiate their imagined sins by marching through towns beating themselves with chains and switches. The church found it easy to raise money by selling indulgences to these desperate people, who were eager to buy their deceased loved ones a shortened stay in purgatory. It certainly seemed that a European golden age had been nipped in the bud.

THE RENAISSANCE

Who can predict when civilizations will rise or fall? We continue our story not with a new civilization in China, Africa, or, perhaps, Central America, but right in Europe, where we left off. From about 1400 to 1700 was the period called the Renaissance, so-named because it was considered to be a time of rebirth of the classical Greco-Roman culture. Interrelated developments in all aspects of life caused the return of progress: the population increased; imperial nations developed; the foundations of modern science and technology, literature, art, and music were laid; the known world expanded to about its present size; democracy of sorts appeared here and there; and Christianity experienced a profound upheaval.

By 1300 the Christian church was sickened by a variety of maladies. Because the monasteries had become rich and fat and no longer served as examples of hard work, frugality, and humbleness, the people could hardly look to them as havens from the cynical and materialistic world. Richest and most splendid of all the church properties was the seat of the Papacy itself. And to make matters worse, both for those who believed that there can be only one true successor to Peter and for those who had to pay the expenses, there were two Popes, one in Avignon and another in Rome. These papal courts exceeded those of most kings in splendor and magnificence. To pay for these courts, the people were squeezed hard, the sale of indulgences was encouraged, and the church properties were administered more for profits than for welfare.

The response of the people to the church's sickness was, on the one hand, a turning away from religion—a secularization—and, on the other, a reform of religion itself. Both of these responses were instrumental in turning society into new directions of progress. The secularization laid fertile grounds for the growth of the philosophy of humanism, the glory of being an individual human being. For humanists, the observation of nature in all its beauty, perhaps even more than simple religious faith, brought revelation and truth. How important this Renaissance spirit was to the development of the arts and sciences cannot be underestimated. In Southern Europe, it took a literate and sophist form because the infatuation with classical Greece and Rome was stronger there than in Northern Europe; there the Renaissance men disdained the vernacular language, even the Latin used by the church, and preferred a classical style of Greek and Latin. But in Northern Europe, the break with the Middle Ages was not as severe. Church scholars continued to be respected, and great universities, which were church-sponsored, were founded in all the major cities. The Renaissance spirit was less imbued with a sense of classical style and more concerned with real research and discovery. However, although the southern Europeans, especially the Italians, could boast of more than their share of artists, and the northern Europeans, more than their share of scientists, the names of great Renaissance innovators in both the arts and sciences, such as Copernicus, Leonardo da Vinci, Newton, Erasmus, Michelangelo, Vasco da Gama, and Machiavelli, constitute an international list.

The reform of religion itself, the Catholic Reformation and the Protestant Revolution, occupies a great many pages of history. From 1300 to the end of the Thirty Years' War in 1648, one war after another was fought over entanglements that involved religion in one way or another. Typically, it was Catholic against Protestant or a Catholic inquisition against Moors or even other Catholics who were considered less than perfect in their faith. But national interests were also involved, and sometimes Catholics would join Protestants of the same locale against other Catholics or Protestants of another area. Out of these entwined threads of religious conflicts, political alliances, personal rivalries, royal marriages, and wars, the fabric of the great imperial powers of the Renaissance, France, Portugal, England, and the Hapsburg lands—including Spain, Austria, and The Netherlands—was woven.

The spiritual content of the reform involved mainly a reaffirmation of the direct relationship between a man and his God and a clean-up of the malpractices of the church. The mood was intensely individualistic, and some students of this period of history, especially the great German sociologist Max Weber writing around 1900, have argued that Protestantism provided the religious sanction for capitalism. Certainly its rationalism, its simplification of religion, and its tenet that God's grace is evidenced by the success and good works of His individual children are all consonant with the spirit of free enterprise and good business practices. Nonetheless, economic development progressed throughout Renaissance Europe and did not divide according to Protestant-Catholic boundary lines.

The pattern of economic activity, however, changed significantly. Since the time of the Greco-Roman civilization and even before, the Mediterranean Sea had served as the main avenue of trade for this part of the world. After the fall of Rome, economic activity had pulled away from the Mediterranean somewhat, but when trade expanded once again during the Renaissance, we might have expected this great avenue to be used again for most of the commerce, combining the sea with overland routes to all parts of Europe as well as to the East. However, the new geographic discoveries changed this pattern. The early Renaissance was the age of explorers, daring seafarers, who, with the aid of better ships and sails, the newly adopted compass, and the financing by kings and queens, set out to find a new route for the spice trade to the East. The new routes ignored the Mediterranean and shifted commercial activity away from the Mediterranean cities to the Atlantic ports: Cadiz, Lisbon, Antwerp, and London.

Spices were very important in those days when salting, smoking, and drying were the main means of food preservation. The use of spices, unbelievably heavy by present standards of taste, made the preserved foods more palatable and covered up the flavor of those that hadn't been so well preserved. During the High Middle Ages the spice trade had taken the European traders only as far as the eastern shores of the Mediterranean, where they met with intermediaries—mostly Arabs—who, in turn, carried on the trade eastward to the mysterious Orient that remained unknown to Europeans. But in 1498 the Portuguese Vasco da Gama discovered the Malabar Coast of Southwest India by traveling around Africa. Five years after his return, spices in Lisbon were only one-fifth as expensive as spices in Venice.

Spain had dispatched Columbus, an Italian, in 1492 to find a new route east by sailing west, and though he did find America, he kept poking around in the Caribbean for that route east until his death in 1506. Magellan, a Portuguese in the service of Spain, succeeded in 1520 by sailing around the bottom of South America, through the strait that now bears his name, and by continuing on to India, where he encountered opposition from the competing Portuguese, who were already established there. Magellan was the first to circumnavigate the world, and from then on, sophisticated maps of the world depicted an orbicular earth. A pattern was, thus, established by the Treaty of Tordesillas (1494) that Spain would get all of the new world (North and South America and the Philippines) except for Brazil, and Portugal would get all of Africa and India. The French, English, and Dutch didn't consider this arrangement binding, and the natives in the newly discovered lands couldn't have been happy with it either. It wasn't the first time, nor the last, that the world was divided in half by two competing powers who were interested in peaceful coexistence.

Although Spain did not get its hoped-for spice trade route, it did make good use of its new-found America. The Spanish church and nobility had just completed the wars to drive the Moors from Spain, and they eagerly turned to the new conquests in America. The church wanted converts; the nobles wanted gold. The natives they found in America supplied both. By 1590, the gold and silver mines of America were pouring about 60,000 pounds (avoirdupois) of silver and 430 pounds of gold into Spain annually. When the church protested the brutal exploitation of the native Americans in the mines, African slaves were imported—it is estimated 100,000 of them by 1560. The gold flowed, and Spain became the most powerful nation in the world.

Mercantilism

Gold played a crucial role in the economic and political structure of the Renaissance. Of course, its inflow eased the liquidity crisis that had been part of the cause of the decline of the High Middle Ages, and commerce was given new life. But it also caused another inflation. From 1500 to 1650, prices tripled, and if any of the poorer nobles had survived the troubled times at the end of the High Middle Ages, they were probably wiped out now. Such nobles and knights were no longer useful anyhow. They had been effective militarily against castles, but the introduction of artillery changed their usefulness. Neither castles nor armored knights could stand up to artillery with which large armies, another new institution, were now equipped. With knights technologically unemployed, even the form of architecture changed—from castles to palaces.

The armies and navies, which were made up of mercenary soldiers and sailors, had to be paid, and only the king had the power to acquire the gold that was needed. In Spain, he got it directly from the mines in the colonies. In other countries, the king got it indirectly by using his monopoly powers to build what was then called a "favorable balance" of trade for his nation, that is, a trade in which more is exported than is imported. To pay for the imports, foreign purchasers had to pay in gold; this gold paid for the large army and navy, which, in turn, secured more colonies for the king; and the colonies paid off the investment handsomely by sending their abundant—and therefore inexpensive—supplies of raw materials to the king's country. With the cost of imports low and with the earnings from exports high, a large, favorable balance of trade was thus obtained. This cycle comes about full swing to more gold imports, a bigger army and navy, still more colonies, cheaper raw material imports, a bigger gap between cost of imports and revenues from exports, and—again—more gold inflows received in payment for the exports. Of course, not every nation at once could be a net exporter; somewhere imports would have to exceed exports. And Spain, with its abundance of gold, played this role. Spanish gold flowed throughout Europe as the Spaniards bought their way to wealth and power. Meanwhile, in their effort to obtain a gold-producing favorable balance of trade, the other European countries were continually developing their export industries.

Encouraging exports, limiting imports, getting the people to work industriously, developing new products, advancing industrial technology, finding new markets and sources of raw materials, protecting commercial property in distant lands, all these activities were intended to bring an inflow of gold to a nation, and they were the substance of what came to be called *mercantilism*. It required a plethora of regulations, tariffs, taxes, subsidies, and government intervention, both economically and militarily. On a national scale, only a strong central government could carry out such complex activities. All through the seventeenth, eighteenth, and even the nineteenth centuries countries that had not concentrated their power in a central government, like Italy and, for a while, Germany, did not share in the mercantilist development of national economies. Kings, of course, tried to get their hands on the gold for their royal treasuries, and to do so they tried every kind of method: they taxed the towns and the nobles; they sold government offices; they debased their currency; they borrowed from the increasingly wealthy bankers; and they sold monopolies for trading with certain areas to such corporations as the Russia Company, East

India Company, and the Virginia and Massachusetts companies. In carrying out such mercantilist policies, the kings were often in conflict with their parliaments of nobles, who were hurting from these methods. In England, the resolution to this conflict resulted in a strong parliament and the makings of a democracy; practically everywhere else it resulted in royal absolutism.

Mercantilism was not a creation of the Renaissance; only mercantilism on a national scale was new. We have seen that during the economic decline at the end of the High Middle Ages, towns and small regions turned to the methods of mercantilism as a desperate move to protect themselves. They restricted imports, encouraged exports, tried to stifle competition through the establishment of monopolies, and attempted to turn all these efforts into an inflow of gold or, at least, to prevent an outflow. The free enterprise that had marked the years 1000 to 1300 with probably the fastest rate of economic progress yet experienced at any time in history was hardly a dim memory by the time of the Renaissance. It is not surprising, because the mercantilist perspective is a natural economic point of view for people to have. For example, every business tries to make its revenues exceed its costs so that it will have profits; likewise, a family will work hard to get a better house, a newer car, a larger bank account, and a college education for the children, all of which are forms of accumulation that can only be achieved by producing more than the family consumes. In a way, we are all mercantilists, even today. But it is one thing to apply this form of thinking—producing more than one consumes or a favorable balance of trade—to a private household or even to the economic conditions of a feudal society, but quite another, as we shall see, to make it the policy of a king or a nation. It completely misinterprets the nature of the whole organism that is a nation's economy.

Nonetheless, the negative effects of mercantilist policy were not to be felt for some time. The Renaissance period was one of rapid economic expansion, which was primarily due to the discoveries, the fresh supply of gold, the new sources of raw materials, the new markets, and the new industries that grew out of these discoveries. Also, mercantilism run on a national scale is less confining than mercantilism on a regional level, for a substantial amount of intranational free enterprise can create a dynamic home commerce and industry. Thus, the mercantilist kings, in order to encourage such a nationally oriented free enterprise, tried to break the power of the regional guilds, built networks of roads, made every effort to prohibit the collection of tolls and tariffs at internal borders—in short, supported industry in every possible way. Even though their intention was to build the nation's export potential and not directly to build the free enterprise system, the latter was in fact what they achieved.

Of all the countries of Europe, England of the sixteenth and seventeenth centuries was the most exciting example of the success of mercantilist policies. The conspicuous development of England's economy began during Queen Elizabeth's reign in the latter half of the 1500s. Before that time, England had lagged behind the countries of continental Europe, culturally, militarily, and economically. But in 1588, Sir Francis Drake won his dazzling victory over the Spanish Armada, which, with its powerhouse of large, cumbersome boats and quarreling seamen who couldn't maneuver in the stormy northern waters, represented what was wrong with a rich but decadent Spain. Now the time was ripe for the hardy, unspoiled, half-barbarous English to venture forth from the safety of their island and seek their fortunes in trade (and piracy) around the world. Meanwhile, Queen Elizabeth, for all her notorious passions and courtships, was careful to tend the garden of economic development at home. It is said that she spent more time touring farms, home industries, markets, and seaports than she did in her royal court. She also carefully guided her state on a reasonably safe journey through the labyrinthine religious conflicts of the day, uniting England in Protestantism, while Spain, The Netherlands, France, and Germany were tearing themselves and one another apart in religious wars.

Still, by the 1600s the world market was dominated by Holland, not by England. The Dutch were now making fat fortunes from commerce and finance when only a century before they had been a poor farming and fishing economy with only a few free towns of middling wealth. Now the Dutch were the chief suppliers of Baltic grains to Spain—a country to which it had only recently been subservient—in exchange for silver and gold. Great banking houses developed that supplied the financial means for trade to the four corners of the globe: furs from Russia, spices from the Orient, and sugar and tobacco from the New World. It was the height of the period called the commercial revolution, which had started at the end of the Middle Ages as the principles of mercantilism were gradually adopted. And Amsterdam embodied the finest flowering of the free merchant town—two or three hundred years after the other towns of Europe had had their heyday. The stolid Dutch trader, uninhibited by religious scruples about usury, unhampered by the need to plead for his business project with a fancy and fatuous royal court full of Pompadour-types (as the French businessmen did), and, above all, unconcerned with high-toned aristocratic living habits, became a legend in his time. For him, profits took precedence over all the other motives.

Perhaps this dedication was his undoing. In France and England, businessmen saw themselves not only earning profits but also building their nations. The advocates of mercantilism in these two countries—who made up kind of a business lobby— argued that their theories and policies would enhance the kingdom. They had, at least to that degree, a nationalistic awareness. By contrast, the Dutch merchants and bankers aspired to little more than feathering their own nests. With profits their only motivation, they thought of little else, and, perhaps like the materialistically successful Mesopotamians two thousand years before them, they ruled their country and their economy with no other purpose than business as usual, which so often results in stagnation.

The English merchants, like those in Holland but unlike those in France, had had easy entrée to political power. They worked in a rather smooth alliance with the artistocrats, who, with all the changes in ruling houses experienced by the English throne during the fourteenth and fifteenth centuries, had achieved a greater parliamentary voice than their counterparts in France had under their divine-right kings. With greater political power came a greater sense of participation and a higher social status. While English merchants envied the elegance in which the rich classes lived in France, the French merchants envied the way English businessmen could marry their daughters off into the nobility.

The most extraodinary proponent of the mercantilist system was the French Minister of Finance for Louis XIV from 1661 to 1683, Jean Baptiste Colbert, who gave his name to mercantilism there—Colbertism. He regarded the entire French nation as the usufructuary of the king, and Frenchmen despised him for his efforts: he made the people work extremely hard; he standardized weights and measures; he initiated controls on business; he canceled many holidays; he showed his dislike for the "parasitic" clergy; and, especially, he introduced the *corvée*, forced labor to build roads.

But adverse public opinion didn't bother the mercantilists or the kings in those days. What concerned them was building a wealthy and powerful nation that could compete successfully both militarily and economically with other nations. And herein lie both the contribution and the error of mercantilism. For the first time in history, the economy, as such, was publicly recognized. Of course, this was intimately connected with the political development of nations themselves. The small feudal manors and monarchies and before them the city-states of Greece and Mesopotamia, even the almost national empires of Rome and Egypt, had all focused their political and economic attention on the central city or the king's castle and had a relatively vague notion of the outside boundaries of the state. The mercantilists turned this around. For them, the most important aspect of the state was its boundaries. The boundaries were the major points of control of the commerce, where the so-called favorable balance of trade could be enforced, and the boundaries delineated the nation. Everyone within the borders of France, for instance, was French, whether he was a Parisian stonemason, a vintner from the Bordeaux region, or a shepherd from Provence. And all of these citizens could be employed in the building of a greater, more powerful, and richer France. This was mercantilism's contribution.

Its error was that a national economy cannot be a profit-making business. A favorable balance of trade that accumulates gold bullion in the hands of rich merchants and kings year after year will at the same time, impoverish the mass of the people. Vast numbers of restrictive regulations, exploitive taxes, and enforced labor choke off the spirit of enterprise and progress. When all international trade is in the hands of rich monopolists, all manufacturing processes rigidly prescribed by governmental decree, and all new products or services prohibited unless they are licensed by a central authority, the people will resign from making extra efforts. Dynamism in the economy, as well as in other aspects of the society, will disappear. And no amount of royal gold will be able to buy the nation out of that predicament.

Nonetheless, during the 1600s and 1700s, England's economy grew vigorously. But Spain missed the main opportunity of the commercial revolution by concentrating on gold instead of production. France was suffering from social ills that would burst forth in the world's most famous revolution. And Holland was stagnating in its bourgeois affluence. Toward the latter half of the eighteenth century, England was actually surpassing her European rivals, and by 1776, a banner year in several respects, she was strong enough to want to discard the rigid shield of mercantilist policy.

CHAPTER 3

The Beginning of Economic Science

Mercantilism was never really an economic theory but a philosophy or point of view. It was the natural outgrowth of the way rulers had behaved since the beginning of civilization, and only its application to a new economy was new. Although it was easy enough to identify mercantilism through the policies of the nations that practiced it and through the writings of the finance ministers, government officials, and merchants who were concerned with it, no one thought of giving mercantilism a thorough-going theoretical exposition. Instead, the first economic theories that were given such an exposition were ones that grew up in opposition to mercantilism. In proposing a change in existing mercantilist policy, the members of this opposition had to be articulate, well reasoned, and convincing. In fact, they were articulate, perhaps even well reasoned, but they were not always completely convincing.

THE PHYSIOCRATS

The first such theorists were called "physiocrats," after physiocracy, the law of natural order. At the time, the middle of the eighteenth century, an interest in the natural sciences was spreading throughout the literate classes, especially in France and England. It was part of the general spirit of the Age of Enlightenment, that chapter of the Renaissance written mostly by Voltaire. Very much in vogue was the concept of natural law, the idea that the universe—from galaxies to atoms, with humans in between—operates according to a magnificent pattern. All one has to do to live successfully in this world is to discover and understand that part of the natural pattern that one is involved with and to live according to its immutable laws. It's still a popular idea today. The founder of the physiocratic school, which applied the natural law to economics, was Francois Quesnay, the court physician to Louis XV and Madame de Pompadour. He saw a striking resemblance between the medical physiology he had learned in his profession, especially the English anatomist William Harvey's theory of blood circulation, and the circular flow of products and money in the economic organism.

According to Quesnay's *Tableau économique* (1758), the ultimate source of all economic productivity and, concomitantly, all wealth was the land. Industry and commerce were considered sterile, mere converters of one form of value into another. Surpluses could be produced only if agriculture was improved, and all segments of the society would prosper as a result. In turn, said Quesnay, the landowners were to pay all the taxes because they were the source of all the wealth—not the industrialists, not the traders, not the peasants. The surpluses, which originated from the earth, would be paid out by the owners of that earth—the nobility.

Table 2 shows how the physiocratic law would work, according to the theorists. If the farmers produced five billion francs' worth of agricultural produce, two billion francs' worth would be used for their own subsistence and for livestock feed and seed. They would sell three billion francs' worth of their product, one billion francs' worth to the landowners for food and two billion francs' worth to the sterile classes of manufacturers for food and as raw materials. The farmers would use the money they earned to pay rent to the landowners—two billion francs—and to buy manufactured goods from the sterile classes—one billion francs. The landowners would then have enough money—one billion francs—to pay for the food they bought and to buy one billion francs' worth of manufactured goods. The sterile classes would then also have enough money from sales of manufactured goods to pay for their two billion francs' worth of food and raw materials. It all fits together very neatly. Everybody gets paid what he contributes to the economy, except the landowners. He con-

Table 2. A physiocratic economic table (billions of francs)

		PURCHASES			
		Farmers	Landowners	Sterile classes	
SALES	Farmers	2 Not sold, used at home	1 Food	2 Food and raw materials	5 Real 3 Money
	Landowners	2 Rent	0	0	2
	Sterile classes	1 Manufactured goods	1 Manufactured goods	0	2
		5 Real 3 Money	2	2	Row totals / Column totals

tributes nothing; yet he gets two billion francs, which he spends on food and manufactured goods. He gets the surplus productivity. That's why, according to Quesnay, he's the only one who should pay taxes. As you can imagine, the physiocrats weren't resoundingly popular with the landowning nobility.

Another major point of physiocratic doctrine was that government should stay out of the economy. Here is where the physiocrats clashed hard with the mercantilists. The former believed that the latter's emphasis on a favorable balance of trade created by a vigorous manufacturing industry, which required a careful regulation of the economy, was precisely the wrong medicine. The physiocrats insisted that manufacturing was sterile, and, indeed, the largely unmechanized manufacturing of that day could have given that impression. Agriculture instead should be encouraged. To this end, all remnants of feudal trade restrictions and mercantilist control over goods should be abandoned. The famous phrase "laissez faire, laissez passer" was coined at this time and remains, to this day, the motto of those who champion a free and unregulated economy. "Let things be the way they will!"

The physiocrats got a turn at bat in the person of Anne Robert Jacques Turgot, who became the finance minister of France under Louis XVI. Voltaire was so happy about the appointment that he wrote, "We are in the Golden Age up to our necks."[1] However, when Turgot started to institute the reforms that the physiocrats and been preaching, the furor from the vested interests, the nobility, the wealthy bourgeoisie, and even from Marie Antoinette, forced his dismissal. Immediately all his reforms were canceled, not to be introduced again until after the French Revolution. The failure of this first attempt to influence national policy was not a good omen for economic science.

Perhaps it shouldn't surprise us. People are seldom convinced by a purely theoretical argument; they usually want something

---

[1] Quoted in Will Durant, *The Story of Philosophy* (Pocket Books, New York, 1953), p. 246.

more factual. And so does science, which requires not only a theory (more accurately, an hypothesis, before the theory has been tested) but also vigorous and continuous testing of the theory in the real world. The physiocrats never bothered to test their ideas. They didn't make any surveys to see if the quantities of production and consumption in the three classes, farmers, landowners, and manufacturers, checked out with their theory. They didn't try to use the statistical data about trade that had been collected rather meticulously by the mercantilists over the years. Nor did they think of working up new statistical series that might have been more useful for their argument. They didn't even construct case studies, which might have at least given them some ammunition to use against their critics. All these tactics are used by economists and social scientists today. The real world around us is the laboratory in which a hypothesis either passes or fails. But the physiocrats were so sure that their ideas were the natural law, because it just made such good sense to them, that they never thought about supporting their theory statistically.

Actually, much in their theory made good sense. The idea of viewing the economy as an organism is a very practical point of view even today. The concept of a circular flow of money through the economy is standard thinking today. Certainly their idea that freer enterprise, given the existing alternatives, would mean a healthier economy has been proven rather conclusively in the intervening two hundred years. But their concept that manufacturing was sterile and that only land was productive was bound to become unrealistic as soon as the Industrial Revolution hit, and so their plan of a single tax on land surplus and their dividing the economy into only those three classes were bound to become unrealistic also.

ADAM SMITH

In 1776 Adam Smith published *An Inquiry into the Nature and Causes of the Wealth of Nations*. This book, one of the two or three economic tracts in the world that actually changed the course of events in the long run, was an immediate best seller. Like the physiocratic theory, it argued forcefully that the way to a healthy economy was through free enterprise and not through the government intervention of mercantilist policies. As manufacturing became more and more important relative to peasant agriculture, mercantilist policy aimed at keeping workers' wages low and their output high. This was supposed to keep the market for imports small, at the same time keeping the low-priced exports highly competitive. In England, the labor force was poorly paid and hard working anyway. No wonder even businessmen, who didn't need mercantilist protection but were still saddled with the regulations, were enthusiastic in support of Adam Smith's free enterprise thesis.

The poor low-pay-for-hard-work conditions of the English workers had several causes, all of them resulting in more workers looking for jobs than there were good jobs available. First, many destitute Irish peasants were flooding into England. Second, the birth rate was high while the death rate was beginning to fall. Third, both the guild system and the mercantilist regulations that protected the skilled crafts were becoming unenforceable as the "putting-out" system spread through the countryside. The putting-out system is often considered the forerunner of the modern factory. In this system a businessman supplies the raw material, such as wool, to the craftsman at home in his cottage, where he spins and weaves the wool, and the next time the businessman visits the cottage to drop off more raw material, he picks up the finished product.[2]

---

[2] Originally the businessman and the craftsman were equal partners in the system, the businessman selling raw materials to the craftsman and buying the finished product from him at a mark-up. But almost always the businessman proved to be a better manager of affairs. When sickness, drunkenness, or other problems caused the craftsman to break the cycle and fail to weave his cloth satisfactorily, he wasn't able to sell anything. That meant that he wasn't able to buy his next batch of raw materials. So the businessman gave him the raw materials on a loan, accepting the craftsman's tools of his trade, his loom, as collateral. If the craftsman failed to pay off the loan, the businessman ended up owning the loom, and the craftsman became a piece-rate employee on the very loom that was originally his.

The largest part of the supply of low-paid, hard-working labor was created by the enclosures. The growing industrial markets of this era also meant growing markets for agricultural products, wool, and foodstuffs. Since the landowning nobles of England were not socially prohibited from actively participating in money-making ventures, they were, in fact, close siblings of the businessman. To take advantage of the growing markets for agricultural produce, they fenced off, that is, "enclosed," the lands on their manorial holdings, the better to clarify whose land it was and to intensify its use. What had been, at least to some small degree, a communal venture, now became clearly separate enterprises. Even the "common" lands, which had been used by all the peasants on the manor as a supplementary resource— a place for herding swine and geese, gathering wood, foraging for fruits and nuts, and hunting—were fenced off. Many peasants could not make a go of it under these new, stringent conditions. To avoid starvation, they flocked to the cities to hunt for jobs. The entire family—men, women, and children—would look for work. Only that way could they hope to eke out a minimum subsistence. As a result, businessmen were assured of an ample supply of low-cost labor to produce those British goods that were well known and demanded around the world.

So although mercantilism was out of favor with many English businessmen and although it always took for granted a very poor standard of living for the working classes, its final death throes were not over until the early 1800s. From 1776 on, Adam Smith's voice was the single most powerful champion of a new direction in economic policy. This man, who was so influential, was more a quiet scholar than a dashing revolutionary. He lived with his mother almost his entire life, earned his living as a professor of logic and moral philosophy (there were no professors of economics yet) and as a private tutor, gave almost all of the money he made from his best-selling book to charity, and had his papers and manuscripts destroyed after his death in 1790. He was known to be a gracious host and had some famous people as close personal friends, notably David Hume. He also corresponded with the physiocrats Quesnay and Turgot, but his social whirl could hardly be called spicy.

The Primacy of Individual Self-Interest

There is no question that Adam Smith was a brilliant intellectual. His main thesis is the foundation stone for the entire superstructure of modern noncommunist economics: that if people are left to do whatever they want out of their own self-interest, within the bounds of decency and some basic legality, the community will experience the greatest possible health and wealth. In other words, the best way for England to be as wealthy as possible is to have every farm and business in England be as profitable as possible. No guidance from the government or any other central authority is necessary. Get rid of government regulations and restrictions on wages, imports and exports, production codes, and so on, and a flood of productive energy will be unleashed, as everybody takes advantage of the best opportunities available to make themselves better off. And their individual successes will become the nation's success.

For those of us who have lived all our lives in a predominantly free enterprise economy, this idea may seem as natural as the sun and the moon. Yet, it was quite revolutionary in 1776, and it still is in many parts of the world today. But if the record of history is any indication of what is the natural state of affairs for mankind, then certainly free enterprise would have to be considered suspiciously unnatural. Even the mercantilists of the sixteen and seventeen hundreds had been preceded by an almost unbroken record of economic enterprise that was anything but free. There had been a few periods when something close to freedom of economic behavior prevailed, as in the High Middle Ages in Europe from 1000 to 1300, when the towns were bursting into economic activity, or in the various city-states of ancient Mesopotamia and the Eastern Mediterranean from 4500 B.C. to 1200 B.C., but the freedom was neither recognized for what it was nor given any credit for the economic health of the community. The Mesopotamians regarded their successful manufacturing and trade, along with everything else, the result of the whims of their gods. The medieval townsmen, as soon as times got bad, turned to manufacturing regulation and trade restriction, pushing precisely the wrong button to counteract the slipping economy. For the rest of history, be it Egypt, Byzantium, or even the Huang Ho River, kings, gods, elites, or rigid social customs ruled and regulated the economy. Those economies that did thrive, did so in spite of, not because of, the restrictions.

In developing his free enterprise theory, Adam Smith broached the problems that have always been the central issues of philosophy: what is it that makes man act? What is the driving force? What is the reason for history, for faith, for truth? Plato taught that man was a political animal for whom questions of justice and ethics were central. The driving force of devout Christians has been salvation and preparation for the hereafter. To the philosopher Kant, a contemporary of Adam Smith, it was the will to power. To Jeremy Bentham human action was explained as a calculated balancing of pleasure against pain, with the object being to obtain the most pleasure possible over the long run. To Freud it was the sex drive that was the basic motive and the ultimate explanation of human action. With each new philosopher, we get a new theory. Yet, in spite of the different explanations, it is clear that a truly creative scientist needs a well-worked-out philosophic foundation on which to build his theories, which explains why Newton and Einstein are considered philosophers as well as physicists and why the doctoral degree in a variety of sciences, chemistry, biology, mathematics, even economics, is called the *Philosophiae Doctor* or Ph.D.

The philosophical foundation of Smith's economics evolved in his *Theory of Moral Sentiments*, published in 1759. The subtitle, "An Essay towards an Analysis of the Principles by which Men naturally judge concerning the Conduct and Character, first of their Neighbours, and afterwards of themselves," summarizes its contents. According to Smith, everyday life gives a man ample experience to know when other people are treating him well and when they are treating him badly. Therefore, applying this experience to himself, he knows when his own behavior toward others is good or bad. Even though, at times, he may act with passion, some part of his consciousness remains an impartial observer of himself and sits in judgment on whether or not his behavior is virtuous or vicious. In other words, Smith would have assured his contemporary fellow Scot Robert Burns that, as far as our behavior is concerned, yes, indeed, "some Power the giftie gie us to see oursel's as ithers see us." Knowing also that bad behavior brings disfavor with one's fellow man and good behavior brings rewards, a man has to think twice about acting badly. In fact, in the long run, good behavior is the only rational choice. Eventually, it becomes a habit that no longer needs to be thought about, and finally it becomes a moral. In short, "Our continual observations upon the conduct of others, insensibly lead us to form to ourselves certain general rules concerning what is fit and proper to be done or avoided. . . . It is thus the general rules of morality are formed."[3]

At first, students of Adam Smith wondered what the connection was between the rather pious tone of his *Moral Sentiments* and the hardheaded realism of his *Wealth of Nations*. There was even talk of a "Smith problem" caused by what appeared to be a 180 degree switch in philosophical perspective. Indeed, there may have been a change in perspective, but the basic idea in *Moral Sentiments*, that it is to man's self-interest to behave virtuously, is the foundation block of Smith's *Wealth of Nations*. If mankind could devise a morality out of behavior motivated by enlightened self-interest, it would seem a simple deduction that an economic morality could be devised out of economic behavior that is motivated by enlightened self-interest. In both the general case and the specific economic case, there is a harmony of interests between the individual and his society.

Not that Adam Smith overestimated the power of this harmony! For example, he recognized that when men act in groups, they do not feel constrained by morality and are capable of vicious acts. Furthermore, his opinion that the "wretched spirit of greed and monopoly" was intense among the merchant and manufacturing classes (some of whom were still firm mercantilists and wanted to protect their advantageous positions) indicates that he had no illusions about the extent of this harmony in the actual body economic. Still, he argued that indi-

---

[3] Adam Smith, *The Theory of Moral Sentiments* (Creech, Bell, & Bradfute, Edinburgh, 1804), pp. 324 and 325.

vidual self-interest would lead to wealth in a nation, especially if the individuals were decent gentlemen behaving in accordance with accepted morality, if there was effective free competition in the market (no one having monopoly powers), and if none of the individuals sought economic advantage through political means.

A Larger Market and the Division of Labor

The wealth that Smith was talking about was different from the wealth the mercantilists had in mind. For the mercantilists, wealth meant gold, great heaps of bullion stored up in vaults. For Smith, it meant what we now call the standard of living. It meant well-fed and happy people, profitable businesses, productive farms, and active trade. In fact, he believed that getting there was more fun than being there:

> It deserves to be remarked, perhaps, that it is in the progressive state, while the society is advancing to the further acquisition, rather than when it has acquired its full complement of riches, that the condition of the labouring poor, of the great body of the people, seems to be the happiest and the most comfortable. It is hard in the stationary, and miserable in the declining state. The progressive state is in reality the cheerful and the hearty state to all the different orders of the society. The stationary is dull; the declining melancholy.[4]

The first rule for acquiring wealth was to have a division of labor. To prove the point, Smith cited an example from a pin factory, where ten men together can make 48,000 pins a day by dividing the job into separate functions: drawing the wire, straightening the wire, pointing the pins, putting on the head, and so on. They had no power-driven machines (this was before the Industrial Revolution) and worked only with primitive tools. Yet, they were experts at their own specialty. If, instead of dividing the process into many separate functions, they had

---

[4] Adam Smith, *The Wealth of Nations* (George Routledge & Son, London, 1898), Book I, Chapter VIII, p. 63.

all tried to make their own pins from scratch, Smith speculates, they may not even have been able to produce one pin a day per person.

Actually, only the most primitive organisms, one-celled plants and animals, try to survive on the face of the earth without some division of labor, and even they usually represent some form of specialization that, in itself, is an implied division of labor— one kind of primitive cell existing only in warm stagnant farm ponds, another existing only in dead wood, still others existing only in intestinal tracts or nerve fibers. As soon as cells join together to form more complex organisms, division of labor becomes a necessity. Some cells form the rigid structure of the plant or animal, some take care of digestion and assimilation, and some concern themselves with reproduction. Just so, when societies are formed from groups of organisms, be they termites, bees, wolf packs or humans, this division of labor is continued, and the more advanced the society, the more thoroughly the functions have been divided into separate specialities. Thus, as an economy advances, seeking always to derive greater and more efficient production from the resources at its disposal, it too develops subdivisions where once a single function sufficed.

Adam Smith's recognition of the division of labor as the basis for a growing economy was well justified. Today, indeed, it is considered by most people as the first rule for the existence of an economy: the greater the division of labor, the greater the potential and need for trade between the separate organs of the economy, the more efficient the economic process, and the healthier and wealthier it will become. Smith reasoned that anything that would impede the free development of trade, anything that would restrict the size of markets, would work to stifle the growth of the economy. This is precisely what he had against mercantilist policy, which, with its many restrictions on prices and regulations of trade, limited the growth potential of industry. The result was a minimal division of labor and, therefore, a minimal efficiency of the economy. More than a century before mass production began, Smith recognized the basic principle underlying its success.

Applying the same principle of freedom to trade with foreign nations, Smith argued that because their economies were more efficient in supplying goods and more capable of demanding them, rich neighbor nations were preferable to poor ones. We can imagine how aghast the mercantilists were at this idea. They always understood trade and military power to go together, just as their merchantmen and their navies did. A rich neighbor would mean a powerful one, and that would only mean unwelcome competition in the East Indies, Africa, and the Americas, where the merchants were trying to establish trading monopolies. Smith's argument was based on a much more sophisticated perspective (and a much more purely economic one) than that of the mercantilists, and even today there are those who do not agree with it. There are still people who feel that everyone else's gain is their loss, who feel that the more profits somebody else is making, the more they are being cheated, who believe that the process of economic exchange is like a football game—one side wins, the other loses. They fail to comprehend that trade makes both parties winners, and if this weren't the case, the loser or prospective loser would certainly not agree to the exchange.

In summary, Smith's system would have everyone free to seek his own economic fortune. Natural self-interest and man's "propensity to truck, barter, and exchange" would see to it that everyone took advantage of his best opportunities. Of course, decency and legitimacy had to be maintained. No special advantages would be given to any one group or person, and a policy of governmental nonintervention in the economy and the maintenance of free and open competition would assure this. The result would be the enlargement of production and markets, increased efficiency, and, as if guided by an "invisible hand," optimum economic growth and wealth. Smith's voice still rings clear to us today.

CHAPTER 4

The Age of
Revolution: 1750-1850

Actually, the revolutions begun in this century of dramatic change 1750–1850 are still going on today. But after one hundred years these revolutions are hardly news so that the next centuries are generally called something else, such as the Iron Age (about 1850–1950) and the Nuclear Age (1950 to the present), or, less universally, the Railroad Age or the Space Age. As we look at this century-long age of revolution, however, let us keep in mind that what is most important about it is what it started, rather than what it accomplished, although it also accomplished a great deal.

To most historians, the century means political revolution, the rising up of the masses of common people against the aristocracies, the assertion of every man's civil equality with every other man. The names Jefferson, Robespierre, Washington, and

Napoleon stand out, and the central events are the American revolutionary war, begun in 1776, and the French one, begun in 1789. But to most economists, the century means a change in the way mankind earned its living on the face of this earth, from simple hand labor and muscle power to gigantic machines and burning fuels. The names Watt, Arkwright, and Whitney seem the most important, and the central event is the Industrial Revolution. Medical scientists speak of a medical revolution; Jenner, Pasteur, and Lister are their heroes, and the smallpox vaccine and antisepsis are their victories. But then there are also the agricultural revolution, which made a population revolution possible, the communications revolution, which began with Gutenberg's invention of movable type in 1436, the transportation revolution, which began in the 1400s with better ships and navigation, and the financial revolution, which reorganized industry and commerce. It was also a century of revolutionary romanticism in the arts and the period when the British empire was established.

Scratch a specialist, and he will tell you of another special revolution. Each revolution, like so many theories and hypotheses, is true in its own way but gives the picture from only one point of view. Just as we need to look at a lot of snapshots in the family album to get a good idea of what a family looks like, to understand fully any one of the revolutions, we need to know what went on in the others.

THE AGRICULTURAL REVOLUTION

In a way the physiocrats would have approved, let's begin with the agricultural revolution. Since civilization overflowed the fertile river valleys and the regularly watered monsoon lands, it has been necessary to rotate land usage between crops and fallow years. We have seen that in the Mediterranean climates in the Greco-Roman world, the pattern was usually one year of crops and one year of fallow on each parcel of land, but that during the High Middle Ages in the wetter non-Mediterranean parts of Europe, a three-year rotation involving two years of crops and one fallow year was introduced. Its use didn't spread very far at that time, but it did serve as an instrument to introduce new crops, especially root crops that could be weeded, thus preparing the field for a grain crop the following year. (Before planting grains, it is important that the field be free of weed seeds since one cannot get into a field of wheat or oats to weed it. The weeding had been achieved by plowing the field repeatedly during the fallow year, killing all the weeds before they could come to seed.)

The Enclosures Acts in England during the 1700s were the key to the agricultural revolution. Not only did they force superfluous agricultural labor into the cities, as we have seen, but the same enclosures that fenced off the land also fenced the animals in, which turned out to be a great advantage. Soil restorative crops, like the legumes clover and alfalfa, were planted during the fallow year, enabling both a three-year root crop-grain-clover cycle, which kept the land producing all the time, and the production of storage food for feeding the animals throughout the winter. (Previously animals often had to be slaughtered and talted for preservation in the fall.) Before the enclosures, farm animals not used for draft had to be herded and, therefore, had so be relatively small and manageable. Selective breeding was impossible, and the animal manure distribution was a random procedure at best. The enclosures made manure management not only possible but necessary since the animals were fenced in, but, more important, it made selective breeding, feed management, and the control of larger animals possible. These changes in field and livestock administration constituted a thorough reorganization of agriculture, and the results were astounding. Food production multiplied geometrically, and from 1750 to 1850 the average animal weights in English slaughterhouses tripled.

What was the spark that ignited this agricultural revolution? We have seen how the English aristocracy, unlike the Continental, had an eye for commerce and trade. They mixed easily with the merchantmen in London, and this must have carried over to their country cousins, who also found it easier to let business intrude upon their traditional manorial life. Furthermore, this was the Age of Enlightenment. Science was not only a new concern of the universities and of the scientists themselves; it was practically a fad. Almost all literate Englishmen were enthusiastic about the marvelous new discoveries and inventions, even to the point of foolishness in all kinds of crazy scientific schemes. Not a month would go by before another scientist would apply for a patent on a perpetual motion machine. Magazines on physical science, nature, geography, mechanics, and similar topics were very popular among the class of men who could read and pay for subscriptions. Whereas the enlightenment in France had an urbane and philosophic hue and in Germany it tended to nurture poets and theoreticians, in England it took on a more practical manifestation, like Boulton and Watt's steam engines and the improvement of farm lands. (In the American colonies, the enlightenment achieved its most stubbornly nontheoretical extreme in the Yankee tinkerers.) Furthermore, innovations in agriculture, industry, and commerce could easily be adopted in England where the power of the guilds had been broken to a great extent and where the parliament so often identified with the new entrepreneurs. In France, where the innovations had to be sanctioned by the crown, entrepreneurs usually got bogged down in the notorious French red tape. In Germany, where the guilds persisted in the towns, the blueprints for new processes were, as often as not, ceremoniously burned to ashes in the town square.

THE POPULATION REVOLUTION

The Growing Cities

The increased agricultural production in England was the prerequisite for the growth of the cities, which was about the only place the peasants could go when the Enclosure Acts drove them off the farms. City life held the promise of adventure, progress, participation in a new age, and, most important, it held the promise of employment. Many of the newcomers had been driven from their rural homes by the new sheep ranching started with the enclosures, which was an integral part of the growing textile industry and which thrived profitably on the infertile lands of northern England, Scotland, and Ireland, where living had been traditionally harsh and the lords exceptionally cruel anyway. But the city also lured those who came from better lands and for whom the old pastoral "merrie England" had provided a more pleasant life than they were likely to find in the raw new cities. In addition to the peasants moving into the cities, there were also the dispossessed cottage industry craftsmen who had lost their trade to the putting-out merchants and had to congregate as piece-rate workers in the new factories, which would soon be mechanized. The migration was probably not a happy event for them. Still, the cities were a great attraction, and, whether out of necessity or out of preference, or both, the people flooded in.

Factory employment grew rapidly in the cities. But, as so often happens in economic history, the cause of the one phenomenon is not directly linked to the cause of the other, even though they are mutually reinforcing; the increasing job opportunities were not coordinated with the increasing number of urban workers. At times, potential jobs went unfilled; at other times, a great many workers were unemployed. Removed from the security of their country parishes, the unemployed roamed the cities, starving or subsisting on charity or thievery.

This urbanization was the beginning of a new trend that has still not run its full course, that is, the turning upside down of the rural-urban population ratio. Since the beginning of agriculture, it took about nine people on the farm to support one in the city. This was so in Mesopotamia, in Egypt, in Rome, and in London before the agricultural revolution. In the economically developed nations today, one farmer feeds as many as twenty or more city dwellers, although this ratio may turn out to be inachievable worldwide in the long run. The Enclosure Acts and the more rational farming techniques of the late 1700s were just the beginning. Labor-saving mechanization, fertilizers and insecticides, and the application of genetics to breeding were to accelerate forcefully farm productivity and the urbanization process a century later.

Some Dynamics of Population Growth

Of course, city growth at this time was due to endogenous population increase as well as migration. The history of the human race up to now has been a history of population growth over the long run. People always were naturally interested in increasing their numbers, perhaps because the human animal believes that large numbers bring security and power; perhaps there is also the simple joy of a big family, tribe, or gang that appeals strongly to the herd instinct of homo sapiens. Whatever the reason, a growing population is the expression, for the aggregate of mankind, of the individual's profound life drive, the will to sustain himself. What self-sustenance is to the individual, population sustenance (and growth) is to the race. (Social scientists often consider this coincidence between aggregate and individual behavior important because when the patterns of the whole and its parts concur in this way, the "Principle of Consistency" is satisfied. This, of course, doesn't prove anything, but it does lend credibility to our observations and leads us to hope that the generalizations deduced therefrom will hold up.)

Throughout history there have been other times when food was abundant, opportunities for earning a living were plentiful, diseases were relatively quiescent, and the population grew rapidly. But there were also times of wars, epidemics, and famines, when the population declined rapidly. Generally, until the early 1700s, the population increased slowly, based on a high birth rate (around 40 births per 1000 people per year) and an almost as high mortality. On the average, only about half the population reached adulthood, which, by the way, represents not only one of the least happy facts of life in the centuries preceding the population revolution but also the biggest single waste of economic resources. Half of humanity was nourished, loved and cared for, and perhaps even educated to some degree but did not become either economically productive or reproductive of its own kind.

Why the population began to increase in Europe, first gradually in the 1600s and then more rapidly in the revolutionary century from 1750 on, has been the subject of recent controversy. Most likely we can explain this upswing simply as the result of the increased "carrying capacity" of the economy. As in the golden ages before, population increases accompanied increased food production, more opportunities for earning a living in the growing trades and industries, and improvements in the social, political, and cultural life that are part of any golden age. So by the 1700s, sensing themselves to be better off, the people began to marry younger and to have more children, thus pushing up the birth rate. But even more important, more of the children survived than before, and the death rate began to decline.

In the decade from 1730 to 1740, deaths in England are estimated at nearly 36 per 1000 per year. By 1811–1821, they had fallen to about 21 per 1000 per year. The effect of such a decline tends to be geometric because it means that more people survive to the reproductive age, thus greatly increasing the population's growth potential. As we have seen, it also means that less humanity is wasted in the grim process of dying before adulthood is reached. Certainly this declining death rate, with its concomitant increase in the efficient use of human resources, is one of the most important clues to understanding the expansion of Western civilization.

The falling death rate in Europe cannot be traced simply to one cause. However, the increasing urbanization of the population played an important role. City construction included sewers and water systems; city ordinances eventually imposed some sort of management over garbage disposal. Access to cheap soap and the increasing use of cotton underwear, which is easier to wash and harbors lice and other parasites less readily than wool, were important health factors. Improved transportation alleviated local famines. The increased food supply often meant a better nourished as well as a larger population.

Also, fewer epidemics raged across this part of the world than in centuries before, but the reasons for their decline were different for each disease. The black rat that harbors the bubonic-plague-carrying louse seemed to become less prevalent in the cities, perhaps because of the improved garbage management and the enclosed sewers. Perhaps the brown rat, which came from the East around 1700, pushed out the black one; diseases spread less rapidly over the countryside through the brown rat because he is more of a homebody, sticking closer to his nest than the carousing black rat, and his lice don't seem to carry the bubonic plague at all. Furthermore, the population may have built up significant immunity to various diseases. This was the case with syphilis, which the Europeans may have first caught from the returning conquistadors, who got it from the native Central and South Americans in the 1500s.[1] At first, the victims of syphilis died an atrocious death, their bodies covered with horrid sores. But by the 1700s, the disease seemed to cause only a rash and a few sores, which ultimately disappeared. When the contractors of the disease died ten or twenty years later from the advanced destruction of their nervous systems, blood vessels, or other organs caused by the silent work of the syphilis spirochete, they usually didn't connect the events. To be sure, plague, typhoid, typhus, smallpox, tuberculosis, dynsentery, cholera, encephalitis, malaria, scarlet fever, diphtheria, and leprosy were still active causes of misery and grief, but they gradually took less and less of a toll on the population.

Medicine's Contribution

Medicine must take part of the credit for the declining death rate, although, until the late 1800s and even the early 1900s, it was still quite medieval and had less effect than one would gather from the list of medical discoveries that were made in this period of scientific enlightenment. The practice of medicine was still more an art or a "mystery" than a science-based profession, and with the rather total ignorance of hygiene, pathol-

---

[1] The conquistadors held up their part of the bargain generously by giving the Indians smallpox, scarlet fever, meningitis, and, worst of all for the Indians, measles. It was these diseases—more than the handful of Spanish warriors— that wiped out the highly cultured Aztec kingdom, forcing the survivors to flee into the mountains and jungles.

ogy, anatomy, physiology or even of the existence of bacteria, cells, and blood circulation, it was long a subject of irrational fads and fashions. In his ribald play *Le Malade imaginaire* (1673) Molière had poked fun at the excesses of these fads, but the way patients were regularly dying because of primitive medicines, clysters, and bloodletting was certainly no joking matter. It was even worse in the hospitals, which were often crowded mainly with the poor and which, because there was absolutely no knowledge of sanitation, were cesspools of disease and death. Postoperative fevers and puerperal fever regularly caused eight of ten hospital deaths.

Against this overwhelming state of ignorance, the new breed of medical scientist had very little effect. Andreas Vesalius (1514–1564), breaking the social taboo against dissecting a human corpse, published a monumental work on anatomy, which was rejected by the practicing doctors. The vaccination against smallpox, first given by Edward Jenner in 1796, did gain some popularity among the wealthier classes but didn't contribute significantly to an improvement in the health of the population. The discovery by James Lind, (1716–1794) the Scottish naval surgeon, that the juice of lemons and oranges prevented scurvy did rid the British navy of that disease after 1795 when ships on long voyages were required to stock lime juice—hence the name "limeys" for British sailors. But the work in bacteriology by Louis Pasteur (1822–1895) and in antisepsis by Joseph Lister (1827–1912) did not have much effect on medical practices during the revolutionary century of 1750–1850. But the groundwork for scientific medicine was being laid, and medicine in the twentieth century was to become one of the most important contributors to human happiness and well-being in history.

The Pattern of Population Growth

Whatever the causes, the population in Europe (including Great Britain and the Scandinavian countries), the United States, and Canada grew more rapidly than ever before during this revolutionary century (see Table 3). The population growth patterns for Europe shown in Figure 2 are recognized as standard and have been repeated in other parts of the world. The pattern may begin with (*top*) a small increase in an already high birth rate, but it really gets moving with a substantial lowering of the death rate. This disparity between the high birth rate and low death rate causes a rapid population increase (*middle and bottom*), resulting from the increased reproductive and economic efficiency inherent in having a larger proportion of the population survive into adulthood.

Table 3. Growth of world population

YEAR	APPROXIMATE WORLD POPULATION	APPROXIMATE POPULATION OF EUROPE, UNITED STATES, AND CANADA AS A PERCENTAGE OF THE WORLD POPULATION
8000 B.C.	10,000,000	–
1 A.D.	250,000,000	–
700	300,000,000	9.0*
1650	545,000,000	18.5
1750	728,000,000	19.3
1850	1,171,000,000	25.0
1900	1,608,000,000	30.0
1950	2,509,000,000	28.1
1960	3,002,000,000	26.2
1970	3,607,000,000	20.6

Source: Demographic Yearbooks (United Nations, New York, 1967), and estimates from U.N. Statistical Office, June 1970.
* Europe only.

Interestingly, the populations in Europe and America that have experienced more than two centuries of increase have also experienced a lowering of their birth rates, especially during the twentieth century. Should the birth rates ever closely match the death rates, at these new lower levels, the populations would

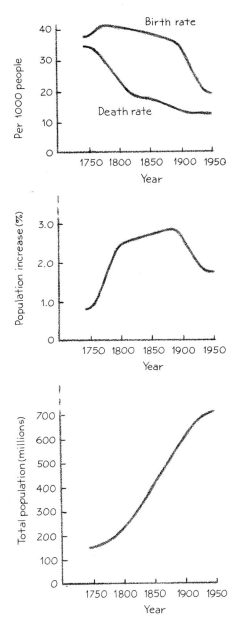

Figure 2. Typical population growth patterns for Europe. *Top:* Approximate birth and death rates per 1000 people per year; *middle:* approximate rate of population increase in percentage per year; *bottom:* approximate total population in millions. (Adapted from a report by Political and Economic Planning, *World Population and Resources*, Allen & Unwin, London, 1955, p. 10.)

once again become more stable. Since Europe and America started on the population increase pattern first, their proportion of the total world population grew from less than 10 percent to about 30 percent by 1900. By then, the other populations of the world were beginning their own growth. If the present growth rate of the world population continues, there will be over 6 billion people to be fed, clothed, housed, entertained, and tolerated by the year 2000.

THE COMMUNICATIONS REVOLUTION

As we have already mentioned, with the increase in population caused mainly by a lowering of the death rate, an enormous improvement in the economic efficiency of the population was achieved. The people lived longer and served many more years as productive adults. Furthermore, the greater longevity of the population fueled the fires of the growth of knowledge that had received their first spark with the enlightenment. The enthusiasm of the upper classes in Great Britain for the new agricultural science, mechanics and technology, and "natural philosophy" spread rapidly to the whole population, especially where the public schools were as good as those in Scotland. Everywhere on continental Europe, Scottish mechanics, inventors, and scientists were sought in order to help develop industries that were striving to imitate the technological progress of the British.

The qualitative improvement of the population would have been impossible without a massive increase in literacy, and this wouldn't have been possible without a technological breakthrough that had happened several centuries earlier, namely, the invention of printing. Because Western languages are written in alphabetic form, they are easily adaptable to some kind of printing or letter stamping reproduction, and so it is not surprising that there was a history of experimentation along these lines. Indeed, wooden type screw presses, involved in a process called xylography, were used in Limoges and Antwerp by 1381 and 1417, respectively. But not until 1454 in Mainz, when Johann Gutenberg first used movable metal type, did the printing process become successful. By this time, cheap paper, manufactured in mills that pounded out the necessary pulp with water-wheel-run trip hammers, was plentiful, as were the necessary oil-based inks.

The demand for printed matter developed quickly. At first, the Protestant revolt and the counterreformation provided a good market for religious tracts, and later the publication requirements of the increasingly democratic politics, the developing sciences, the burgeoning commerce and industry, and the increasingly literate masses kept the presses humming. In the 1500s, tens of thousands of books a year had been printed, but in the 1700s and 1800s, when the screw press was being replaced by the more rapid mechanical lever press, that many books could be printed in a month. The process was further accelerated by the cylindrical press introduced in London in 1812. It made possible the penny newspapers, which attained massive circulation, and, at the same time, made an important industry out of advertising.

The communications revolution was now at full blast. Delivering the mail, which had been the business of a few private express companies, became the function of national agencies. The volume of letters carried per year in France, for example, increased from 4,000,000 in 1830 to 358,000,000 in 1869, only thirty-nine years later. The telegraph, generally credited as the invention of Samuel Morse in 1844, was widely used only a decade later, especially by the railroads. In 1868 the typewriter was improved to the point of being quite useful. And in 1876 Alexander Graham Bell introduced the world to his boon and bane, the telephone.

From these beginnings, communications have taken a rapidly increasing proportion of mankind's interest and energies. New media, such as radio, movies, and television, were introduced, and all the media have continually improved and grown in importance (with the exception of the telegraph, whose few improvements have not prevented it from falling behind into obsolescence). Many diverse industries have grown out of the basic communications industries: electronics, pulp wood, Hollywood, and public relations, to name a few. Colleges and universities are designing new communication science curricula. Social critics and philosophers find great sport in examining all the nooks and crannies of the communication phenomenon. Marshall McLuhan, for example, has analyzed the evolution of communication from simple characters, words, and sentences— which give us only a visual message—to the present expansion of communication to both a visual and aural message—through the medium of television. He believes that the form of the written message determined our way of thinking and our social organization, perhaps even our whole way of life and that the new media of communication have been and will continue to affect our present and future thinking and life style in very new and, perhaps, even revolutionary ways.[2]

There has been another more important spin-off from this communications revolution. Printing is indeed the mechanical production of writing, but it does not mechanically *reproduce* the writing process. Rather, with the stamping of whole pages at a time instead of drawing them letter by letter, communications was taken in an entirely new direction. Photo-offset printing and the Xerox machine are its latest forms. It is surprising that this initial mass production technique, printing, is such a sophisticated and imaginative departure from manual techniques. Many later mechanical inventions, for example, most of the textile working machines, were simply mechanized versions of the original hand process. As such, they were not nearly as revolutionary technologically as the printing press, although they were enormously important to the Industrial Revolution.

Today the mechanics of mass production seem more often a printing type of operation than a "mechanical fingers" operation that reproduces the processes of hand labor. The use of mechanical dies to stamp out numerous identical and interchangeable parts is a central concept in modern production technology. In that sense, our cars and refrigerators are "printed," printed on steel instead of paper, and the phenomenal efficiency of modern

---

[2] Marshall McLuhan, *Understanding Media: The Extensions of Man* (McGraw-Hill, New York, 1965).

industry owes much to the technological breakthrough achieved by the early printers five centuries ago.

Still, the most important contribution of the communications revolution has really been the improvement in the quality of life for the whole population, that is, its educational effect, resulting in vastly increased efficiency in human affairs. No longer is it necessary for a person to be present, both in time or place, for communication to occur. Interpersonal communication via mail, telegraph, or telephone can proceed very much faster and at a greatly reduced cost than the persons themselves could achieve if they had to travel toward each other to establish face-to-face contact. And public communication via newspapers or broadcast, in spite of all the jokes about the speed with which rumors travel, could not possibly be matched by face-to-face contact as a distribution system. Of equal importance, many of the mass media are highly efficient means of information storage and record keeping. The use of libraries and the keeping of business records originated with the first civilizations in Mesopotamia, but the new technology of the communications revolution gave it an entirely new mass dimension. Indeed, the accumulation and storage of information is still easier today than its retrieval: we have good printing presses, but no reading machine has yet been invented!

THE TRANSPORTATION REVOLUTION

Highways and Carriages

Perhaps less dramatic but just as important, transportation also underwent a revolution in the century from 1750 to 1850. The great global explorations of the early 1500s and the commercial revolution of the 1600s and 1700s had been based on technological breakthroughs in navigation and shipbuilding, but travel on land had been unchanged for centuries. The best roads were still the few ancient highways built by the Romans, whose carriages were heavy and slow. The dangers from highwaymen and the exploitive tariffs and tolls even exceeded the difficulties caused by the poor roads. But when, largely because of the efforts of the mercantilists, the security of the roads and the freedom from exploitive customs were assured, it became obvious that the poor condition of the roads was one of the major remaining impediments to commerce.

The standard first-class road, the highway, was still built of cobblestones or large rock slabs, just as the Roman roads had been. These were expensive to build and difficult to repair, although they were very durable. A cheaper kind of road construction was sought, however, and roads made of gravel—first a layer of coarse gravel, then smaller gravel, and finally very small gravel or even clay on the surface—were found to be very useful. The roads were raised in the middle so that rain water could run off, and ditches were dug along either side so that they would remain reasonably dry. This kind of road construction was developed simultaneously in several places, but the Scotsman John McAdam (1756–1836) is usually credited with this new type of road. The macadam type of construction, with a few improvements, such as a hard surface of asphalt or concrete, is used for almost all kinds of roads today, from country lanes to superhighways.

With better roads, better vehicles could also be developed. Carriages, which used to be of an all-purpose design, now became specialized. Surreys, buckboards, berlines, phaetons, gigs, and broughams crowded the streets and highways as never before. Generally, they were more carefully built than the older carriages, lighter yet stronger. The suspension systems made use of new eliptical springs; the windows were often covered with plate glass instead of just curtains; and a remarkable concern for elegance crept into the styling. Some technological improvements helped set the stage for the motorized vehicles that were soon to follow, like the just-mentioned precision craftsmanship in carriage building, the new suspension systems, and also the first use of grease cups to lubricate the axles. Some carriage builders, like H. and C. Studebaker of South Bend, Indiana, would utilize this technology in the automobile industry.

But perhaps the most important contribution of this first stage of the transportation revolution was the preparation it gave society for the very drastic changes to come: railroads, automobiles, ocean liners, and airplanes. The better and cheaper roads and the improved carriages had democratized transportation. Travel was no longer the privilege of the rich or a function left exclusively to teamsters and liverymen. It became a source of convenience, efficiency, and pleasure for the masses, providing a sense of geographical freedom that is still considered extremely important today. (Ask any young adult. He will tell you that getting his driver's license was a far more important event than being confirmed in his church or becoming old enough to vote.)

Canals

The building of canals was another development of the transportation revolution, especially in England and then in the United States. Rivers were made more navigable; locks were built; and canals were strung between these inland waterway systems. The first canal in the United States was built in 1794 in South Hadley, Massachusetts, on the Connecticut River. It was soon followed by the more famous Middlesex Canal in 1804 and the Erie Canal in 1825. For the movement of heavy bulk goods, water transport is by far the most efficient, and some economists argue that the United States would have a more efficient economy today if canal building (and, presumably, canal technology) had continued to the present. But canal transport is slow even in the summer, and in the winter, when the water freezes, it doesn't move at all. Although time is money, this slowness may not have prevented canals from being the most efficient transport for a great variety of goods in the 1800s or even now, but businessmen are often victims of a certain amount of irrational impatience. Speed has a tendency to be reassuring; it becomes an end in itself. And the railroads, by the latter half of the nineteenth century, put an end to most inland canal building. Of course, the important connecting canals for ocean shipping, such as the Suez, Panama, Kiel, and Corinth canals, and, most recently, the St. Lawrence Seaway, were still to be built.

Railroads

But it was the "Rocket" that became the crowning glory of this first century of the transportation revolution. The Rocket was a steam locomotive built by George Stephenson that ran between Manchester and Liverpool in 1829 at the fantastic speed of 31 miles per hour. From that point on, there was a steady stream of technological improvements: in the locomotives, the couplings of cars, the roadbed under the rails, the rails themselves—which were changed from cast iron to steel—the construction of bridges, and brake mechanisms, to name a few. George Westinghouse perfected his vacuum air brake in 1868, and the standardization of the track gauge led to the establishment of the railroad as the prime mover of the Industrial Revolution. The first railroad lines were built to provide a means of hauling coal within mine compounds. But soon lines were built to connect the mines with the markets, and gradually others were built that were emancipated from the coal mines entirely, such as those built in the 1830s connecting Paris to its suburbs St. Germain-en-Laye and Versailles.

In England and the United States, the railroad lines were built wherever businessmen put them, and a hit-or-miss pattern full of duplication and inadequacy tended to develop. In Europe, an effort was made to plan more carefully. Friedrich List (1789–1846), one of the first great German economists, designed a railroad system that was intended to help overcome the economic backwardness of some of the more provincial states of Germany. Goethe, that ultimate source of quotations for German literati, had alluded to the coming of the railroad when he said that there was no doubt of Germany's eventual political unification; "iron ribbons," he wrote, would soon tie the nation together. In Austria, a sixty-mile stretch from Vienna to Bochnia that began operation on July 7, 1839, was given the auspicious title of "Kaiser Ferdinand Nordbahn," to lend a sense of national grandeur to the project. It was a clever public relations touch by Solomon Rothschild, who, like many other financiers, expected to make a fortune out of railroads and actually did.

Despite the fact that railroads grew at a fantastic rate, they were not universally welcome. Society has always been chary about innovations, and the railroads, with their thundering locomotives, belching steam, sparks, and soot, blowing their whistles, and roaring through the once peaceful countryside at unheard-of speeds, gave many a brave citizen second thoughts. Even before the age of ecology, medical authorities worried about what the speed might do to people's sanity and what the damp air in the tunnels would to to their lungs; moralists worried about possible sex orgies on the trains caused by the excitement of the speed and noise; military men worried that riding trains would weaken their soldiers; more realistically, farmers complained that the trains scared their livestock half to death, and some counties in England insisted that a postilion ride fifty paces ahead of the locomotive to warn the local inhabitants with trumpet blasts of the approaching abomination.

Less than a century later the automobile would cause a similar reaction. But the "tin lizzie" eventually caught the people's imagination and endeared itself to them. Cars could be fun, and, besides, one could own a car himself, even if he had just an average income. But railroads were owned only by the very rich, and they had their biggest impact on business, industry, and the economy. They were not directly as strong a democratizing influence as the automobile. Still, the Duke of Wellington grumbled that railroads did tend to debase the aristocratic gentility of English life because they "will only encourage the lower classes to move about needlessly."[3]

THE FINANCIAL REVOLUTION

Business Organization

The means for obtaining a living are not only those that originate from man's relationships with his external environment;

---

[3] Frederic Morton, *The Rothschilds* (Fawcett World Library, New York, 1963), p. 98.

they are also derived from his relationships with his fellow man. We have seen, in discussing the theories of Adam Smith, that increased production is accompanied by an increasing division of labor. The ways in which labor is organized in productive institutions change as the complexity of the processes increases. At first, the family and the tribe were adequate for the basic economic activities of farming and hunting. But with the beginning of trade and the development of cities, the establishment of business organizations became a necessity. These firms were, at first, simply extensions of the family organization, what today we would call proprietorships. The businessman or proprietor, then as now, be he a craftsman or some sort of merchant, owned his own tools and shop, made his own decisions, kept all the profits for himself and his family, and suffered any losses that occurred. Indeed, the proprietorship and the family farm are different only in that one is thought of as a manufacturing or trading business while the other is thought of as the business of growing crops.

However, as economic aspirations became more grand, one family was no longer an adequate organizational base. The problem usually was that one man alone (one family alone) was not able to amass all the tools necessary for the larger business undertakings. For instance, the medieval merchant did not have enough time and energy by himself to build, nor enough money to buy, a sea-worthy sailing vessel to run the spice trade to the Orient. So the partnership, which is a proprietorship for two or more men, was born. In its modern form, the partnership is a legally established business in which the relative shares of the partners in the ownership and the profits or losses of the business are carefully delineated. If one of the partners dies or is otherwise seriously incapacitated, the partnership is dissolved.

But even the partnership was unable to take full advantage of all the new opportunities of the time, and businessmen searched for something better. We have seen that in the High Middle Ages the development of double-entry bookkeeping, with its attendant change in accounting perspective—from the proprietor or partners themselves to the business itself—made it possible to account for the size of the business's assets. Thus, the business owners could determine their share of the assets, as well as their proportion of its profits or losses. This new accounting arrangement made possible the joint stock company, an organization in which usually more than two or three businessmen take part, because a record could be kept of what was happening to the original investment in the business. At first, like the proprietorship and the partnership, the joint stock company did not protect the investor against losses larger than his original investment. The result was that no matter how tempting it was, a businessman did not want to join in a new venture if he was liable to lose not only what he put into it, but also part or all of his family's fortune, should the business incur debts larger than its total assets.

To get around this problem, the concept of limited liability ownership was created. This was the final step in separating a business from a man's personal or family fortune. Under limited liability, a participating investor could lose only what he had originally invested; his personal property, house, and landholdings remained unattachable. On the Continent, especially in France, this institutional innovation was built into the partnership structure. "Sleeping partners," that is, investors who did not participate in the managerial process of the business and who were not held personally responsible for it, were given a legal limited liability status. In England, limited liability was eventually built into the joint stock company structure, freeing shareholders of the firm from any personal liability at all. In the United States, the word "corporation" (or "incorporated") is used instead of the British "limited," both terms meaning limited liability.

Whatever the name, the effect was to liberate the flow of investment from many people into the sizable accumulations necessary to take advantage of the new business areas that were opening up through trade with the newly developed colonies and trading outposts of the commercial revolution. After the "South Sea Bubble"[4] of 1720 and other similar experiences with

---

[4] An overoptimistic business outlook, together with a mass hysteria at speculation, drove the price of the stock of the South Sea Company up from 126 pounds in late 1719 to 1050 pounds in mid-1720. In September 1720, the euphoric bubble burst and the market crashed, causing great financial loss to the company's numerous investors.

investments in nonexistent business ventures, the joint stock company fell into disrepute as a form of business organization. In many places it became legally restricted. But when the textile mills, the iron foundries and steel mills, the railroads, and the other great opportunities of the Industrial Revolution presented themselves a century later, the limited liability joint stock company, incorporated as a separate legal entity (corpus), was recognized as the only organizational structure that would allow large enough amounts of money to be amassed to get these new businesses off the ground. The legal restraints were gradually removed during the early 1800s, and a flood of new limited liability joint stock companies and corporations were registered as legal entities.

To facilitate further the flow of investment funds into the corporations, markets were established where ownership shares, or stocks, could be bought and sold. These markets were very informal affairs at first but became more and more institutionalized as their function became more important. For instance, in London the stock exchange was founded in Jonathan's Coffee House in the early 1700s. By 1773 it had come up in the world sufficiently to meet in a coffee house named after itself, the Stock Exchange Coffee House. In 1802, the business of the market had become so important that there was no time left for coffee, and the home of the market was moved into a building quite matter-of-factly called the Stock Exchange. In New York, there wasn't enough business in stocks to organize a formal exchange until 1792, when twenty-four professional stockbrokers agreed on the commissions they would charge their clients for the trading they did when they met in the shade of a buttonwood tree along Wall Street, which was their marketplace. Two years later, business was good enough for them to move indoors.

Growing insurance companies also served as the means for channeling dispersed sources of capital into the new investment opportunities. Insurance of commercial ventures, of ships and cargoes, and of the lives of the ship captains had been common practice since the High Middle Ages. The Industrial Revolution, however, encouraged the purchase of insurance throughout the entire economy and society. The new mechanized industries that were developing between 1750 and 1850 were so large that a few good friends could no longer bail out a businessman whose plant burned down or who experienced some other misfortune. Dealing with risk had to be on a much larger scale and much more dependable. Furthermore, the old family, parish, and community ties that a person could depend on to keep body and soul together when he was down and out were rapidly disappearing as industrialization and other revolutionary forces were wrenching society out of its accustomed patterns. The answer was a rational and institutionalized insurance, a contractual agreement that, in exchange for the payment of an annual fee, a specified sum of money would be paid to an injured business or person in the event of any clearly delineated misfortune.

English and Scottish private insurance companies led the way, the first of these beginning operation in 1762. Other Western nations soon followed. In the 1880s, under Bismarck, Germany established government-operated insurance plans for the working classes that included sickness and industrial accident insurance and a limited form of what is today called social security. Not only did these insurance operations make life more secure and the establishment of big businesses, especially risky ones, possible, but the accumulated annual fees, the premiums, for this insurance made a sizable contribution to the supply of investment funds: insurance firms invested most of this premium money in stocks and bonds, in loans to new or expanding businesses, or for the purchase of real estate.

Banking, Money, and Gold

Another institution that played a major role in the financial revolution was the bank. Something like banks—and certainly the idea of extending credit—had existed wherever trade had flourished since the beginning of civilization. But with the gradually increasing use of money in the High Middle Ages, with the spread of mercantilism, and now in this period of industrial revolution, the banking function became more formalized and institutionalized. The first modern banking houses in Europe were often managed by rich merchants themselves. Banking was a natural adjunct to their trading business. They received deposits of gold and silver in their vaults as payments for goods that they sold, but they also received deposits simply for safekeeping. In exchange for the gold and silver they guarded, they issued vault receipts redeemable in the specified amount of the precious metals. The services of other secure vaults, typically provided by goldsmiths, silversmiths, and royal exchequers, were also used in the same way.

Because vault receipts were more convenient to carry around and use in buying and selling, they soon began to circulate as money. The more the receipts circulated and the less they were redeemed, the safer it was for the merchant's banking house, the goldsmith, silversmith, or the royal exchequer to print and issue more vault receipts than there was actually precious metal in the vault. These extra receipts were usually circulated by the vault-owner banker in the form of interest-earning loans and investments made to businessmen and the nobility who needed to borrow funds. This practice of keeping only partial reserves of gold and silver in the vault against the vault receipts in circulation was and is the reason why banks are a profitable business. Their profits come from interest earned on loans and investments. It is also the reason why they occasionally go bankrupt, because, obviously, the system works only as long as not everyone tries at once to redeem his vault receipts, that is, his paper money, in gold or silver.

The same caveat applied to currency issued by other agencies. Kings and national governments often minted full-valued coins out of gold and small denomination coins out of other metals. They also issued paper money in payment for government debts, money that was usually intended to have a limited life because it was expected to be redeemed in the foreseeable future for gold or silver. This paper money also circulated among the general public but usually at a lower value than its actual worth (a discount from the face value), and the weaker the king or the national government, the weaker the value of the paper money and the larger the discount. Human nature being what it is, even for kings and national governments, the tendency was always to issue more paper money than there was gold or silver to redeem it. Even the supposedly full-valued coins sometimes circulated at discounts because the kings or national governments would occasionally try to make their money supply stretch a little further by melting down the coins as they received them and reminting them, adding more of a cheap metal alloy in the process.[5] All of these tricks, whether with paper money or with debased coinage, tended to expand the money supply faster than the supply of goods to be bought, and the history of all the monies ever issued is overwhelmingly one of price inflation, to the point that the monetary unit is just about worthless and goes into oblivion—and often with it the government that over-issued it.

Such experiences have perpetuated mankind's faith in pure gold, at times even to the point of superstition. Not even silver has been considered a completely adequate substitute for gold, perhaps because it became more abundant or because it has so many nonmonetary uses. Times of social and political upheaval, especially, bring out the gold fixation in people. Even today, when order has been brought out of the mad confusion of many different kinds of money and many unsafe banks that once plagued the businessman, when only national governments or central banks issue money, when this issue is carefully managed in every major nation of the world, independent of the gold supply, and when there is not nearly enough gold in the whole world to redeem every dollar, franc, lira, mark, etc., in circulation anyway, still there are people who cry doom every time a nation's gold stock decreases or the ratio of gold to currency decreases. These extremist members of the "currency" school of thought would prefer money to be backed 100 percent by, and be redeemable 100 percent in, gold. The more reasonable majority of the currency school would like to have at least as much gold backing as possible.

By contrast, the members of the "banking" school of thought

---

[5] This is essentially what has happened recently to the solid silver alloy dimes, quarters, half-dollars, and dollars in the United States. They have to be minted now as "sandwich" coins, consisting of thin layers of silver alloy on the outside with a core of cheap copper on the inside, because the solid silver alloy coins were becoming more valuable than their face value. If they would work in vending machines, the coins could just as well be made of plastic today.

would rather allow the quantity of money to expand or contract as the needs of the economy dictate. The extremists among them would remove all arbitrary limits to the money supply. Even the more reasonable members argue that money is more an instrument to further other ends and less an end in itself. They view money as the servant to economic growth, full employment, and stability, and they want to be able to have control over the quantity of money. They would "back" the currency in any good securities—usually government bonds—and would have the government or its official agent, the central bank, issue checks and paper money into the economy by buying these securities with them, rather than buying only gold. Of course, this gives an unwise or unscrupulous government a practically limitless ability to expand the money supply since the supply of good securities need never dry up. For example, should the government need to raise some money for a war or other project, it could print some bonds and sell them to the public (mostly rich individuals, banks, insurance companies, etc.), who could, in turn, make a quick profit by selling them to the central bank at a higher price. The central bank would be able to pay for them with money simultaneously created and based on the very bonds just purchased. Thus, the government and central bank working together would have expanded the money supply, and all of the new money—except for the quick profits of the bond-buying and -selling public—would be in the hands of the government. This handy one-two punch at monetary stability is precisely what worries the members of the currency school about the banking school. It is an effective team play, but it ends in inflation.

Central banking had its beginning with the establishment of the Bank of England in 1694, Napoleon's Bank of France in 1800, and the First and Second Banks of the United States in 1791–1811 and 1816–1836, respectively. While these were originally private commercial banks, they tended to exercise control over the other banks and the money supplies in their respective countries. They become the lenders of last resort: the banks to whom other banks turn when they want to borrow money to make up for a shortage in their reserves. Typically, central banks are semipublic institutions even today. The Federal Reserve system in the United States was established in 1913 as an autonomous agency of the government, and the Bank of England, although nationalized in 1945, operates almost as independently of the government as before. The independence from governments is intended to prevent the banks from becoming mere "printing presses" for issuing less and less valuable currency, which may be politically expedient at times but is ultimately economically disastrous.

Since in the major countries of the world today only national governments or central banks can issue currency, the ordinary neighborhood bank doesn't need to keep gold in its vault any more. The gold can be kept almost exclusively in the vaults of the national government or its central bank, and, indeed, in the United States it is kept entirely in the United States Treasury vault at Fort Knox and in the vaults of the Federal Reserve system. In theory, it is used to "back" the American dollar, that is, the dollar could be redeemed in gold at the exchange rate of one ounce of fine gold for 35 dollars at a Federal Reserve bank if there were enough gold to redeem all the dollars that are in circulation. (This holds true for all other national currencies today also.) However, that is not the case, and it has been made illegal for American citizens to exchange their dollars for gold or to own large amounts of gold bullion for monetary purposes. In effect, for Americans the dollar isn't backed by anything except faith or, perhaps more precisely, habit. It is fiat money, whose value depends on the ratio between the quantity of money in circulation and the quantity of goods for sale. All the gold held by the United States government can be used only to back the dollars held by foreign central banks, which are still allowed to redeem their dollars in gold under normal circumstances. Perhaps it is important that it should be this way; foreigners might not trust our money as readily as Americans-in-residence would, and since they aren't a captive audience, unredeemability might make them unwilling to accept dollars in payment for anything. That would hurt America's international trade.

In recent years, even the amount of foreign-held United States dollars and stocks and bonds, which can be rapidly turned into dollars, has increased beyond the size of our gold supply. Thus, an international run on the dollar could presumably wipe out our supplies of gold entirely. (See the section on International Trade and Payments in Chapter 9.) Our monetary authorities assume (*hope* might be the better word) that this won't happen because the dollar has more appeal than gold. After all, a dollar invested in a profitable American industry can earn a tidy dividend; a dollar spent on American products is a good investment; but gold doesn't do anything: it just lies in somebody's vault.

Then what do the commercial neighborhood banks do, if they no longer store gold in their vaults or issue currency? In essence, they continue to do what they have always done: they accept deposits and make loans and investments at interest. The only difference is that their reserve, instead of gold, consists of currency stored in the vault and behind the tellers' windows and kept on account with a central bank, where it may be withdrawn in the form of currency on short notice if needed. The deposits, instead of coming in as gold or currency, come in as currency and checks brought to the bank—typically on payday— by the people who have checking accounts there. And the loans and investments are made by issuing checks or, rarely, by paying out currency. In fact, currency has taken the place of gold as the ultimate medium of exchange, and checks have usually replaced currency as the money of everyday exchange. There has been a kind of pyramiding effect, where the money we use is more and more one step further removed from the gold than before. The banks still hope that not all of their depositors will want to withdraw their accounts at once because the large proportion of their money, about 75 percent, has been loaned out and invested at interest, which is, as always, the main source of the banks' profits.

As we can see in the Pyramid of Credit illustrated in Figure 3, checking accounts, called demand deposits by bankers, constitute about 75 percent of the money supply for the public and businesses; the remainder is currency—paper money and coins. Savings accounts in banks and savings and loan companies

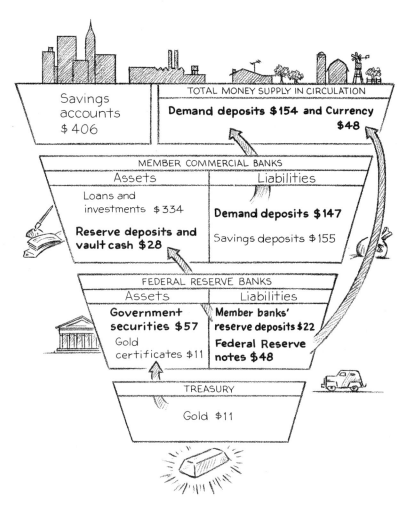

Figure 3. Pyramid of credit (billions of dollars). Because this diagram is a simplification with marginal amounts omitted, assets don't equal liabilities, nor do the amounts connected by arrows equal each other. Amounts are from mid-1970. (*Federal Reserve Bulletin*, Federal Reserve System, Washington, D.C., July 1970, vol. 56, no. 7, Tables A-12, A-17, A-19, A-37, A-38.)

aren't considered available money because, according to the letter of the law, withdrawals may be postponed by a waiting period. They are sometimes called time deposits (as opposed to demand deposits) for this reason. But, of course, savings accounts come very close to being used exactly like money. At the next lower level in the pyramid, the commercial banks use vault cash and deposits held by the Federal Reserve banks as reserves for the demand deposits of their customers. On the next lower level again, the Federal Reserve banks, in turn, use government securities as the legal reserve or legal basis for the Federal Reserve notes (money) issued and the member banks' deposits. Although no longer required to do so by law, the Federal Reserve system also holds about 10 billion dollars worth of gold, largely in the form of gold certificates, as an asset and as a vestige of the gold base of our monetary system. However, this gold has little influence on the entire monetary structure, and even as an international medium of exchange its usefulness is waning. The amounts of credit shown in bold type in the pyramid are the primary determinants of the ultimate quantity of money, and the arrows show the progress of this credit up the pyramid, with liabilities from one level connecting to assets in the next higher level.

We may note that the partial reserve system used by the commercial banks introduces a potential instability into the total money supply. For example, when the government creates new money with its treasury-central bank mechanism described above, this new money will most likely be deposited in the commercial banks. These, following standard operating procedures and staying within the legal limits decreed by the Federal Reserve Board, will lend out about 75 percent of it to borrowers, who will naturally spend it. (The remaining 25 percent is held in reserve on account with the Federal Reserve bank or in the vaults of the commercial banks.) The people and businesses which receive the money when it is spent will, in all likelihood, again deposit it into banks, where, let's say, 75 percent of it will be lent out again, and so on. In this way, a new one hundred million dollars will eventually mean an increase in the money supply as follows: $100,000,000 + 75,000,000 + 56,250,000 + 42,187,500 + 31,640,625 + \ldots = 400,000,000$ dollars. If the Federal Reserve Board would allow 80 percent to be lent out again each time, with only 20 percent being kept in reserve, the new 100,000,000 dollars would result in a 500,000,000 dollar increase in the money supply. This geometric progression can work in reverse when there is an initial withdrawal from the total money supply. As a result, the partial reserve system of banking has often been accused of having a destabilizing, now-inflationary/now-deflationary, effect. Here also the currency school would prefer the maintenance of total or, at least, larger reserves, turning banks into checking-account-servicing and vault-renting agencies.

But partial reserve banking is also the key to the potentially beneficial monetary economic policy of a central bank. Since partial reserve banking allows small changes in the quantity of money to be amplified into large ones, the instruments that make the small changes also become powerful, and the central bank has these instruments. For example, should the central bank want to encourage and expand economic activity, an increased money supply would help turn the trick by making it easier for businessmen and consumers to borrow at lower interest rates. So, as already explained, the central bank could create money by buying government securities. It could also encourage the commercial banks to expand the money supply by making it attractive to them to increase their reserves by borrowing from the central bank's reserves at a lower interest rate. Of course, these new commercial bank reserves would soon find their way into new loans and investments and, in the familiar sequence, be redeposited and lent out again, and so on, to create the new amplified quantity of money. The central bank's interest rate for this lending is called the "discount rate" or the "bank rate," and it is often considered a barometer of the central bank's policy intentions.

The central bank could also create a large potential for an expanded money supply by merely changing the commercial banks' reserve requirement. As shown in the previous example, changing the reserve requirement from 25 to 20 percent can increase the money supply by 25 percent. Of course, should the central bank want to rein in an overheated economy, it can use these instruments in reverse: it can sell securities, raise its discount rate, and raise the reserve requirements for commercial banks. In all the advanced free enterprise economies, these are the essential tools of central bank economic policy. The central bank makes decisions about the sales and purchases of government securities almost daily; the discount rate is changed less frequently—sometimes not for many months; and years can go by before the reserve requirements are changed.

Monetary systems in the world are still not completely neat and standardized. For example, there are many banks in the United States that do not belong to the Federal Reserve system and, thus, do not keep part of their reserves deposited with a Federal Reserve bank nor abide by its regulations. These non-member banks are large in number, over half the banks in the country, but are small in significance since they contain only about one-sixth of the total deposits. Therefore, most of the deposit accounts, which are the bases for the checks that are written—the most important kind of money used today—are under the jurisdiction of the Federal Reserve Board. But savings accounts have been rising at a rapid rate of growth especially in recent decades and are now more than twice the size of demand deposits. While, theoretically, savings accounts are not considered available money, they can generally be easily withdrawn, and, thus, they do, in fact, constitute a form of money or something very near to money.

Credit cards are now beginning to replace checks as a medium of exchange. In many situations, they are both more convenient and more acceptable to the seller since they provide a guarantee of safety. With credit cards, the pyramid of credit grows another level (not illustrated in Figure 3): the cards are backed by the creditability and acceptability of the checks with which the monthly credit card bill is paid; checks are backed by the faith in the currency; and currency (only in the traditional sense) is backed by gold. Gold, of course, is backed by nothing more substantial than faith in its scarcity.

And there is speculation that there are still more levels to be added to the credit pyramid. An electronic money card, which will be used in place of credit cards and all other forms of money, even coins, sounds like science fiction but is being seriously considered. This card, when presented to a machine at one's place of work or at the supermarket, will automatically credit or debit one's account at the bank. With this and all the other new media of exchange confusing the structure of our total money supply, it may be small comfort that the obsolete United States Note, the last remaining "Greenback" dollar bill of the Civil War era, was discontinued in 1966 and that the demise of the Silver Certificate dollar bill occurred in 1968. A few of the latter may still be found in circulation; one must look carefully for the label "Silver Certificate" on the face side of the bill where it now says "Federal Reserve Note." The institutions of money and banking do not follow any physical principle or natural law that makes them rational and orderly. They are man-made creations, and they come in almost as many colors, sizes, shapes, and varieties as man himself.

The financial revolution, with its limited liability joint stock companies and its corporations, its stock markets and insurance companies, its banks and its more adequate kinds of money, was a critically necessary ingredient in the development of Western commerce and industry. Where these financial institutions don't exist or where they don't function effectively, as, for example, in most underdeveloped economies today, the lack usually presents an insuperable obstacle to development. In these economies, whatever money is available for purchases is not always readily acceptable; whatever savings are accumulated cannot always find the proper channels into productive investments; and whatever new industrial technologies are available are often too risky or too large to be undertaken.

When the financial machinery breaks down in developed countries, as it did in the Western nations during the Great Depression of the 1930s, no amount of effort to get the idle factories and workers producing again will be successful until the financial machinery is repaired. It is painfully frustrating both in developed economies suffering a temporary depression and in underdeveloped economies to see the physical opportunities for production and growth—the factories, the farms, the technology of industry—so close at hand, yet so hard to reach. It probably will come as no surprise that just as in our personal lives we do virtually everything within the context of some institutional framework, that production also must function within such a framework. The institutions established during the financial revolution constitute that necessary context.

THE INDUSTRIAL REVOLUTION

This whole age of many revolutions is usually called simply the Industrial Revolution, and we have freely used this expression throughout our previous discussions. The changes in methods of production that constitute the Industrial Revolution are often considered the single most important aspect of the entire age, the aspect from which most of the other revolutions are derived. Certainly, for economists this industrial revolution is central. It meant the use of machines, metals, engines, chemicals, and the building of whole new factory districts where once hand labor, simple tools and wooden implements, and a green rural countryside prevailed. It was a watershed that separated history into two parts: the age of biological primacy and the age of mechanical primacy. It was probably the biggest single change in the pattern of civilization since its beginning many thousands of years before. The Industrial Revolution, like the other revolutions of this century, is an ongoing struggle in most of the world today, but it had its first campaign in England.

Textiles

We cannot be sure exactly with what industry it began, but the textile industry seems about the best place to begin our story. The putting-out system had advanced through most of the textile industry by the early 1700s, resulting in a substantial division of labor between the various spinning, carding, weaving, dyeing, and other processes. Most workers performed in their own homes and were paid for their product on a piece-rate basis. This was a powerful incentive to increase their productivity, and since they often lived outside of towns and out of the reach of guild production regulations, which were weak in England anyway, they could tinker with their spinning, weaving, and carding machines to their heart's content. Many of the improvements on the simple machinery were minor and remained isolated events, but the traveling agent, who brought each worker his materials and picked up the products, served as the means for communicating the news of better improvements.

The first major improvement was John Kay's flying shuttle, invented in 1733. This device consisted of hand-operated mechanical hammers that allowed one man to throw a shuttle across a width of cloth that was much wider than he alone could normally handle. In other words, the flying shuttle allowed one man to accomplish the work of two, and its use spread quickly.

The thread for weaving was still spun in the old fashion way, however, until the invention by James Hargreaves of the famous spinning jenny, which he patented in 1770. This machine was also hand-powered at first, but it produced much more thread per man than the old spinning wheel method. In 1769, Richard Arkwright patented a water frame (a water-powered spinning machine) that made such a strong thread out of cotton that cloth could be woven without the addition of wool or other threads for strength. And by 1785, Edmund Cartwright developed a mechanically powered loom that could keep pace with all the new abundance of thread coming off the spinning jennies and water frames. In 1793 in the United States, Eli Whitney invented the cotton gin, which removed the seeds from the cotton bolls mechanically and thus supplied the voracious appetite of the efficient new water frames that made 100 percent cotton cloth practical.

From the time of the American Revolution to about 1830, the English cotton manufacturing industry increased its output a hundredfold. Already by the beginning of the 1800s, it represented about one-third of all British exports. For the young United States, cotton also grew enormously in importance. Shortly before the Civil War, over half the exports from the United States was unmanufactured cotton, valued at about 745 million dollars, compared with 167 million dollars for the exports of manufactured goods, 157 million dollars for wheat and flour exports, and 87 million dollars for unmanufactured tobacco exports, the three next largest export categories. So much cotton was used that the oil pressed from the cottonseeds picked out of the boll by Whitney's gin became an important type of oil for lamps by the 1820s. The left-over cottonseed cakes resulting from the pressings were, at first, fed to livestock, and a lively export trade in these cakes soon developed. The dairy farmers on the relatively poor soil of Denmark were important customers because the cakes were so rich in nutrients that, not only did they contribute substantially to Denmark's thriving livestock, but the enriched animal manure contributed to the improvement of the country's soil conditions. Today, the Danes chuckle at the fact that their rich soil was imported from the American South, via cottonseed cakes and the bovine alimentary canal.

Factories

All the machines that made the growth of the textile industry possible performed the skillful hand-and-finger functions of the old methods mechanically, and they performed them more rapidly and more accurately than hands could. The operator of the machine was reduced simply to cranking wheels or moving levers back and forth. The next step was to replace his muscle power with mechanical power, typically water wheel power, at first. Not only did the machines lend themselves easily to this mechanization, but the structure of the putting-out system itself led to this development. It had already turned the independent textile craftsman into a piece-rate worker and had gradually but inevitably transferred his tools and equipment into the hands of the putting-out agent. When he saw the economic feasibility of applying mechanical power to his looms, if only they could be centrally placed around a water wheel, the agent, now a factory manager, moved them into buildings that became the first industrial factories in the world. Soon, all textile machines were installed in factories. Indeed, mechanical power was such an advantage that in order to stay competitive with other producers, businessmen had to organize factories as quickly as possible. Mill towns, as they came to be called, sprang up at most water wheel locations and grew rapidly. The erstwhile cottagers

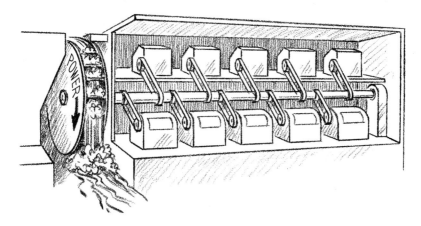

Figure 4. Basic architecture of a factory. The central power source serves all machines simultaneously through pulley power takeoffs (cutaway view).

crowded into the quickly built living quarters that clustered within short walking distance around the mill; and new workers, evicted from their peasant lands by the Enclosure Acts and attracted by the promise of wages for unskilled labor, also poured in in great waves.

Engines

But water wheel power would never have been sufficient for something as cataclysmic as the Industrial Revolution. Factories would have to be built where there were no waterfalls; a new source of power would be needed. And it was not long in coming. As early as 1708, Thomas Newcomen put his steam engine to work to pump water out of coal mines. It was a cumbersome and inefficient machine, using enormous amounts of fuel and water, which were easy enough to come by at the coal mines, and involving the repetitive opening and closing of valves by hand. Worst of all, the Newcomen engine had to be heated and cooled with each cycle of the piston because its power was derived both from the steam pressure in the cylinder pushing out the piston and the atmospheric pressure pressing the piston back as the steam in the cylinder was condensed by water cooling. In spite of its difficulties, however, it was the best that was available, and it worked.

But in 1765, James Watt introduced his vastly improved version of the steam engine. It eliminated the need for alternately heating and cooling the engine, had automatic valves to regulate the steam flow, and was much closer to the modern steam engine of today. Even his first models were four times more efficient than the Newcomen engine, and the Watt engines continued to become more powerful, more efficient, and less cumbersome. It is important to note that much of the success of Watt's steam engine is due to the happy merger with the wealthy button and buckle manufacturer Matthew Boulton, who was a brilliant businessman and in close contact with the coal miners and ironmongers of the Birmingham area in England. Together, they produced engines that were tailored to the needs of industry while at the same time constructed according to the latest metal-working techniques. This merger typified the technological dynamism of the realistic and practical men for whom England was famous during this period. By 1850, the British were producing about 11,000 horsepower from water wheels and 71,000 horsepower from steam engines.

From the standpoint of engineering, the steam engines of Newcomen and Watt pointed toward new directions. Water wheels and wind mills, both of which had been used to some extent for centuries, are essentially turbines, which produce a rotating power directly. The steam engines with their cylinders and pistons are a very different kind of machine; they involve many more moving parts, much closer machining of parts, and produce reciprocating power. It might be argued that the production of reciprocating power was an imitation of the back-and-forth sawing action of human elbow grease power, and, indeed, the first Newcomen engine applied its reciprocating power directly to a reciprocating piston pump. But the steam engines were employed mainly in substituting for water wheels, which required that their reciprocating motion be converted into rotating motion. To this day, virtually all reciprocating engines, which include mainly gasoline and diesel engines, must first convert reciprocating power to rotary power before the final power application can be made. To make matters worse, even the best reciprocating engines are inherently rather inefficient because of the energy lost in stopping and starting a piston every time it goes back and forth. Engineers point out that these engines are essentially trying to break themselves apart, and, in this context, they champion the superiority of turbines and the new Wankel rotary-piston engine for automobiles. Yet the steam engine and its gasoline and diesel offspring supplied the majority of the power for the first two centuries of the Industrial Revolution.

While the steam engine and even the water wheel were great improvements over the simple hand-driven machines, the extreme centralization of this power never sat well with production engineers. The main belt drive of the factory not only tyrannized the workers, but it also tyrannized the organization of the production process. If decentralized sources of power could be found so that the separate machines could be operated and located independently of one another, production could be made much more rational. In some cases, the smaller internal combustion engines fit the bill. But the usual solution was to interpose a second power stage: from steam to electricity to (electric) motor, or from diesel to compressed air to air tools. These improvements, especially since World War II, have led to the common "corn field" factory design, in which a factory is only one story high, covers a large acreage of land (maybe a former corn field), and is surrounded by parking lots—because the workers too have found a mechanical means of decentralization. This new spread-out factory is not only more efficient, but it is also a much more pleasant, safe, and healthy place to work. It is not the final solution, however, because this modern factory design extracts an increasing cost in land use as open land becomes less abundant and as the pollution caused by the commuting workers' automobiles becomes more severe.

Iron and Steel

To talk about the mechanization of industry and steam engines without mentioning iron and steel would be leaving out half the story. Industrialization could not have progressed without the development of new and better materials, which are the building blocks for any new industries. The first textile machines were primarily made of wood, but, as soon as mechanical power was applied to them, it became quite clear that stronger materials would have to be used. Of course, the steam engine itself is inconceivable without metal. The state of iron technology in the early 1700s consisted of smelting the iron ore in furnaces fired by charcoal and either using the iron as it came from the furnaces— forming it into the desired parts by pouring it into molds and letting it cool, resulting in "cast iron"—or hammering it while it was red hot, a process that removes some of the impurities, resulting in a kind of low-grade steel called "wrought iron." Cast iron contains substantial quantities of carbon, silicon, and sulfur. It is brittle but useful in parts that have to be rigid, but it may be bulky. Wrought iron is purer; it is malleable and tough and can hold a sharpened edge relatively well, but the way it was made limited it to small pieces.

The smelting process itself was typically a small operation because it had to be moved frequently to be near fresh stands of timber that could be made into charcoal. The furnaces themselves had to be small because the charcoal pieces were too fragile to support large quantities of iron ore and the limestone that was also needed in the smelting process to flux the ore as it was being deoxidized. Coal, which might have supported a larger furnace, didn't burn well enough in the confines of the smelt furnace to create enough heat.

By the late 1700s in Britain, the forests that were within reasonable proximity to the iron ore were nearly depleted. As early as 1709, a Quaker ironmaster named Abraham Darby had developed a process of iron smelting that used coal in the form of coke, that is, charcoaled coal. Experimentation with this method and others was increasing as the forests dwindled, and in 1828 coke came into its own as the most practical and economic fuel for smelting when J. B. Neilson of Glasgow used a blast of air preheated with coke to blow the furnace, instead of relying solely on the coke or charcoal burning within the furnace. The iron industry moved to the Midlands of England,

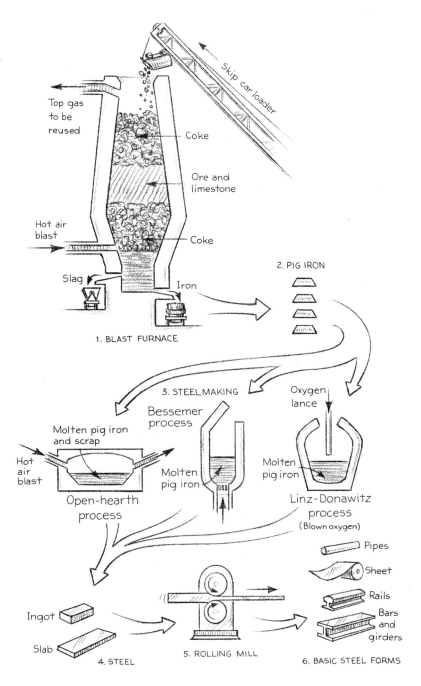

Top gas
to be
reused

Coke

Ore and
limestone

Hot air
blast

Coke

Slag

Iron

1. BLAST FURNACE

2. PIG IRON

Skip car loader

3. STEELMAKING

Bessemer
process

Oxygen
lance

Molten pig iron
and scrap

Hot
air
blast

Molten
pig iron

Molten
pig iron

Open-hearth
process

Linz-Donawitz
process
(Blown oxygen)

Pipes

Sheet

Rails

Bars
and
girders

Ingot

Slab

4. STEEL

5. ROLLING MILL

6. BASIC STEEL FORMS

Figure 5. The making of iron and steel.

where it would be nearer the coal sources, since four times as much coal as iron ore was needed to charge the blast furnaces. Following the same pattern of settling near sources of coal, young iron industries established themselves in the Ruhr, Silesia, and Lorraine areas of Europe and in the Pittsburgh area in the United States. And the industry as well as the individual blast furnaces grew larger and larger.

All during the Industrial Revolution, the most pressing need was for better grades of iron. In 1780, James Watt devised a steam hammer that could make wrought iron mechanically in larger quantities and in larger pieces than could be made by hand hammering. More importantly, in 1784, Peter Onions and Henry Cort simultaneously developed the puddling process, which stirred a pool of molten iron. This stirring action tended to burn off the impurities in the iron, thus making a kind of wrought iron without hammering. For over half a century, this was to remain the most important method of making steel, until Henry Bessemer introduced his converter in 1856. The Bessemer converter is a pear-shaped vessel containing molten iron and blown with very hot air injected at the bottom of the vessel. It rapidly (in about half an hour) burns off most of the impurities, and a good grade of steel results. The converter works especially well with iron made from ores that are low in phosphorus, but, unfortunately, most of the ores are high in phosphorus. In 1866, Sir William Siemens first used the open-hearth process, which he later refined with the help of Pierre Martin. It allowed the use of iron from high or low phosphorus ores and scrap iron as well, but because the process consisted of blowing hot air over the top of a pool full of molten iron, it took ten times longer than the Bessemer process. To this day, however, some of the finest and most specialized steels come from the open-hearth process because the length of time allows careful adjustments in the alloy content and other metallurgical properties of the blast.

About ten years after the use of the first open hearth, the Bessemer converter was improved by the Thomas-Gilchrist process of lining the converter vessel with a magnesium lime-stone firebrick, which absorbed the excess phosphorus in the high phosphorus ores. This improved Bessemer process became the most common method of steel production and until recently was the basic technology of the world's most important steel areas. Since World War II, steelmaking methods have increasingly switched over to the Linz-Donawitz process, which uses oxygen-blown converters. In this process an oxygen lance is inserted into the Bessemer-converter-shaped vessel from above, and oxygen is blown directly on top of the molten iron. It makes a high grade of steel, metallurgically controlled by an electronic computer, and at the speed of the Bessemer process. In 1870, annual world crude steel production was about 12 million metric tons; by 1900 it was about 40 million metric tons; by 1950 it had shot up to 161 million metric tons; and by 1968 the world production of crude steel was 529 million metric tons.[6]

Improvements in the technology of working with the iron and steel developed, on the whole, from the small inventions of tinkerers rather than of scientists seeking grand technological breakthroughs. Especially in the development of machine tools for cutting, drilling, and grinding iron and steel, the previously developed skills of the precision implement industries, such as clockmaking and gunsmithing, were very useful. Machine tool centers grew up in those areas where such previous experience existed; for example, southern Germany's clockmakers became the machine toolmakers of modern Germany. They brought the tool industry, along with their beer and sausage, to Cincinnati and Milwaukee in the United States, when they settled there in large numbers in the latter half of the 1800s. Basic to all iron and steel working, other than casting iron, was the development of the rolling mill for forming the large bars, girders, sheets, and so on, that could be used directly or refined even more. The first rolling mill for forming iron plates was developed by Henry Cort in 1783 in England. John Wilkinson had already devised a drill for boring cannon in 1756, and by the turn of the century technology was well enough advanced to construct a great many new tools, including nail- and screw-making machines, lathes, and drill chucks. Many of the machines were also power driven.

[6] *Statistical Yearbook 1969* (United Nations, New York, 1970), and N. J. G. Pounds, *The Geography of Iron and Steel*, 4th ed. (Hutchinson University Library, London, 1968).

In other industries, mechanical technology was advancing too. The power-driven circular saw, which was first used in 1777, and the band saw, introduced in 1808, had a revolutionary effect on the lumber and wood-working industry. Although propellers had been used for more than a dozen centuries in windmills, they were not used to drive boats until 1836. The year 1845 saw the first turret lathe, and compressed air tools were used in coal mining by 1852.

Chemistry also contributed its share to industrialization, both by increasing the body of knowledge about mankind's natural environment and by the invention of efficient and practical processes for manufacturing essential industrial chemicals. In the 1770s Antoine Lavoisier propounded the theory of combustion; in the early 1780s Henry Cavendish discovered the chemical composition of water; and in 1803 John Dalton submitted the theory that matter was made up of atoms. In a more practical but equally important vein, in 1746 John Roebuck made the production of low-cost sulfuric acid possible, and Charles Macintosh invented bleaching powder in 1799. Nicholas Leblanc found a way to make soda ash from salt and was awarded a prize for his discovery by the French Academy of Sciences in 1783. And so it went through the first century of the Industrial Revolution and beyond.

Fund Processes and Flow Processes

From the very beginning of the Industrial Revolution, technologies and institutions were sought that would make the industrial processes flow as continuously as possible. Today we speak of *fund* processes and *flow* processes of production to distinguish between things that are made in batches, like cookies and books, and things that are made in a continuous output, like heat for a home in winter or the supply of electricity and water. Fund processes are by far the most common, and the majority of all the commodities made by mankind throughout history have been made in batches, at least at first. Agriculture, because of the seasons, is a fund process that transforms seeds into harvest in yearly batches; the medieval craftsman made a pair of shoes or a farm wagon one at a time for customers who had ordered the commodities. The merchants who sailed to the Orient in the spice trade of the commercial revolution both organized their own trips and invested in them, and when the boats returned after many months, they divided the profits or losses and then closed their books. In a very real sense, even many of the most important biological functions of our own bodies are "fund" processes; we eat three batches of food a day, inhale and exhale in batches; even our hearts beat rather than hum, indicating that they work on single batches of blood at a time.

But fund processes are inefficient in many ways. They often have to be organized from scratch each time, like the trading venture to the Orient just mentioned. With each batch, materials have to be accumulated and prepared, the machines have to be cranked up, and the entire production process is confronted anew. Once a fund process is begun, little can be done to change it qualitatively or quantitatively; it must be either carried on to completion or abandoned. Flow processes, on the other hand, are more subject to constant control. They require new organization only in the beginning, waste no energy in shutting down and starting up, and present a continuous flow of experience that lends itself to finer adjustments and greater accuracy in the production process. The more the process flows, the more the division of labor and the greater specialization in plant and equipment are possible. The moving conveyor belt of mass production is a dramatic symbol of the effort to make processes flow. Here workers perform only one function with very specialized machines on the commodites that parade by on the production line. It is very much more efficient (but more boring) than when a craftsman made a pair of shoes all by himself.

New industrial institutions, such as the corporation, were devised to accommodate commercial and industrial ventures that were ongoing affairs, rather than just one-shot undertakings. Production methods were improved to make the batches larger and larger until they approximated a flow, such as the blast furnaces, which could be charged continuously with new ore, coke, and flux from the top, so that a single heat (batch) could go on for six months, until the firebrick furnace lining was worn out. New flow technologies were invented that replaced fund technologies, like the continuous strip paper mill, introduced in 1799, and the cylindrical printing press, introduced in 1812, which lowered the cost of printing so much that newspapers were made possible. Today, steel rolling mills are being built that form the basic steel parts in a continuous strip; some brewers are making beer in a flow process that eliminates the funds of the settling tanks; the fierce keening of jet engines has almost completely replaced the staccato roar of piston motors at major airports; and while our hearts are still beating out their funds of blood, the latest electric wrist watches hum instead of tick.

CHAPTER 5

The Age of
Classical Economics

If the Industrial Revolution, along with its many adjunct revolutions, did any one thing, it eliminated any doubt that there was, indeed, a separate institution in society called the economy. No longer could the structure of civilization be regarded as an integrated and undifferentiated whole, where work and play, love and marriage, war and peace, and wealth and poverty were regarded as part and parcel of one grand scheme. The world was being viewed now as a body politic, as a social structure made up of various parts, and as an economy, and man himself was being fragmented into a citizen and voter, a worker during the day, a husband and father or wife and mother during the afternoon and evening, perhaps a member of a labor union one night a week, and a child of God on Sunday. The trend was to bring the ultimate degree of division of labor, the most thorough fracturing of man and his society, and with it would come the highest level of productive efficiency but also accompanied by anxiety and yearning for a lost wholesomeness.

Every kind of science was enjoying a full harvest of respect during this age of revolution, even though many sciences were still embryonic. And economics came in for a greater share of this respect than ever before or since. Perhaps, the reason for this esteem was that economics was developing rapidly along rather quantitative lines, in the statistical sense; that is, economists tended to count things: money, profits, costs, labor hours, numbers of products, exports and imports, population, birth rates, exchange rates, and interest rates. Thus, their theories seemed more realistic and their policies more practical than those in the other areas. At any rate, quantification is essential to scientific development, and while other sciences have since caught up with and even surpassed economics in this respect, the progress of economics as a science continues to depend largely on the development of its mathematical usage and quantitative analysis. Another reason for the high status of economics among the sciences was that it shared in the glory of the phenomenal progress of industry. While medicine, chemistry, biology, physics, and other fields were just beginning to implement their new knowledge in the everyday world, the economy was burgeoning forth with uninhibited gusto. The science associated with this phenomenon was considered very special.

DAVID RICARDO

Today it is generally agreed that one of the first scientific economic analysts was David Ricardo (1772–1823). He was an Englishman born into a family of well-to-do immigrant Dutch Jews, the third of seventeen children. At age fourteen, he entered his father's stockbrokerage business and learned the trade. However, when he was twenty-one, he married a Quaker woman and joined the Unitarian church, for which his father disowned him and banished him from the family business. But young David was able to borrow funds from business friends, started a brokerage of his own, and soon was richer than his father. Reconciliation followed. By the age of forty-three, David Ricardo had retired from business and devoted himself to economic studies and, a few years later, his membership in Parliament. His major work on economics, *The Principles of Political Economy and Taxation*, appeared first in 1817. It was revised in its third and final edition in 1821.

Iron Law of Wages

In spite of his personal success, Ricardo did not cast an optimistic eye on the economy, as Adam Smith had. To Ricardo, the natural course of events seemed always to stabilize the economy at the level where the mass of the people—the laborers—were earning just enough money barely to keep alive and where businessmen were making very little, if any, profit. Instead of seeing a bright future in the division of labor, the expansion of markets, the freeing of productive energies, and the increased wealth of a nation à la Adam Smith, Ricardo thought that in the long run population increases would supply so much labor that wages would be forced down to a subsistence level. When they went below subsistence, the population would decrease and wages would be adjusted upward accordingly. His "iron law of wages" worked immutably: even though, at any one time, wages might exceed subsistence and the people might enjoy a slightly brighter standard of living, the economy would always gravitate toward this stationary state of subsistence, and profits would also sink lower and lower.

To economists, this outlook suggested a new emphasis. If the economy always tended toward a stationary state, where population, production, prices, and wages remained in a constant relationship to each other, then one is bound to ask how the income in this economy is distributed. In other words, if the size of the pie becomes fixed, who eventually gets the biggest piece? Ricardo deduced his answer from an analysis of the determinants of *value* and *rent*. Let's look at each in turn.

Labor Theory of Value

The value of a commodity can be determined by various standards. For example, if the commodity is a rare and irreplaceable painting by Rembrandt, then its value and price on the market is determined by its scarcity. Often, many commodities are temporarily scarce and irreplaceable in this way, like water during a drought or wheat after a bad harvest season, and their prices will be temporarily higher than average. But in the long run, what determines the relative values of the vast majority of commodities that are not abnormally scarce and that can be produced and replaced every day is the number of labor hours it takes to make them. For example, if it takes fifteen hours of labor to make a pair of shoes, from cows to leather to finished product, and if it takes thirty hours of labor to make a suit of clothes, from sheep to wool to cloth to the finished suit, then the suit will cost twice as much as the shoes. This *labor theory of value* is the basis for the rest of the Ricardian analysis. One might ask: what about the productivity of machines that would come to replace so many hours of manual labor in the next decades of industrialization? Ricardo could only answer that machines embodied the labor expended on them when they were made, and were, thus, merely reservoirs of labor value. One might also ask: what of the influence of natural resources? Ricardo would say that they were the fixed "original and indestructible powers of the soil," and as such, natural resources were not active value determinants.

Even though Ricardo was never completely satisfied with his labor theory of value, he still maintained that in the absence of a better explanation, the *relative* price of the vast majority of all products sold is ultimately determined by this theory, including the price of labor itself. If it takes many hours of labor to support the life of a laborer, then wages will have to be high. And, conversely, if it takes only a small amount of labor to keep him alive and working, then wages will be low. Of course, says Ricardo, it doesn't make any difference to the laborer whether wages are high or low. He is on a subsistence standard of living in any event. The question is: what makes a laborer's upkeep require many hours or a few hours of labor? The answer: the cost of the food he eats. And what makes the price of food high or low? The answer: the productivity of the land that it is grown on. If the land is highly productive, then high yields of grains and other food crops can be had with very little work, but if the land is poor, dry, and rocky, then the farmer must sweat many hours for his meager harvest.

Theory of Rent, Income Distribution, and Population

We know, of course, that throughout any one country there is both rich and poor farm land, but the price of each one of the basic foodstuffs is about the same everywhere. Surely, a farmer who has to work longer hours for his bushel of wheat can't sell it for more than the farmer who owns the richest bottom land in the country. What does occur, in fact, is that at any one time the prices are generally the same all over the country, but to the poor farmer they represent a return only for his labor. For the highly productive farmer, the prices also represent a return for his labor, but since he doesn't need to work as hard per bushel of wheat, the price also represents a gratuitous income for him called "economic rent." The owner of the rich land receives a rent; the owner of the poor land receives nothing except wages for his labor. The larger the population, the more food will have to be grown, the more land will have to be put under cultivation, and, assuming that the best land is always put into use first, the more labor will have to be applied to the extra land to get a bushel's worth of yield. This will drive up food prices and land rents received by all but the most recently added farmers. The higher food prices will necessitate a higher subsistence wage for the workers. Figure 6 illustrates this situation symbolically.

Now we can tie all the factors together with a big blue ribbon. The higher wages will tend to shrink the profits of the industrialists and make them less and less eager to expand their businesses. New savings and new investments will cease. The increased cost of food is assurance that the population is struggling along on the barest subsistence standard of living and that there will be little chance for an expanding population. Only the owners of rich farm land can enjoy the situation because they are receiving high rents. But this high rent income has no place to go. It cannot serve as a spark to fire up the economy again. The very nature of

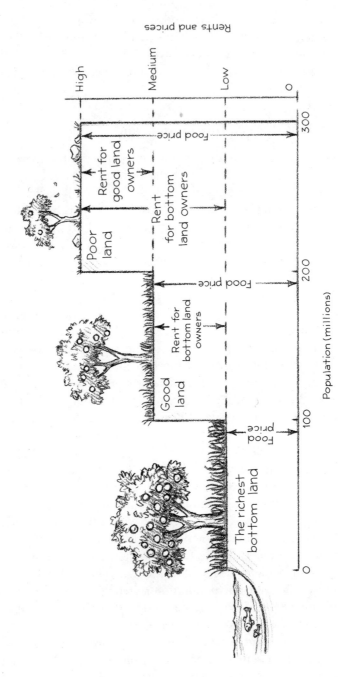

Figure 6. The determination of the rate of rent by the price of food and the size of the population.

rich farm land is that it is in limited supply; therefore, the receivers of rent cannot buy any more of it. They won't want to invest in the profitless businesses they see around them. All they can do is spend their income on consumption and live high on the hog—which is what they seemed to be doing in the England of Ricardo's day. And that is how the total pie gets divided up.

Times had changed in the fifty years or so since the French physiocrats developed their theory that land was the ultimate source of all value. Perhaps the development of manufacturing industry made Ricardo appreciate the role of labor more than Quesnay or Turgot did. Perhaps it was simply that the French were more agricultural and the English more industrial to begin with. At any rate, it is interesting that both the physiocratic theory of value and Ricardo's labor theory of value concluded that it was the landowner who was left holding the bag that contained whatever surplus the economy could produce.

Is there any hope that the stationary state may be avoided? Yes, said Ricardo, if inventions that increase productivity occurred often enough and if the population exercised powerful restraint on the urge to procreate, neither of which was a good bet. In the end, it seemed to Ricardo that the stationary state was inevitable. Of course, our experience since his time has proven him dead wrong on that point, but, as a theory, it still has validity on several levels of operation. For one, there may be an ever-present force that pushes the economy toward a stationary state that is obscured in reality by other stronger forces, for example, the just-mentioned restraint in population growth and technological advance. In this sense, it may be like the gravitational attraction between the moon and the earth: we notice it only in the way it causes tides in our oceans. It has never succeeded in pulling the two bodies together because other, stronger forces work to keep them apart. Yet, this gravitational pull must be considered a real force.

For another, the stationary state is a most useful concept in scientific thinking. It is difficult to imagine a movement in any direction that continues indefinitely without a starting point or an ending point; it is as unsatisfactory to the human mind as the idea of an infinite universe. We prefer to think that rivers flow down to the sea, where they end, that children grow up to be adults, that clocks run until they are completely unwound, and that the economy changes and grows until it hits the stationary state. Furthermore, to do any quantitative measurements and calculations, benchmarks have to be established, which, in themselves, supply a sense of definiteness. It is impossible to find the value of an unknown value, x, in a function, unless the function happens to be an equation (or part of a system of equations) that can be "solved," balanced so that all the uneven values that would cause an ongoing change have been evened out. To put it yet another way, we humans find it hard to conceive of a continuously dynamic reality. We prefer to think of dynamics as only a temporary aberration from a clearly defined static state. We have a movie film mind that prefers to understand motion as a change from one static state—from one still picture—to another rather than to try to understand motion purely on its own terms. So also in economics, the stationary state serves as the final equilibrium in the economic equation.

Theory of Comparative Advantage

Although Ricardo was less optimistic than Adam Smith about the long-run future of his economy, he did agree with Smith that free enterprise and free international trade would create the best of possible worlds, even if he thought the best possible still wasn't very good. He understood the essence of a free market economy when he argued that only this freedom of enterprise and trade would achieve the optimum allocation of labor, capital, and resources consistent with the existing level of technology and the social customs of the day. Only this freedom could create the true community of nations on which all hopes for international peace rest.

> Under a system of perfectly free commerce, each country naturally devotes its capital and labour to such employments as are most beneficial to each. This pursuit of individual advantage is admirably connected with the universal good of the whole. By stimulating industry, by rewarding ingenuity, and by using most efficaciously the peculiar powers bestowed by nature, it distributes labor most effectively and most economically: while, by in-

creasing the general mass of productions, it diffuses general benefit, and binds together, by one common tie of interest and intercourse, the universal society of nations throughout the civilized world.[1]

In this period of the early 1800s, mercantilist opinion was still going strong. Indeed, throughout history, the arguments for restrictions on free trade, based on theoretical, ideological, or military grounds or merely on the special pleadings of a group with vested interests threatened by competition from outside, have always been loud and long. Smith answered these arguments with a general statement on the benefits of free enterprise and trade. Ricardo answered them with carefully analyzed computations of benefits and costs. He used the following hypothetical case to make his argument.

Suppose that the total possible trade between two countries, say, England and Portugal, consists of wine and cloth and that one country, Portugal, can produce both of these products more efficiently—with fewer labor hours—than the other. Wouldn't efficient Portugal export both wine and cloth to inefficient England, making England pay for its imports with gold until its treasuries were bankrupt? Not at all! says Ricardo. Trade is not determined by the absolute advantage in total economic productivity that one country has over another; rather, it is determined by which commodities are produced relatively more efficiently than other commodities within the same country. We illustrate this point with Portugal and England as follows:

LABOR HOURS NEEDED FOR PRODUCTION

Product	England	Portugal
One bolt of cloth	100	80
One barrel of wine	120	80

Clearly, Portugal is more productive per labor hour and could

---

[1] David Ricardo, "On Foreign Trade," *The Principles of Political Economy and Taxation* (Richard D. Irwin, Homewood, Ill., 1963), p. 71.

export both wine and cloth to England for gold if the English would accept that arrangement. In the long run, this one-sided export would not be acceptable to the country paying the gold. In fact, what accounts for trade is that the English notice that they can buy one barrel of wine in Portugal with the money they receive from the sale of one bolt of cloth there. In England itself, one bolt of cloth brings only five-sixths of a barrel of wine. Any self-respecting merchant would see a chance to clean up a tidy profit here and would export cloth to Portugal and import wine from Portugal. By the same token, a Portuguese merchant will notice that one barrel of wine will exchange for one-and-one-fifth bolts of cloth in England whereas it will only exchange for one bolt in Portugal. Therefore, he will export wine to England and import cloth from England. The Portuguese and the English merchants agree with this example: the former export wine, the latter export cloth. Any other direction of trade would be down-right unprofitable.

This trade could continue forever, except that the combined English and Portuguese demand for wine might force less and less efficient Portuguese vineyards into production, causing the labor hours needed for a barrel of wine to rise to, say, 96. At this point there would no longer be any profit in the trade. (One bolt of English cloth would exchange for five-sixths of a barrel of wine in Portugal, just as in England.) In the same way, the combined demand for English cloth may increase the labor hours input per bolt to, say, 120, again ending the profitable trade. But until either of these effects takes place (and this might never happen), trade between Portugal and England presents a good opportunity for profit.

Ricardo's "theory of comparative advantage," as this analysis is called, explains more than just international trade. It governs the economic relationships between regions within a country, between groups of people, and even between individuals. For example, suppose a medical doctor is also a very good typist. It takes him eight hours a day to treat his patients but only three hours to type up all the bills. The best typist he can get takes twice as long, six hours, to type the bills. Should he hire the typist? Of course! Because he should do what he can do best, namely, treat his patients. It would take the typist an impossibly long time (let's just say 100 hours) to treat the patients, because he or she has never been trained in medicine. So let the typist type, and both the doctor and the typist will profit from the exchange. The doctor can get all his daily typing done by the typist in exchange for only six-hundredths of a day's doctoring. Or putting it another way, the doctor can exchange one day's worth of doctoring for $16\frac{2}{3}$ days' worth of typing with the typist ($100 \div 6 = 16\frac{2}{3}$). He would only get $2\frac{2}{3}$ days' ($8 \div 3 = 2\frac{2}{3}$) worth of typing done by doing it himself for one full day. The typist can get a full day's medical treatment or its equivalent with only sixteen hours of typing.

Although the theory of comparative advantage is based on Ricardo's labor theory of value, that is, that labor hours are the only costs of production, it is still applicable to modern economics because labor is, even today, the largest single cost of production in finished and most semifinished goods, and it is a reliable figurative symbol for relative values. Nonetheless, we must keep in mind that the theory explains only that *both* parties to the trade benefit but not *how much* each is benefited.

Ricardo's theory of rent, which we have already seen applied to the explanation of the distribution of income (pp. 121ff) has survived particularly well in another context. In general terms, the theory of rent states that any factor of production that is not reproducible, that is, only available in its original supply and available for production whether or not it is paid for, will receive an income—if it receives any at all—that is called rent. Thus, natural land, which is not reproducible but which is always available in its original supply, is such a factor, and the income of a landowner is called rent. Herein lies Ricardo's point: this income will be large or small not according to any efforts by the owner of the rentable factor, but according to the demand for that factor. Furthermore, because such rentable factors are in limited supply, they will absorb any excess income that the productive process is able to produce. Specifically, Ricardo theorized that landowners are able to extract all the surplus income produced in the economy because they are sitting on the most important unreproducible factor of production. They hold the trump card.

There are other factors that also come close to the ideal of original and unreproducible, for example, a beauty queen's figure, a concert violinist's extraordinary musical ear, or oil concealed under a piece of Saudi Arabian real estate. But, whether land, beauty, talent, or underground oil, all of these factors need development in order to become fully useful; therefore, the income they earn isn't purely rent. But part of their income must still be explained as a rent payment to that original and unreproducible quality that made that one woman a beauty queen, that one violinist a virtuoso, and that one Arabian sheik a millionaire. Any factor of production that contributes something unique, original, and unreproducible receives part of its income not in payment for productive efforts but simply as a payment for itself, which may be termed an economic rent. How big will this rent be? That depends on the demand for beauty queens, concert violinists, and Arabian petroleum, just as the demand for land, via the demand for food, determines the land rent.

HENRY GEORGE AND THE SINGLE TAX

Rent theory can tell us a lot about why certain factors of production earn the income they do. Often this income may seem unjustifiable. Why should one Arab sheik be rich and the others poor, just because the former was lucky enough to have oil below his stretch of sand? Or, in another case, why should the descendants of the original settlers in the rich farm lands of the American Midwest enjoy a rent income from their inherited land? Or, again, why should a musician with an inherited talent claim his rent income as his own? In fact, in the late 1880s this was an important political issue, and the American economist Henry George (1839–1897) proposed a reform in which all pure land rent would be taxed away. This "single tax," as he called it because it would do away with the necessity of all other taxes, would eliminate the economic distortion that results from taxes on productive efforts, such as taxes on incomes and accumulated capital, and, in a sense, would return all the original value of the land to all the living citizens of the United States forever. The farmer wouldn't be excessively burdened because none of his land improvements or investments or the results of his efforts would be taxed. Only the pure rent, the income of the land-lord, would be taxed away, and the agricultural prices would rise to shift the burden of this tax on to those who consumed the products of the land. All of which makes very good sense. At least, it's an idea with strong appeal to those people who don't happen to be landlords.

Still, Henry George's ideas were not particularly popular at first, and he couldn't find a publisher for his book *Progress and Poverty* until he agreed to pay for the printing plates out of his own pocket. With the publication of this book in 1879, the single tax idea caught on rapidly. By 1881, a pirated paperback edition was a best seller. The English, especially, with their strong anti-landlord and anti-landed-aristocracy sentiments, found George's ideas an interesting alternative to the socialistic meas-ures that they were inclined to institute as reforms. In 1886, George came in second in a three-way race for the mayorality of New York City, ahead of a young and up-and-coming Republican named Teddy Roosevelt, but that was the closest single taxing ever came to political power.

The single tax idea is hardly heard of any more. The social problems it was supposed to have solved have disappeared or changed so much that people don't get very excited just about economic rents. Sometimes the function of an economic rent may even be considered virtuous. Take, for example, the so-called "quasi-rents," like the income from new inventions that are momentarily only available from one source, incomes generated by trademarks, brand names, product designs that are the ex-clusive property of only one producer, and incomes resulting from works of art. These are the rent-like payments to factors of production that are only temporarily unreproducible or are often regarded as sources for greater economic development.

Countries even encourage the development of such incomes through the patent and copyright laws that make the period of potential quasi-rent receipts longer than it might otherwise be.

THE LAW OF DIMINISHING RETURNS

Underlying Ricardo's rent theory is a concept that is basic to economic science; that is the idea of diminishing returns. The law of diminishing returns states that in any functional relationship, the more one quantity is increased while all other quantities remain unchanged, the more the returns from the use of this quantity diminish. What this meant to Ricardo was that the larger the population, with land being constant, the less food per person could be grown, even though more total food might be grown. Increasing the number of farmers without increasing the acreage would result in a less than proportionate increase in crops. Stated in general terms, ideal proportions may not be exceeded without causing a deterioration in the rate of returns. It applies to industrial processes as well as to problems of population. It applies to the quantity of vermouth in a martini and to the number of green apples eaten by the neighbor boy. Both Aristotle and Confucius had this law in mind when they counseled temperance and moderation.

The essence of the life process itself may be seen as a running battle between diminishing returns and optimum proportions. That is, we sleep until the last hour in the morning gives us barely enough rest to justify being in bed. Then we wake until our fatigue in the last hour suggests we might get better returns from sleep. We eat to correct the disproportionate lack of food commonly called hunger. We eat until we are satisfied that more food wouldn't help. As soon as we stop eating, we begin to erode this optimum proportion until the returns from doing something other than eating have diminished so far that we must stop and have lunch. Three times a day we create and destroy this optimum.

The idea of diminishing returns and optimum proportions

certainly occurred to Fra Pacioli when he devised the system of double-entry bookkeeping, in which the proportions of the various assets and the various liabilities of a business were made clearly visible in the balance sheet. Productive processes, be they biological life processes or economic ones, aim at achieving optimum proportions, but the processes themselves destroy some of the values on which this optimum proportion depends.

It would appear to be a never-ending cycle, and this is one way of looking at both life and the production that sustains life. Only death of the organism, disbanding the functioning institution, business bankruptcy, or whatever word best describes the end of any particular process will allow the process of striving for an optimum proportion to cease forever. Yet, optimum proportions can be reached during the process, especially when we restrict our area of concern to economic production and consumption or some other less than universal optimum. For example, psychologists define homeostasis as a state in which all motives and drives are equally balanced with one another so that the person remains psychically stable. Likewise, ecologists describe a goldfish bowl to be in the homeostatic state if the plants and fish are able to balance each other in their needs for food, oxygen, carbon dioxide, and so on. This is precisely the kind of balance Ricardo had in mind when he postulated the ultimate stationary state. However, more interesting than the optimal state itself is the process of getting there. In this process, various forces and quantities come into relationships with one another, reach temporary equilibriums, and are ruled by the law of diminishing returns.

Modern economists have amended the law of diminishing returns to include the possibility of increasing returns before diminishing returns set in. To put it in more concrete terms, the youngster eating ice cream may enjoy the second spoonful more (get a higher rate of returns of pleasure) than the first spoonful, and the third spoonful more than the second, as his appetite is whetted. But, eventually, each additional spoonful will bring diminished returns. Of that we can be sure, and for that reason the law is often called the law of *eventually* diminishing returns.

132

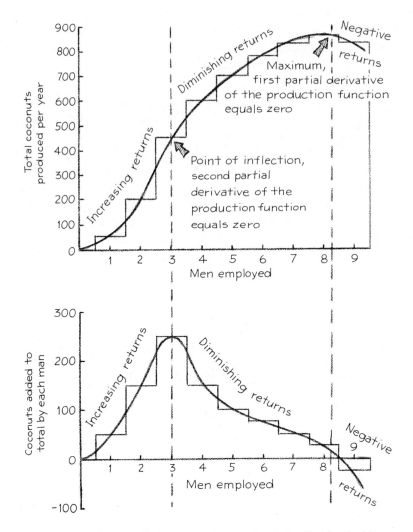

Figure 7. The production of coconuts on a South Pacific island with different levels of manpower.

This relationship is clearly shown in Figure 7, a hypothetical case in which an increasing number of workers is placed on an island in the South Pacific to harvest coconuts.[2] At first, as their number

---

[2] The coconut island became a traditional example in courses by the late Edward H. Chamberlin, Wells Professor of Political Economy at Harvard University.

is increased, efficiency is increased through the division of labor, and the total coconuts harvested increases at a more than proportional rate. Soon, however, the additional men add proportionately less to the coconut total. In fact, a point may be reached where additional men may actually decrease the total, presumably because they trample the young coconut trees or get in one another's way so much that they can't get any work done. Notice that in this hypothetical case, because the coconut trees are assumed to be the natural growth on a tropical island, all factors of production (land and capital) except labor are presumed to be constant. But the theory would apply just as well to any other factor, if all the rest were held constant. (See the following Mathematical Note.)

Mathematical Note

The same production function depicted in Figure 7 can be expressed in mathematical terms, and for economists with a fluent understanding of this most useful language, it is often more convenient than geometric presentations. The production function is generally expressed as

$$P = f(L, R, K)$$

where f is the function, production, P, equals some function of labor, L, land resources, R, and capital, K. In this particular coconut island case, the land resources and capital are held constant and only the labor input is varied. It may interest the reader already familiar with the calculus that without specifying the actual terms of the function and assuming that it is continuous (smooth, unbroken, not step-by-step), we can state that the boundary between the stage of increasing returns and the stage of diminishing returns will be at the point of inflection in the production function, where the value of the second partial derivative of the function is equal to zero.

$$\frac{\partial^2 P}{\partial L^2} = 0$$

The boundary between the stage of diminishing returns and the stage of negative returns will be at the point of maximum height of the production function, where the value of the first partial derivative of the function is equal to zero.

$$\frac{\partial P}{\partial L} = 0$$

Thus, in mathematical language, we have said quite a bit about the relationship between various quantities of a factor of production and the resultant levels of output, indeed, everything that we said in Figure 7. And we haven't yet specified any of the actual quantities in these relationships.

Anybody interested in learning more than the most rudimentary ideas in economics should become familiar with this kind of mathematical language. The French mathematician Antoine Augustin Cournot (1801–1877) was one of the first to apply mathematics to economic analysis and with a sophistication that was far ahead of his time. Today, a great deal of the science is written that way, and a very large proportion of economic research is an attempt to find the actual numbers that will transform the general statements into precise formulas that will most accurately describe past behavior and predict future behavior.

MALTHUS AND THE THEORY OF POPULATION

The law of diminishing returns was given a particularly pessimistic twist at the hands of the Reverend Thomas Robert Malthus (1766–1834), curate in the Church of England and professor of political economy. Although he didn't use these terms, he saw the whole world as a coconut island with its limited land area. As the human population increased, food production per person would diminish until there would be hardly enough food to keep everyone alive. As Malthus put it, even with heroic efforts, the productivity of agriculture can be increased only arithmetically, but population, if it reproduces itself without restraint, will increase geometrically. Clearly, a few generations of geometric increase will outrun the food supply, and those who won't starve to death will live on the brink of starvation.

After writing a few shorter pieces on the subject, Malthus turned his theory into a best-selling book, *An Essay on the Principle of Population*, first published in 1798. Its unhappy theme caused Thomas Carlyle, a contemporary of Malthus, to call economics the "dismal science." When all the other arts and sciences of the day were opening up new and glorious vistas, Malthus was prediciting our perdition. Ricardo's iron law of wages and his theory of rent were based on the same idea of the economy ultimately stabilizing on a subsistence level, but the Malthusian emphasis was particularly grim. He saw as the only limit to a geometric population increase the deadly discipline of disease and starvation. Preventative checks, such as postponed marriages, sexual continence, a greater number of unmarried men and women, and a strict adherence to sexual morality, were quite unrealistic in Malthus's opinion, and birth control was abhorrent to him on moral grounds.

In a way, his theory was right. All living things on this earth must ultimately abide by the limits of their food supply. Occasionally we hear of a bad winter or a long drought that causes mass deaths from starvation among herds of animals or flocks of birds in a particular area, and it has even happened among humans. But the normal situation of living things seems to be, if not abundance, at least not such a constant teetering on the brink of starvation. Adequacy of the food supply seems to be the long-run condition. In other words, while the Malthusian limit of the food supply is, indeed, a barrier to population expansion, most species of the biosphere are not constantly throwing themselves against this barrier. Predators, territorial crowding, instinctual reactions, and a variety of other limitations, just now beginning to be studied with intensity, function before the food barrier is reached.

Today, with the birth control methods that Malthus considered so vile, humans do have a considerable ability to restrain their reproductivity. When given the choice, most families have fewer children than their unimpeded reproductive capacity would give them. Life is simply more comfortable and more economical that way. And when families find their present standard of living threatened, they will make a strong effort to avoid compounding their problems with another mouth to feed. For example, restraint is clearly at work when, nine months after a major strike was begun in a town's main industry, the maternity ward of the town hospital is operating at half the normal patient load. This decrease happens even when a substantial proportion of the population does not use birth control devices because of religious reasons.

Many people wonder why Malthus constructed such a pessimistic theory. Some students of population say that his pessimism is not unfounded. They claim that homo sapiens have a particularly voracious sexual appetite, untempered by the seasons of the year or any other natural restraint. Only the rather ineffective inhibitions of religious morality and social conventions may give him pause in his libidinous pursuits. Thus, he is one of the few species that can endanger his own existence in this way. Without dwelling on this argument, let it suffice to comment that sex is not to be entirely equated with reproduction in this or any other case. Furthermore, in rates of reproduction over time, humans are pikers in comparison to, let's say, fruit flies or sun fish or the legendary rabbit.

Other students of Malthusian theory claim that his pessimism was a response to the unalloyed and probably rather irritating optimism of Malthus's father, who believed in the perfectibility of man and society along the lines of the then popular William Godwin. Perhaps for Oedipal reasons, perhaps for the sheer delight of going against his Godwinian old man, young Malthus seemed to make it his life's work to refute his father's rosy outlook. It also seems that a certain amount of puritanical zeal fueled his hellfire wrath against promiscuity and immorality. Overpopulation becomes just retribution for our sins. Whatever our psychoanalysis of Malthus himself or of the human race consists of (and let us be advised against taking such psychoanalysis too seriously), we can be sure that economic theories, like theories in all the arts and sciences, have their origins as much in the subjective motivations of the mind as in the objective observation of phenomena.

The record of history since Malthus's time both substantiates his population theory and disproves it. As examples against the theory, we can list the economies of developed countries, including the nations of Western Europe, North America, and Japan, where food production has increased, population growth is under some control, and the standard of living, in terms of the consumption of marketed goods at least, is high and improving. As examples for the theory, we can cite large areas of the remaining world that are still quite similar to the pre-industrial agrarian world that Malthus knew and wrote about. They include, especially, the poorest parts of Africa, Latin America, and India. Here, humanity has been threatened by its own reproduction. Every increase in agricultural production is more than offset by a larger increase in the population. The standard of living, already painfully low, is falling even lower, and without food shipments into these areas from the wealthy economies of the world, the grim Malthusian reaper would already be claiming his toll.

Recently developed new varieties of grains, particularly rice, wheat, and corn, promise some very substantial relief from this problem. Startling reports about the strains of rice developed with Rockefeller and Ford Foundation money at the Los Banos experimental station in the Philippines, strains that have increased yields up to fifteen times—to $8\frac{1}{2}$ tons per acre—have led optimists to herald a "Green Revolution" that will end food shortages for all time. But, at best, this new agricultural productivity will provide a welcome breather, during which time population control measures will have to be introduced, or the old Malthusian forces will extract their toll once again, and this time on a much larger population.

True Malthusians say that the Western economies are just postponing their ultimate fate, which will descend on them when they run out of new agricultural technology or when they have despoiled their environment completely. The non-Malthusians, on the other hand, argue that the unhappy experience of the undeveloped countries is merely the result of an unfortunate coincidence of events: the increasing longevity of the population brought about by twentieth century hygiene and medicine, the disruption of old patterns of culture because of contact with the Western nations and industrialization, and the persistence of the old ways of farming. They argue that as soon as birth control is introduced, as soon as cultural adjustments are made to the new influences from the West, and as soon as modern farm technology is instituted, the problem will cease to exist. So, between the pessimism and the optimism, "you pays your money and you takes your choice." But it is also possible to withhold judgment. Stationary states, Ricardian, Malthusian, or otherwise, have a way of being forever put off by the dynamic, ongoing events of history.

JEREMY BENTHAM

To Jeremy Bentham (1748–1832) the most important "returns" to be derived from economic activity were those which came from the avoidance of pains and the accumulation of pleasures as perceived by the individual while producing and consuming. A truly unique person, Bentham studied Latin at the age of four, graduated from Oxford at the age of fifteen, was the friend of several generations of English economists, and willed his entire estate to the University of London with the stipulation that his stuffed and dressed skeleton be seated at the meetings of the University's board. (It sometimes is.) Bentham theorized that the force that makes man act is his search for the greatest happiness, which he carries out by finding pleasure and avoiding pain. Anything instrumental to this search is said to have a positive utility. For example, food, clothing, money, leisure, and security have utility for man in this sense. Work, inconvenience, discomfort, and insecurity have a negative utility. However, Bentham's pleasure-pain calculus is not simply hedonism. He carefully points out that man has been so conditioned by his society that he can also get positive utility from behavior that benefits society, not just himself. Thus, the most Platonic idealist is motivated by his search for pleasure, which, in his case, is best satisfied by being idealistic, which ultimately is for the good of society. But Bentham's theory of pleasure tends to empty tautology: people do what they do because they want to do it. Not very enlightening!

His application of the law of diminishing returns, however, sheds more light. Bentham's theory specifies that the utility obtained from any one commodity is subject to diminishing returns with each additional unit of that commodity, or, more directly stated, it is subject to diminishing marginal utility: "the quantity of happiness produced by a particle of wealth . . . will be less and less at every particle; the second will produce less than the first, the third than the second, and so on."[3] We have already explained the theory of diminishing marginal utility in our description of the diminishing pleasures of spoonfuls of ice cream. In Ricardo's time this concept was applied primarily to the returns from factors of production and not to the utility derived from commodities consumed. Bentham's contribution was to extend the theory into a general philosophy of behavior, including, especially, consumer behavior. Ultimately, he hoped that his calculus of pleasure and pain would make an exact science out of politics and morals.

Even though he failed at this ultimate objective, his theory of diminishing marginal utility did have a tremendous impact on the social issues of his time and still does on those of today. The most important aspect of his theory is that an extra dollar of income brings less utility to a wealthy man than it does to a poor man. Poor people have always known this, but they have never before had such a convincing rational theory to support them.

This relatively simple idea is the basis of the economic egalitarianism found in socialist theory and virtually all reform politics today. It is the underlying assumption of the progressive income tax, used today in practically every developed nation, which taxes the rich proportionately more than the poor. It is the usually unspoken justification for all institutions that redistribute the national product from low marginal utility uses to those that will bring higher marginal utility, whether the institutions are established within a governmental, religious, social, or charitable framework.

According to Bentham's theory of diminishing marginal utility, the social good is increased by any policy that secures the highest possible marginal utility from the productive efforts. Many of the reforms that this genteel and scholarly man advocated are con-

---

[3] W. Stark, ed., *Jeremy Bentham's Economic Writings* (Humanities Press, New York, 1952), Vol. I, p. 113.

sidered radical even today: he designed a model prison that would reform criminals rather than punish them; he advocated public works to provide employment for the unemployed; he advocated free trade and competition; and he thought of a great number of other social, legal, educational, and parliamentary reforms. Even his concern for the greatest good for the greatest number was itself somewhat heretical at that time, and, to some people it still is today.

What Bentham contributed to economics was not so much an advancement of the science as a reminder of the importance of the human motive in the economic system. Ricardo and Malthus had applied the law of diminishing returns to the relationship between land—the natural resources—and the supply of food and other products. Bentham applied the law to the relationship between the economic product and the consumer; in the process, he had examined the motives of this ultimate consumer. Adam Smith had also concerned himself at length with the causes and nature of man's behavior. But Ricardo, Malthus, and most of the other economists who followed them had little interest in this basic question. For them, it seemed self-evident that man's economic behavior was motivated by some sort of self-interest, a profit motive in the most general sense. It wasn't necessary to pursue the matter further. Only Bentham, along with Adam Smith and Karl Marx and a very few others, pursued the matter, and economic science is the richer for it.

JOHN STUART MILL

Classical economics reached its peak and its end with John Stuart Mill (1806–1873). The story of the extraordinary childhood and education of this Englishman at the hands of a brilliant, egotistical father has become legendary. At the age of three he had begun to learn Greek; by the age of eight he was learning Latin; by twelve it was algebra, geometry, and the calculus; by thirteen, political economy; in his teens he edited and published Bentham's works; by nineteen he was writing his own scholarly articles; and at twenty he had a nervous break-down. A major work, *Principles of Political Economy*, first published in 1848, served as the definitive textbook on the subject for forty years. Yet, all through his life, the sensitive and gentle Mill always attributed his greatness to someone else: first, his father, James Mill, then his wife, the former Mrs. Harriet Taylor, whom he loved for twenty years before her husband died and he could marry her. This humble quality is noticeable in his work, which brims with a humanitarianism and an empathy for the poor that is unusual for a scientific theoretician and is, perhaps, especially unexpected in a theoretical economist.

Mill's contribution to economic science was less the creation of new ideas than the clarification and synthesis of old ones. Every science benefits enormously from having such a person come along every few years to edit, organize, and articulate its theories. These people become the master teachers of the next generation; their names are included among the great in science; and their writings have a long and influential reach. In Mill's *Principles*, the various classical theories of value, diminishing returns, rent, production, international trade, population, and growth were systematized and neatly divided into five parts: "Production," "Distribution," "Exchange," "Influence of the Progress of Society on Production and Distribution," and "On the Influence of Government." Even in such an heroic compendium of established economic science, he was able to sharpen and polish many rough edges.[4]

Mill also helped reintroduce a brighter optimism to the "dismal science." Unlike most of his predecessors, he argued that by improving environmental conditions, the nature of man him-

---

[4] For example, by using an analysis of demand intensity, which anticipated Alfred Marshall's concept of elasticity (see Chapter 7), Mill improved on Ricardo's theory of comparative advantage. He showed how much each party to international trade benefits, which Ricardo was unable to do (see p. 127). For instance, assuming an increase in production efficiency with a concomitant opportunity for a price decrease, the producer gains most if the demander has an elastic demand, that is, if he will buy a great deal more at the lower price. The producer gains least if the demander has an inelastic demand, that is, if he will buy very little more even though the lower price was more favorable to him.

self would gradually improve and the final stationary state toward which economies tended would be peaceful and mild. As he wrote in Book IV, Chapter VI, of his *Principles:*

> I cannot, therefore, regard the stationary state of capital and wealth with the unaffected aversion so generally manifested towards it by political economists of the old school. I am inclined to believe that it would be, on the whole, a very considerable improvement on our present condition. I confess I am not charmed with the ideal of life held out by those who think that the normal state of human beings is that of struggling to get on; that the trampling, crushing, elbowing, and treading on each other's heels, which form the existing type of social life, are the most desirable lot of human kind, or anything but the disagreeable symptoms of one of the phases of industrial progress.[5]

---

[5] John Stuart Mill, *Principles of Political Economy* (Longmans, Green & Co., London, 1881), p. 453.

CHAPTER 6

Accelerating Social Change

WORKING CONDITIONS AND CITY LIFE

Writing in 1859 in England about the 1780s in France, Charles
Dickens began *A Tale of Two Cities* with, "It was the best of times,
it was the worst of times, . . . the period was so far like the present
period," and distilled the essence of the age in that one sentence,
admittedly a sentence whose 120 words ran on for the entire
first paragraph of the book. It was the best of times, we have
seen, because with the vastly increased carrying capacity of the
land—and the agriculture and industry on it—the population of
England and other countries similarly touched by the Industrial
Revolution increased rapidly. The life expectancy at birth, which
had been roughly thirty years in 1750, increased to forty years by
1850. (It is about seventy years today.) Urban populations grew,
proportionately even faster than the total, and entire cities

cropped up where there had been only open fields a little more than a generation earlier. To be sure, many of the new city dwellers had been forced off their traditional rural lands by the enclosures, but many others came to seek the glamor and high wages of the city. Knowledge, literacy, geographic mobility, and opportunity for advancement, which had been the private domain of only the rich and the titled, became increasingly available to the masses.

But it was also the worst of times. The rapid changes brought about a breakdown of the traditional social order, which continues even into our own times. Families that had worked together in the pre-industrial days were broken up, with each member going his own way, to return home together only at the end of the long and wearying work day. The small towns and parishes, the guilds, and the relationships between landlord and peasant that had served as the basic institutions of mutual aid for the people during so many centuries gave way to the burgeoning, impersonal mill towns that had no leadership or traditions and that were heartlessly indifferent to the well-being of the inhabitants. A worker's home labor, which at one time had provided the simple needs of his life, the food, clothing, and shelter for his rural family, was now replaced by the piece-rate wage, which would decrease his income with every day, even every minute, that he faltered at his toil. With the family and community structure weakened, any period of crisis or major change— for example, unemployment, sickness, death, childbirth, marriage—had to be dealt with on an individual or family basis. Assistance might be forthcoming from sympathetic neighbors, but there were no institutional guarantees of such aid. Those who were hit hardest by this social change were the poor, who had no cushion of wealth to fall back on. What good did the slightly higher income from factory work do them if they were unable to keep body and soul together during a temporary unemployment? A very large proportion of the working class population found themselves eventually unable to make ends meet and had to appeal to the meager and often demeaning charity provided by poor laws. These laws may have prevented a revolution in England, but they did so at the expense of a demoralized and emasculated work force.

The higher incomes in the cities were also largely spurious. Though wages may have increased, so did prices, and historians are confused about whether the average standard of living really did increase or not. The times in England from 1800 to 1850 seem to have been generally good, but the age of revolution and after, on to the start of the twentieth century, shows no clear record of an increase in real income for the majority of the laboring masses. What the record *is* clear on, however, is the rapid growth in population. The phenomenal increase in economic productivity and in total national income was mostly gobbled up by an ever-increasing number of mouths. Of course, the new industry did indeed make fortunes for those who could capitalize on the opportunity, but the standard of living of the burgeoning masses remained for the most part unchanged.

Even if the wages in industry were higher than those for farm labor, they would have to be balanced against the extra cost extracted from the workers by the discomforts of urban industrial living. In their old life, the rural peasants had fresh air and sunshine, space to live in, and their heavy toil was not unhealthy. Men, women, and children, all had to pitch in to work from sunup to sundown, whether on the farm or in the cottage industry. And on the farm they worked together as a family, and somehow the picture of a young child doing menial farm chores does not seem as tragic as that of a young city child working in a factory.

In the cities, all the nonmonetary benefits of rural life were absent. The fetid, sulfur-fumed air blocked out the sunshine; the factory cramped every physical movement; the work was unhealthy and dangerous; living space was minimal in the noisy, filthy, and crowded tenements; and the entire family—men, women, and children—still had to work, and not as an integrated unit but at separate jobs. Transferring from the countryside to the city in order to earn a living seems to involve a deterioration of all aspects of life. Whether this is because the living and working conditions of the city are just more visible than they are in the rural areas, or whether they are, in fact, the negatives of urban life is open to question.

At the same time in the nineteenth century, the populace of relatively urban England is considered to have been better off

than the populace of relatively rural France. Even if the Englishman ate only bread and water all year, curing his resulting heart-
burn by eating pieces of chalk from the Cliffs of Dover, he was
still living better than the Frenchman. In fact, the Englishman
did occasionally get cheese, porridge, and skimmed milk. Tea
was popular and inexpensive. Yet, urbanization seems to have
caused increased alcoholism and "strawhouses"—inns where
anyone could get gin-drunk and sleep it off on fresh straw provided free by the innkeeper—neither of which indicated a con-
tented or comfortable people. And we might note that about
a century later, when the city dwellers were able to afford it,
they emigrated again—this time to the suburbs.

Working conditions in the factories were, in most cases, abys-
mal. In the search for ever cheaper labor, children in pauper
and orphan homes were farmed out to the mills, where they
were worked, beaten, and starved unmercifully. The parishes
that administered the children's homes were glad to get rid of
them and were paid a fee for their use. The factory foremen,
who accepted the children as "pauper apprentices," themselves
received a wage that was determined by how much work their
children turned out relative to the cost of maintaining them.
In every way, the system worked against the children, and they
had absolutely no voice in the matter. If they lived to adulthood, which was not very likely, they grew up physically
stunted, mentally retarded, often morally depraved, and completely incapable of doing anything productive except serving
the one machine to which they had been set as children. Early
reports cite the case of the apprentices at the mill in Litton,
competing with the pigs to get at the hog swill in the troughs.
Instances of sadism, perversion, and the torture of little children
and their attempts at suicide to escape this hell have also been
reported.

The factories bred disease. The air in cotton mills was filled
with fluff that caused serious lung infections. In the flax mills,
where the spinning was done with wet fibers, the workers were
usually soaking wet. No thought was given to ventilation, and at
night the smoke from candles made it even worse. In Manchester,
the first epidemic of "factory fever," a type of typhus, broke out

in 1784. It spread rapidly to other industrial districts and led to many deaths. Machine safety provisions were unheard of, and workers that had fingers and limbs crushed or missing were a common sight. The children were especially susceptible to accidents at the end of their fourteen-, sixteen-, and even eighteen-hour day, when, completely exhausted, they became careless. Boys and girls slept together in crowded, filthy dormitories, the beds never left empty as the night shift replaced the day shift. Venereal diseases, especially syphilis, raged like a prairie fire.

The relentless logic of the profit motive led to more and more children and women being employed in the factories, where small hands and endurance counted more than skill or strength. The workshops of Sir Robert Peel in Lancashire alone employed more than a thousand children. The children and women received a much lower wage than the men, sometimes only one-sixth as much, and the children would occasionally be given only their food in payment. This rush for profit also worked to the disadvantage of the men, who were frequently passed over by the employment of cheaper labor and had to depend on their wives and children for the family income. Any workers who failed to perform their duty, for whatever reason, or who simply displeased the foreman were fired on the spot. The newly mechanized industries depended on a steady and reliable work force, which meant that absenteeism was not tolerated and that workers had to be reliable seven days a week, fifty-two weeks a year. Warnings, such as, "If you don't come in Sunday, don't come in Monday," were posted on billboards to remind workers that a day of rest, even the Sabbath, was not their lot.

Not only were the men, women, and children being exploited by the long hours and inhuman working conditions, but they were also being victimized by all kinds of fraud. For example, if they had their own watches, they were not allowed to wear them at work and were forced to abide by the foreman's less than objective interpretation of time. In some cases, where there was a factory clock, it would miraculously run faster during the lunch break, which was the only pause in the long day. During the working hours, the foreman could make the workers go faster by accelerating the main source of power for the machines, the steam engine, or water wheel. Driven by fierce competition from other factories, justified in his actions by the new philosophy of laissez faire, and uninhibited by any of the niceties of humanitarianism or sympathy, the employer ran his factory to get the most out of his investment. What happened to the employees' lives was irrelevant to him.

THE BEGINNING OF DISSENT

The power of the capitalist over the worker seemed absolute. Yet the first rebellion was not directed against the capitalist employer himself but against his machines. Then, as now, the workers were confused about the effect of mechanization on their welfare. They believed that the machines took their jobs away and that by destroying the machines they could regain the good old life. They were in no condition to appreciate that although machines caused unemployment of the men directly replaced by them, they would, by being more efficient, bring lower prices of the commodities they produced. These lower prices would stimulate a larger quantity demanded of those commodities, and the result would be a larger demand for labor again. Mechanization does not have to bring a decrease in employment if the workers are mobile enough to respond to the new employment opportunities that are created. Furthermore, by lowering prices or increasing wages or both, mechanization increases the total real income created by the economy, which can be (but may not be) distributed to the workers. The first Neanderthal man "mechanized" by using a stone or a stick implement to hunt his game, and, ever since, mechanization has usually meant an improvement in man's ability to deal with his environment. But there have always been groups, such as the guilds of the Middle Ages and some labor unions of today, that would rather protect their vested interest in the old and sometimes inefficient ways of the past, rather than take a chance with new, more mechanized means of production.

After a mob of workers stormed and destroyed a mechanical saw mill near London and spinning jennies in Lancashire were broken up, a law was passed in 1769 making the destruction of machinery punishable by death. Still the workers rebelled. In 1779, they destroyed engines near Bolton; by 1796 some factories had to be protected by garrisons of troops; and from 1811 to 1816, the Luddite movement, named after a half-witted Leicestershire worker who thirty years earlier had gained notoriety by destroying stocking frames, spread terror throughout the English Midlands, wreaking revenge against their employers for the prevailing unemployment and low wages by destroying their machines. In France, the workers were throwing their wooden shoes, sabots, into weaving machines—thus the origin of the word, sabotage. English workers also petitioned Parliament for legal protection against these "labor-saving" machines that seemed to cause them so much hardship. They reactivated the guild arguments that the machines depreciated the quality of the goods, but to no avail.

THE LABOR UNION MOVEMENT

More beneficial to the workers than these waves of rebellion against machines was the development of labor unions, which tackled the problem at its source, namely, the absolute power of management. But the idea of a combination of laborers against this absolute power had a difficult birth. Many of the factory workers were employed nominally as apprentices, and they first had to realize that their apprenticeship was, in fact, a fiction. In no way did it involve training for a higher level job, let alone the ultimate achievement of the master's degree in a skilled trade, as it once had. This remnant of the guild practice had long been abused by the employers, who hired hundreds of apprentices at minimal wages under the guise that these workers were receiving training for their future life's work. When the "apprentices" would have been ready for their mastership after at least seven years of toil and not before the age of 21, they were put off with the intermediate degree of journeyman. Originally, journeymen were supposed to travel from master to master in other cities to learn the refinements of their trade before settling down to their own shops as established masters. But for these industrial journeymen, mastership was not theirs to have, for they did not travel and were kept in their journeyman status. Nor was it even feasible in the newly mechanized factories to continue the old apprentice-master structure because it was more suited to a shoemaker's shop or a village bakery than the new industrial age.

The new industries needed unskilled, untrained, homogeneous workers by the thousands, and once the workers realized that they could not deal with their employers on the personal basis of the handicraft shop, they began to organize combinations that would bargain collectively. The first of these appeared in the woolen industry in England in the early 1700s. By the 1780s, they were strong enough to resist wage decreases with strikes. In Philadelphia, in 1794, the Federal Society of Journeymen Cordwainers (bootmakers) was a functioning union, probably the first in the country, although union development in America and on the Continent was generally about a half century behind that in England.

Almost immediately laws were passed to make labor unions illegal. In France, the Chapelier Law of 1791 was passed. In England, it was the Combination Acts of 1799 and 1800. In the United States, the courts in effect outlawed unions by finding them guilty of criminal conspiracy should they engage in any "trouble-making" activities, such as strikes, slowdowns, or other such protests. Courts of law and, to almost the same degree, legislatures tend to be conservative, behind the times, and suspicious of new social phenomena. But the development of unions could not be stopped, and as industries grew larger and more dominant in the Western economies, so did the unions.

Just as the structure of industry evolved from the small local factory to the large, national organization, so did unions become national. And as business cycles brought alternately good times and bad times to business, the unions also experienced upswings and downswings in their fortune. When business conditions were good, factories were running full tilt, and wages were relatively high. This afforded workers the cushion on which to entertain thoughts of improving their lot, and unions increased. When times were bad, workers were happy to hold a job at any wage, and unions decreased—even disappeared in some cases. Revolutions, whether political, military, economic, or social, cannot be fought from the worst possible conditions. Only when the hardships that spawned the revolutionary motive are somewhat ameliorated can the revolution itself begin.

For the unions, the revolution was an on-again-off-again affair. Their organizations were much more fragile and vulnerable than the businesses they were fighting. Then, too, they were constantly the victims of legal harassment, even after the repeal of the Combination Acts in England in 1825 and in France the Chapelier Law in 1864, and even after the case of the Commonwealth (of Massachusetts) vs. Hunt in 1842 set the precedent in the United States that unions were not conspiracies if they did not commit unlawful acts. The legal estate was still on the side of the employer, and union action was effectively squashed by criminal proceedings and court injunctions. In the United States, even the Sherman Antitrust Act of 1890, which was supposed to outlaw business monopoly, was used as an effective weapon against unions in its first trials. The courts continued to obstruct union activity until finally the Norris-La Guardia Act of 1932 came to labor's legal rescue. It clearly declared many anti-union activities illegal and, most important, it severely limited the courts' freedom to enjoin strikes.

Of course, management had developed its own tactics inside the factories to break the unions. These included industrial spying, to ferret out the union members and then fire them; the "yellow dog contract," which made workers pledge not to belong to a union—a contract that was enforceable in the federal courts until the Norris-La Guardia Act outlawed it; and the establishment of "company unions," management-dominated organizations to divert the employees' unionization potential. Employers also refused to recognize already organized unions and, therefore, to sit down and bargain with them (which they still do today). But they did recognize them enough to hire armies of police and armed guards to break up strikes and to protect the plant and equipment. To the employers, unionists were simply dry-land mutineers and were resisted with a righteous wrath.

The unionists were equally persistent in their crusade for the dignity of the working man. As one would expect, this conflict invited violence, and in England from the early 1700s on, strikes led to riots and riots to bloodshed. A few of the worst confrontations in the United States were a railroad strike in 1877, the steel strike at Homestead in 1892, the textile strike in Lawrence, Massachusetts, in 1912, and the notorious Chicago Memorial Day Massacre in 1937. But bullets, bombs, and the injury and death of policemen, workers, and innocent bystanders accompanied a great many labor-management disagreements. Especially in the Appalachian mining towns, often insulated from the outside world, the heat of conflict became dangerously high, and from the 1870s to the 1930s, the area was a scene of continuous guerilla warfare.

The union movement didn't struggle completely alone. In 1891 Pope Leo XIII issued the encyclical *Rerum Novarum*, which strongly encouraged the social-reform-minded Catholic clergy that had been working with workers and socialist groups. This encyclical also serves as the foundation on which modern Christian Socialist and Catholic Socialist parties were built. Intellectuals and persons with strong social consciences championed the union movement. In the first half of the 1800s in England, Robert Owen gave the unions substantial moral and material support. He welcomed them into his own spinning mills, which were the largest and best equipped in Scotland at the time, and his son, Robert Dale Owen, supported union growth in America, as did Frances Wright, the first American women's suffragist, and Thomas Skidmore, a brilliant pamphleteer. Many of their ideas were considered utopian, but they had a strong influence on the growth of early unions.

The first, large, national union in the United States, the Knights of Labor, was a creation of these socially concerned interests united with the working classes. The leader of the Knights, T. V. Powderly, called his union's amalgam of political reform, economic progress, and agrarian revolt the "Great Upheaval," and it seemed a formula for success. With an important railroad strike in 1886, the union won recognition and collective bargaining rights from Jay Gould, the powerful financier, and membership increased to 700,000 workers (out of a total non-farm labor force of about 11,000,000). But after the rise of the American Federation of Labor under Samuel Gompers in the 1880s, its influence rapidly declined.

A similar fate befell the Industrial Workers of the World— or Wobblies, as the members were called—which was founded in Chicago in 1905. It organized all kinds of unskilled labor, preached a militant socialistic doctrine, fought one successful but violent strike, the Lawrence textile strike of 1912, and then faded from the scene after World War I. The problem with both the Knights and the I.W.W. was that while they were successful at conducting strikes, they were weak at collective bargaining. Also, organizers often didn't stay around after a strike was over because they were off organizing in other places; dues weren't collected regularly; local chapter offices were poorly organized; meetings weren't held often enough; and too many of the members came from different trades and economic classes. But the harassment of left-wing groups before and after World War I was also a major factor in their demise.

Samuel Gompers, the founder of the American Federation of Labor, believed that a successful union could develop and last only if it was steady and businesslike and not given to dramatic excesses. From the time of its founding in 1886, the AFL stood for "bread and butter" unionism and opposed the great upheaval or social ideals of the Knights of Labor and the I.W.W. Instead, it was to be a loose federation of the tightly organized trade unions of cigar makers, carpenters, machinists, garment workers, and so on. It would negotiate for better wages, better hours, and better working conditions, the holy trinity of the AFL, by means of collective bargaining with management. The AFL would provide financial support and legal and nego-tiating skills for these trade unions and serve as a focus for the national labor movement. Whereas the labor unions in Britain and Europe used a great deal of political pressure and ultimately became the main support of socialist governments, the AFL concentrated on purely economic means and ends. Addressing the AFL convention in 1903, Sam Gompers told the Socialists in attendance, "I am entirely at variance with your philosophy. . . . Economically, you are unsound; socially, you are wrong; and industrially you are an impossibility."[1] To this day, American labor is philosophically conservative. This may be the cause of serious problems for unions today, but in the late 1800s and early 1900s, it was the foundation on which the AFL flourished. By 1900, the AFL had about one million members in its affiliated unions, and by 1920, it had about five million, representing 25 percent of the nonfarm labor force.

But after 1920 union membership began to decline. It was clear that the AFL, dominated by trade unions, each of which was jealous of the other's separate craft jurisdictions, wasn't doing enough to gain membership in the large manufacturing industries, where unskilled and semiskilled workers predominated. Led by John L. Lewis, the tough and fiery president of the United Mine Workers, and aided by new government legislation, especially the National Industrial Recovery Act of 1933 and the National Labor Relations Act of 1935, which guaranteed workers the right to organize into unions of their own choosing, efforts at unionizing these large industries were begun. When Lewis's Committee for Industrial Organization unionized about one million workers in six different industrial unions, the challenge to the established trade unions of the AFL was too great, and these industrial unions were at first suspended, then expelled from the AFL. But there was no turning back. Retaining the magic letters, CIO, the Committee renamed itself in 1938 the Congress of Industrial Organizations, declared its independence of the AFL, and proceeded to unionize Bethlehem, Republic, and United States Steel, Ford, General Motors, and Chrysler, General Electric and Westinghouse, Goodyear and Firestone, and many others. Both the CIO unions and the AFL unions grew as prosperity returned after the Depression and the government developed a more favorable attitude toward them. In 1955, with old wounds forgotten (and some old leaders

---

[1] *AFL Convention Proceedings 1903*, pp. 188–198.

replaced by a new generation), the AFL and CIO joined to form the AFL-CIO. Membership was over 16 million and comprised almost one-third of the nonfarm labor force.

But after World War II the government's attitude toward unions began to be less favorable and was reflected in legislation passed in the forties and fifties. Already in 1947, spurred by the wave of postwar strikes in 1946, the legislature passed the Labor-Management Relations Act (Taft-Hartley Labor Act), which prescribed standards of conduct for the unions that severely limited their bargaining tactics. Primarily because of the financial corruption of the Teamsters union, the government also pushed through the Labor-Management Reporting and Disclosure Act of 1959 (Landrum-Griffin Act), which required a higher degree of financial virtue of the unions. But federal restrictions on union activities were not their only problem. It became increasingly difficult to organize the remaining nonunion workers. Today, the bulk of unorganized workers are farm laborers and white collar workers, most of whom have been resistant to unionization. Furthermore, unions have remained true to their conservative philosophy and have rarely been in the vanguard of movements for racial integration, rights for women, environmental protection, or international understanding. Except for a few dedicated personalities like Cesar Chavez, who is organizing the predominantly Chicano farm workers in California, union leadership generally wears a dark business suit and behaves very much like the businessmen with whom they bargain. In 1965, ten years after the formation of the AFL-CIO, its membership had slipped below 16 million. Since then it has grown again, but very slowly.

COMMUNES, COOPERATIVES, AND UTOPIA

Whatever the problems, the union movement proved to be the most effective force to countervail the unrestrained abuses and excesses of the rapidly growing industrialism. Unions play an important role in virtually every free market economy today. But other instruments were also tried. The same phalanx of intellectual and social-welfare-minded persons that influenced the early years of the labor movement also experimented with radical departures from the existing industrial pattern. Most of these experiments were strongly sweetened with social uplift motives, belief in the perfectibility of the human race, and a rather unrealistic vision of a possible utopia that balanced the sense of outrage at the injustices of industrial conditions at the time.

Among the first social experimenters were Henri Comte de Saint-Simon (1760–1825) and Charles Fourier (1772–1837) in France. In a way, Saint-Simon was a socialist who was born too soon. He argued that the only valuable contribution made to society was made by the working masses, ironically the poorest class. The aristocracy, the clergy, and bureaucracy were useless "plaster and gilt." Work and industry should be given not only their full share of the economy's production, but they should also make the major decisions of government. The parlimentary government should consist of three chambers: invention, review, and execution. Industry should be organized on as large a scale as possible. Saint-Simon's followers, as is so often the case, became fanatical and dogmatic champions of his philosophy, but Saint-Simon himself found little resonance for his ideas in a France that had not yet fully entered the Industrial Revolution.

Although Fourier also lived before France's full industrialization, his ideas were actually tried out in several countries. He argued that the social ills of the rapidly changing and growing economy could best be solved by forming cooperative communities called *phalanges* (or *phalanxes*) which he planned meticulously in every detail. All the families would live, work, and consume together, everyone getting a fair share of the total product, and no one living with less than the minimum of subsistence. In the United States alone, forty of these phalanges were organized, the best-known one being the North American Phalanx in Red Bank, New Jersey, which lasted from 1841 to 1846. All of these failed, but they had an important influence on social philosophy, and the idea never died out completely. The Chinese communists have experimented with it on an immense scale. Examples of communal living and a communal organization of part of the economy can be found in many older and newer institutions, for example, primitive tribes, religious monasteries, Israeli kibbutzim, Quaker work camps, and the many new family-type living groups cropping up across our country.

Robert Owen (1771–1858), a utopian in England, nurtured Fourier's idea of the cooperative into bloom. We have already seen that he was interested in helping the early labor unions develop, but he was really interested in a much more radical departure from existing economic convention. He argued that human nature could be improved by perfecting the environment in which people lived and that management could accomplish this job while making a profit to boot. And he proved it. He bought a mill in New Lanark, Scotland, whose workers, most of whom lived in poverty, included five hundred pauper children, some of whom were only six years old but who, nevertheless, kept the machines running twelve hours a day and six days a week. With Owen's reforms instituted, the minimum work age was ten, children went to a free school from ages five to ten, and there was even a nursery for pre-schoolers. Comfortable housing was built, the company store sold fuel and food at cost, the twelve-hour work day was reduced to ten-and-a-half hours, and wages were high for the times. Workers were compensated for unemployment and sickness, and an old-age pension was set up. Fines and punishments levied on workers in the factory, which was standard procedure at the time, were abolished, and adult educational and recreational facilities were established.

The employees of the New Lanark mill worshipped Robert Owen. And the mill made profits, of which he and his partners kept only 5 percent. The experiment seemed a success, and largely because of his influence, some factory reform legislation was written into law in Britain. But when he established a colony based on the same spirit of cooperation in New Harmony, Indiana, in 1825, he lost almost all of his fortune in three years. His other colonies in Britain also failed. But part of the cooperative movement hung on and finally succeeded. The Rochdale Society of Equitable Pioneers, founded in 1844 in Rochdale,

England, by his followers, became a highly successful consumers' cooperative and is one of the larger retailers in Britain today.

Consumers' cooperatives, farm cooperatives, mutual banking and insurance companies, and many other forms of cooperatives remain as a viable alternative to the conventional business organization. What the different kinds of cooperatives have in common is that they pool the capital investment, on which the cooperatives are built, from among their customers. These, then, "own" the cooperative and share in its profits. The advantages are that widely dispersed, small amounts of savings can be accumulated into a large enough sum to establish a business operation; likewise, managerial talent may be tapped from a class of people that wouldn't normally be given this opportunity; and the cooperatives are managed in the interest of the customer-owners themselves. At first, the spirit of social reform and uplift pervaded the cooperative movement, but today cooperatives are quite sober, businesslike, and generally undistinguishable from conventionally owned businesses. They do enjoy certain tax advantages in some countries, the United States included, which give them a competitive edge seriously resented by the rest of the business community, but most cooperatives operate in markets that are ignored or avoided by conventional businesses so that the area of conflict is not large.

The Anarchists

The economic philosophers who hoped to find their utopias in communes or cooperatives believed in the necessity of imposing some kind of strong institutional structure on the economy. The anarchists, on the other hand, believed that the best structure was no structure at all. They seemed to have a Rousseauesque yearning for a more natural and simpler way of life and believed that whatever cooperative working together might be needed could be spontaneously organized, like a frontier barn-building: no formal institutionalized structure was necessary. Pierre Joseph Proudhon (1809–1865), one of the first anarchists, preached that any form of government, whether it be a monarchy or a democracy, was primarily concerned with serving the privileged classes, that property was merely a form of theft, that there was very little justification for the inequalities in wealth and income, and that all these institutional structures impeded the free intercourse between individual humans—the only source of value and productivity in society. Proudhon's anarchy was never accepted, and although he did succeed in organizing a "People's Bank" in Paris in 1849, which was to be kind of a commodity exchange operating on credit, he was arrested for revolutionary sympathies before the bank could begin to function. The other anarchists that followed in the next decades achieved no more success than Proudhon, and the movement became generally discredited by the bomb-throwing excesses of its fanatics. Yet, the anarchist point of view strongly influenced those libertarian economists, philosophers, and social critics who were and are, still, suspicious of large governmental powers. Strangely enough, as we shall see below, anarchist thought also influenced the economists, philosophers, and social critics that leaned toward the communist ideology.

KARL MARX AND THE BIRTH OF COMMUNISM

Of all the dissents from the existing order created by the Industrial Revolution, none was as sophisticated, as grand, or as influential on the course of history as that of Karl Marx. That the record so far seems to show that his dissent was based on error doesn't diminish his achievement. Like no other economist— like no other human being, for that matter—he is virtually the sole inventor of an economic, social, and ideological system that is followed by roughly one-third of the population of the world today. This would be reason enough to study Marx and communism, but he is also an important contributor to economic science, which is our concern here.

Karl Marx was born into a respectable, but not rich, German Jewish family in 1818. His childhood seems to have been normal, and when he was seventeen, he entered the University of Bonn to study law and follow in his father's footsteps. When he found law boring, he entered the University of Berlin, where he concentrated his energies on philosophy, literature, history, and art, although he remained nominally a student of law, to please his father. Marx became a very serious and hard-working student, so much so that his father implored him to stop overworking himself, enjoy life a little, and have some beer with the boys. But Karl would not relent, and, according to his exasperated father, he would build philosophic systems for himself during the day, only to tear them apart during sleepless nights, until he was less sure of himself than when he began.

Marx's economics, when he finally was ready to put it all together years later, was based on a completely systematic and carefully specified philosophic foundation. For this effort, he is to be lauded. Too much scientific study, economics included, is carried on without any regard for the basic premises on which the study builds. Assumptions are accepted as given, hypotheses are taken as facts, and, even worse, the researcher himself is often unaware of the philosophically questionable, underlying premises that he has blithely taken for granted. Not so Marx! If anything, his philosophic foundation had too much, rather than too little, influence on his scientific economics.

After getting his doctoral degree from the University of Jena in 1842, he applied for a lectureship at the University of Bonn but was turned down for being too radical for this relatively bucolic school. The University of Berlin, which appreciated his brilliance and did not fear his radicalism, also would not accept him because he was too inexperienced. At age 24, with the academic world apparently closed to him, he began to edit a liberal, workingman's newspaper in the industrial Rhineland of Germany, but a year later the paper was suppressed because of his radical views. Later, he edited other similar papers, free-lanced as a reporter and writer, served in Paris as European correspondent for the New York *Tribune*, but seldom did he earn a regular income for very long. His writings were too revolutionary for the many governments that were experiencing unrest at home—there was a revolution in France in 1848, uprisings in Austria, Italy, and Germany, and strong public dissent in Switzerland and England. So Marx traveled a lot. In 1845 he was expelled from Paris, in 1848 from Brussels. Then he went to Germany, back to Paris again, and finally he landed in London in 1849, where he lived until his death in 1883. From 1849 on, Friederich Engels, his intellectual companion and collaborator, supported Marx and his family, whose not infrequent poverty contributed to the death of three of his six children.

Marx was not much of a revolutionary activist. He did join the League of the Just, a German workingman's association, and the Communist League in 1847, one year before he and Engels wrote the *Communist Manifesto*. Although, through these experiences, he did get an inside view of the conditions of the working classes in several countries, the scholarly and bourgeois Marx had very little in common with the crude and uneducated proletariat. From 1864 to 1879, he also represented the German workers in the International Working Men's Association (the First International), which met in London, but his main work during all his years there was done in the British Museum, writing his magnum opus, *Das Kapital*, which has since become the bible of the communist world. Marx published the first volume in 1867. The remaining two volumes were published posthumously by Engels.

In order to understand Marx's communism, we must understand that, above all else, his theories are designed as a complete philosophic and scientific system. At the same time that Richard Wagner was composing operas, which he expected would be both the apex and the ultimate end of all musical, dramatic, and artistic expression, and at the same time that Charles Darwin was writing *The Origin of Species*, in which he expounded nothing less that the evolution of life on earth, Marx was developing a theoretical system that would explain the basis of world history and would predict the ultimate outcome of it all. It was the age of Romanticism, and only very grand ideas would do. At the very time when all the forces of change were fragmenting the social and physical aspects of human life so that little remained of the traditional, wholesome, and unified context of man's world, these men were building systems that were intended to explain the totality of experience, integrate the universe, and bring the march of time to a logical conclusion.

At the heart of Marx's system is his philosophy of dialectics, which he adapted from Hegel's philosophy. Both were in agreement that reality is only discernable when there is movement, that the most basic fact of the universe is change or action. But Hegel, a philosophic idealist, argued that reality, that is, action or change, existed only in the mind as an idea. Marx, a philosophic realist, argued that reality existed outside of the mind, that change or action in physical events is the only reality, and that the mind merely perceived the reality external to it. This idea of reality Marx found easy to apply to economics. After all, he was one of the last great classical economists, a "close cousin" to John Stuart Mill and David Ricardo. With them, he believed that the value of commodities is determined by how many labor hours went into their production. This value was a built-in characteristic of the commodities themselves, not a mental evaluation of them. Therefore, Marx argued, it followed that if economic value is inherent in the commodities themselves, then philosophic reality must also be inherent in the external, material world. Finally, Marx concluded, since change or action can only be defined in terms of movement relative to something else, all reality can only be defined in terms of something that is opposite. In Hegelian language, every thesis exists only in relationship to its antithesis. When the thesis and antithesis conflict, action and reality are created. Ultimately, the conflict is resolved in a synthesis of the opposites. But this synthesis is not the end of action and reality because it is itself a new thesis—with its attendant antithesis. And on and on it goes.

To appreciate the philosophic validity of dialectics, we don't need to search for profound and sophisticated examples. Dialectics make good sense when we realize that all of the measures of our reality are relative. How can we explain north, except in relation to its opposite, south? How can we define white, except as the most different from black? Heavy vs. light, fast vs. slow, hot vs. cold, virtue vs. vice, many vs. none—these and many more are the measures of our reality. It's a compelling argument. Reality is called into existence by the dialectic. Without stress from the conflict of opposites, the entire world—our whole universe, in fact—would be a bland, amorphous, changeless mass of homogeneous nothingness, in which time would not flow and the idea of reality would be irrelevant.

But, no matter how convincing a philosophy may be, it can never serve as more than a framework of basic premises within which scientific study is carried out. We must understand this relationship in order to appreciate how philosophy and science work together. On the one hand, a philosophy attempts to speak about the universe, but it is itself a creature of limited scope and endurance. In the last analysis, no human has the omniscience to experience the total, infinite universe in order to *deduce* absolute generalizations. Instead, the philosophic process is inductive. From the experiences that he gathers during the fleeting moment that is his life and from the tiny niche that is his entire environment, the philosopher induces generalizations about the universe. He has drawn a sample from which he makes implications about the whole. All of our knowledge is inductive, in this philosophical sense.

On the other hand, the scientific process imposes an additional discipline on the search for knowledge, which is that wherever possible, deductive processes should be used in place of inductive ones. Scientists have the task of selecting small areas of experience for careful and total observation, making accurate deductions, and expressing the deductions in a form in which they may be tested again and again for accuracy. If these scientific deductions survive repeated tests, they are installed as building blocks in the philosophic framework that, as a whole, still remains primarily inductive. This is the mutual relationship in which philosophy and science can work in harmony. Should the inductive philosophic "truths" be made to take precedence over scientific observation in the specific areas where the scientific deductive process is possible, then the purpose of philosophy is abused and the benefits of science are forfeited.

When the philosophical framework is particularly grand and compelling, the temptation is strong to let it impose its schemata on the scientific process. This was Marx's undoing. Once his philosophic system was established, his economic science lost its objectivity. It merely served to substantiate the already established philosophy, putting the cart before the horse and turning the philosophy into an ideology. Under these circumstances, scientific testing, which attempts only to disprove, to destroy a previously held truth, and, perhaps, to clear the way for a new, more accurate, tentative, hypothetical truth, may be perverted into hypocrisy. Dogmatic fundamentalism replaces reason, and the body of human knowledge becomes rigidly fixed and eventually irrelevant to man and his environment. There is no question that fundamentalism is comfortable, and it is unlikely that any of us are completely innocent of invoking it. But it does seem tragic that Marx, who had done his philosophic homework so much more diligently than most economists ever do, should have made this error, an error compounded many times over by his followers, and the consequence—communism today—is awe-inspiring.

History à la Marx

According to Marx, the history of mankind is determined by the way man has produced the commodities that are his means of life, and that way has always involved a class struggle between those who actually produce the commodities and those who own the means of production. In the *Communist Manifesto*, written by Marx and Engels and first published in 1848, they argued that throughout history,

> Freeman and slave, patrician and plebeian, lord and serf, guild-master and journeyman, in a word, oppressor and oppressed, stood in constant opposition to one another, carried on an uninterrupted, now hidden, now open fight, a fight that each time ended, either in a revolutionary reconstitution of society at large, or in the common ruin of the contending classes.[2]

In short, history is determined by the reality of having to produce our material needs and the struggle between the rich and poor in the process of producing them.

This interpretation of history is called "dialectical materialism" and is graphically illustrated in Figure 8. Through the

---

[2] Karl Marx and Friedrich Engels, *Manifesto of the Communist Party* (International Publishers, New York, 1948).

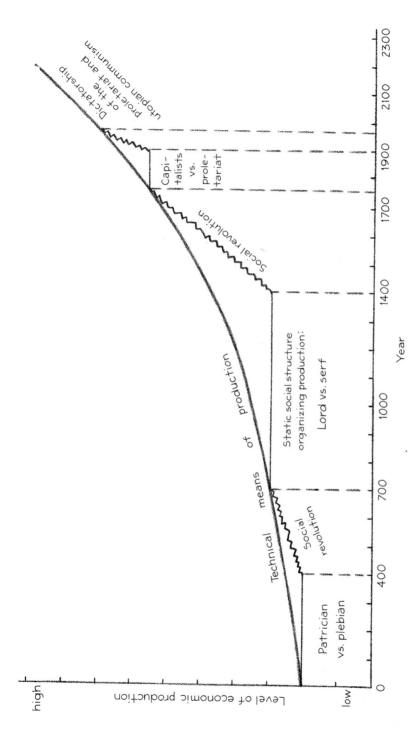

Figure 8. Marxist stages of history.

years, as new inventions and new discoveries are made, the techniques of production change and improve slowly but continuously. However, the actual methods of production don't follow this course of persistent change because one class of people has a vested interest in maintaining the status quo. This is the class that has grown rich, the class that owns the means of production. Originally, there may not have been a rich class and a poor class because the workers and the owners of the means of production together formed a social structure that exactly matched the needs of the existing technical means of production. But as the technical means improved, it was possible for the workers to produce a surplus value over what they needed to sustain themselves. However, the surplus did not accrue to the workers. It went to the owners of the means of production, who became very well satisfied with the system that allowed them to exploit the workers in this way. The rich class used every means at its disposal—the government, the military, the church—to insure the continuation of the social structure. The only way for the workers to break out of this yoke of increasing exploitation was and is to revolt. The *Manifesto* closes on the message:

> Let the ruling classes tremble at a Communistic revolution. The proletarians have nothing to lose but their chains. They have a world to win.
> Working men of all countries unite![3]

Of course, Marx's main interest was in his contemporary society. He saw the capitalist owners of the new industries getting richer and richer while the poor, exploited working masses lived lives of wretched destitution. Clearly, the social structure that organized the mode of production was wildly out of tune with the technical means of production. Marx believed that capitalism was ripe for revolution. In fact, according to Marx's theory, the very success of capitalism was the handwriting of doom on the wall. This is the way Marx saw it happening: The capitalists were exploiting the workers so suc-

---

[3] *Ibid.*

cessfully that much more was being produced than the workers could buy back with their dismal salaries. This surplus value enabled the capitalists to enjoy some high living, but most of it was spent on new machines for the factories. These machines would eventually cause unemployment among the workers and allow the capitalists to press wages down even further. According to the labor theory of value, to which Marx was ever faithful, machines don't produce any new value—only live labor does. So, with increased mechanization, less and less surplus value could be skimmed off the total production of the economy by the capitalists, and profits would fall. With falling profits and overproduction of goods, a business crisis—a depression—would set in. This would wash out the smaller capitalists and leave the larger, stronger ones to pick up the battle again more fiercely and more destructively than before, after the depression is over. Crisis would follow crisis in an ever-worsening pattern, leaving fewer but more monopolistic capitalists and squeezing the workers more and more cruelly each time. And soon comes the revolution!

Marx was not concerned with how the revolution actually happens and how communism is to be established afterwards, but Vladimir Lenin (1870–1924) and others have filled in some of the theoretical details. As the capitalist crises become successively worse, foreign markets would be eagerly sought by the monopolistic capitalists as an outlet for their overproduction. Colonies would be developed by the capitalistic nations, and soon, as conditions continued to get worse, these imperialists would begin to war with one another over these colonial countries. Now the proletariat will take charge of their own destiny. They will have been organized and armed by the capitalists to sacrifice themselves in the cause of their oppressors. Instead, the workers of all nations will unite, turn their weapons against the capitalists, and inherit the world that is rightfully theirs.

In a rather different version of the same revolutionary process and in a new interpretation of Marx that is becoming increasingly important in the world, China's Mao Tse-tung (born 1893) explains that the capitalists of North America and Western Europe are exploiting the peasants of Asia, Africa, and Latin

America, rather than the traditional industrial proletariat. These peasants will organize and arm themselves and, using their own countryside as their staging areas, seize or destroy the big cities that are the cancerous outposts of corrupt capitalist domination. According to Mao, then, communism can grow directly out of a *peasant* economy, although the inspiration for it is still created by the advanced depravity of the capitalist monopolists.

What happens after the revolution Marx's followers are less clear about. A dictatorship of the proletariat is to be imposed on the entire society. Labor will receive the total productivity of the economy, and there will be no exploiting class that owns the means of production. The ultimate synthesis of the material dialectic seems to be approaching at this stage, and there will be no basis for theoretical antitheses, political opposition, or even open discussion. The dictatorship of the proletariat is the only true and realistic way. Democracy, majority rule, or even an honest difference of opinion with the dictatorship can only be considered subversive treason in the scientific Marxist state because in the true Marxist state everybody agrees with one another. The government, which is the ruling instrument of the dictatorship of the proletariat, rules the classless society of workers on their behalf. The economic socialism and the collectivism that the state imposes on the people are efforts to remake them into more perfect human beings so that they can eventually achieve pure communism. In pure communism, the state will have withered away, there will be no coercion, no exploitation, no conflict, and no crime. Each person will consume only what he needs and produce whatever he is able to. Utopia will have arrived.

Of course, it didn't turn out that way. Capitalism didn't die. The rich got richer, but the poor didn't get poorer. Mechanization continued, but profits didn't fall. There were periods of economic depression and serious unemployment, but not quite for the reasons that Marx expected. Individual businesses did grow larger and some monopolies did develop, but small industries were not eliminated.

At times, especially in the 1930s, it looked as if Marx's predictions would come true after all. The advanced capitalist nations were in a severe depression, unemployment was critical, one world war had just been fought—largely over territorial rights—and a second was being planned, and it seemed that conditions were ripe for a communist takeover. Many people in these nations joined communist parties at this time; admittedly, though, they were always a very small proportion of their total populations. But when the great expansion of communism did take place after World War II, it was not the result of a revolution in the decadent capitalist countries. It was the result of a takeover by Soviet Russia of its next-door neighbors, and, in China, it was the result of the victory of communist cadres over the Nationalist cadres.

There is less chance today than ever before that capitalism will ripen until it bursts into a communist revolution in developed nations. Instead, contrary to Marxist doctrine, the appeal of communism is primarily to underdeveloped countries. The communist emphasis on materialism, on industrial development, on the overthrow of the old leaders and the establishment of a dictatorship by the poor gets a resonant response from the poor peoples of Africa, Latin America, and Asia, who feel they have been cheated of their due by colonialism, rich landowners, or the entrenched ruling groups in their particular countries. They are too embittered by their poverty to be concerned about the possible loss of individual freedoms or the enforced collectivization, which they see as improvements over their lot. The idea of a bloody revolution seems like their last desperate means to remedy their exploitation. Some sympathetic intellectuals find the Marxist system appealing because of its sophisticated philosophy and economic science and for its humanitarian intention to improve the lot of the more wretched of the earth.

Communism's Problems Today

No communist nation today pretends to have achieved full communism. The People's Republic of China, the Democratic Republic of (East) Germany, the Union of Soviet Socialist Republics, and so on that constitute the communist world consider themselves to be just over the revolution and into the dictatorship of the proletariat. They are in the process of remaking their societies by instituting socialist reforms and eradicating the last vestiges of capitalist ways of thinking such as private ownership of productive enterprises. There are substantial differences in the organization and character of the various communist countries, but generally in all of them the communist party has taken over all of the major decision making functions, not only in political and governmental matters, but also in the economic and social arenas. State monopolies, albeit in the name of the people, replace private enterprise. Giant collective farms and state industries are controlled by a central planning agency, which sets production targets for the economy as a whole and for the various industries. Money is still used to facilitate the flow of goods and services, but prices, wages, and the quantities of goods and services produced are determined by the planning agency. With such a concentration of power, there has been a tendency to use force. Life in these socialist-communist countries is often made harsh and terrifying by a secret police, a conspiratorial communist party, and a power-conscious elite in government. The often inhuman means that are used to enforce the system are considered justified by the ends—the ultimate good of the people, the eventual achievement of pure communism.

However, communist countries have scored some important successes, notably in the Soviet Union, where there has been rapid economic development. Industrialism and economic growth had already begun in Russia at the time of the communist revolution and takeover of the country, which began with the mildly democratic revolution of March 1917, continued with the communist (Bolshevik) revolution in November,[4] and ended with the formal establishment of the Union of Soviet Socialist Republics in 1922. The bitter civil war that lasted from 1918 to 1922 and the first groping economic policies of the new government actually destroyed much of the progress that had been achieved. There was even a short but severe famine in 1932. But the economic plans, which consistently favored heavy

---

[4] This was called the October Revolution because the Julian calendar was used in Russia until 1918.

industry and were rigidly enforced by Stalinist totalitarian methods, bore fruit. At the expense of the mass of the people, who were kept virtually at a subsistence level of existence, industrialization proceeded at a pace probably unequaled by any other nation at that time. By World War II, the Soviet Union had enough industrial might to mount a remarkable war effort. Since that war, the Russian accomplishments in space, in industrialization, and even in the improvement of their own standard of living have become well known.

It remains to be seen whether a similar industrialization can be achieved by Chinese communism. The Chinese experiments, the communes, the "Great Leaps," and the internal cultural revolutions, with which they had hoped to achieve a degree of pure communism even before the Russians, wasted much of China's productive energies and resources. Perhaps they believed that these violent agonies were the only way the traditions of thousands of years could be expunged. Since 1970, a more stable and less revolutionary tone has prevailed in China, evidently with the result that economic productivity has improved greatly.

The main dilemma of contemporary communism is the conflict between the original communist dogma and the realities of the twentieth century. For example, the puritanical zeal, the religious sense of a worldwide mission that the early communists had, is being replaced by a more narrow national patriotism that has splintered the international communist bloc. In Russia, where the communists once believed themselves in the vanguard of a total world revolution and considered all capitalist nations their mortal enemies, they now speak of peaceful coexistence. With the increased standard of living, many workers no longer identify with the proletarian solidarity necessary for the class struggle. Rather, they tend to assume positively bourgeois, middle class aspirations, such as a house, a car, an education for their children, vacations, and privacy. Also the technical complexity of running modern industries has brought about a class of technicians and administrators who are not as interested in the communist dogma as they are in performing their functions efficiently. They are impatient to take over more and more of the decisions and, in some of the East European countries, seem to have won important leadership positions. As education is improved in the communist countries, the people are demanding new freedoms to act and to express themselves with an individualism that seems unbecoming for a faithful communist.

Even the physical sciences contribute to the communist dilemma. The Yugoslavian communist Milovan Djilas writes, "What can the unfortunate physicists do, if atoms do not behave according to the Hegelian-Marxist struggle or according to the uniformity of opposites and their development into higher forms? What of the astronomers, if the cosmos is apathetic to Communist Dialectics?"[5] The days when the biologist Lysenko could try to impose dialectical materialism on wheat seedlings and set back Russian agriculture by twenty years in the process (because under Stalin no other philosophical premise for research was allowed) are over in most modern communist countries today. But some of communism's fervor and charm disappeared with them.

The rest of the world has generally cheered the recurring periods when the communists have discarded some of their dogma. These moments have been called "thaws," with the implication each time that a springtime of new freedoms and fresh opportunities will soon come. These thaws have often involved a substantial amount of decentralization of economic control and even the reestablishment of something like the profit motive in some sectors of the economy. But the conservative pressures of orthodox Soviet-style communism have not yet let these thaws become a full-fledged spring, as evidenced by the tragic Russian invasion of Czechoslovakia in 1968.

At the same time that Westerners have been applauding the various thaws in the communist countries, some observers feel that the United States, a staunch opponent of communism, is, itself, experiencing a trend toward collectivization in many of its institutions, which makes it look more and more like a socialist country. So there is speculation that propelled by the

---

[5] Milovan Djilas, *The New Class* (Frederick A. Praeger, New York, 1957), p. 130.

exigencies of the twentieth century, the two most powerful nations of the world are actually drawing closer together economically. In some sense, the United States has been a step
ahead of Russia in some of Marx's objectives. Proportionately,
American workers receive a greater share of the total national
product than do Russian workers, not because Americans believe in the labor theory of value or try to be good Marxists,
but because proportionately less of the national product is
siphoned off for new capital investments and national security.
America does not adhere to the Marxist principle of a classless
society but because, in the more advanced American economy,
the mass-produced consumer products must necessarily be accessible to the broadest possible segment of the population, a
reasonably affluent middle class becomes large enough to make
the rich and the poor classes minorities.

The main cause of the communist dilemma, however, is
communist theory itself. To begin with, the economic and materialist emphasis makes an interesting philosophy but is a naive
oversimplification of reality. Honor, freedom, religious beliefs,
and many other values have affected the course of history. These
other values will continue to be important, especially when economies become so advanced and affluent that consumers will be
too jaded to be interested in materialist motives. (Admittedly,
this isn't a problem in communist countries yet.) Applying
Marxist philosophy to the practical problems of running a country is bound to lead to problems, and the more rigid the dogma,
the more serious the problems. As time goes on, the dilemma
will get worse. The economic conditions of the Industrial Revolution, which were a spur to Marx's theories, were very different from the conditions that prevail in either the developed
or underdeveloped economies today.

By comparison with communism, it certainly seems fortunate for the free enterprise economies of the world that they
have no comparable philosophic system and ideological dogma
to struggle with. When it comes to matters of principle, ideology,
or commandments of faith, the less specific they are, the better.
In that sense, even the Ten Commandments are not as timeless
and universally applicable as the simple Golden Rule.

THE EMERGING "ISMS" AND THE
FIRST SUCCESS OF CAPITALISM

Karl Marx saw little good in reform-minded socialists. In his opinion, all gradual improvements in the conditions of the working classes were temporary and all reforms in the structure of the capitalist economy were merely palliatives that would only prolong the agony of the class struggle. He argued hard and long for the necessity of revolution, not reforms, among his socialist and communist colleagues. But by the later 1800s, an active campaign for reforms to improve social and economic conditions was under way. Industrialism had spread from the United Kingdom to Germany, France, northern Italy, Belgium, Sweden, and the United States, and these countries easily accounted for the majority of the world's manufacturing by 1870. In every one of these countries, active groups of concerned citizens, including workers, socialists, reformers, democrats, intellectuals, and even some conscience-stricken capitalists, began to campaign for adjustments in the industrial economy. The age of ideology was beginning, and a wild bouquet of "isms" was coming into full bloom. From the 1820s to the 1850s, the English language had heard the words liberalism, radicalism, socialism, conservatism, individualism, constitutionalism, humanitarianism, monarchism, nationalism, communism, and capitalism for the first time. Toward the end of the nineteenth century, these often clashing isms were beginning to influence the environment in which they were growing.

Progress in industrial reform was slow and sporadic at first, even though the parliaments of France and Germany had, by the 1880s, some socialist members who were committed to reform. In fact, much of the progress came as a defense against the socialists and reformers rather than because of agreement with them. As early as the 1860s, Bismarck, the Prussian of "blood and iron" fame, not one of the most democratic and liberal rulers of his day, made a deal with the socialists and instituted a social security system consisting of sickness, accident, and old age insurance. It was the world's first such insurance, and for many decades it was the world's most comprehensive system.

In doing so, he stole the thunder from the German socialists, most of whom were followers of the nonrevolutionary Ferdinand Lassalle, and they cooperated with Bismarck rather well from then on. Marx was, of course, disgusted by this "cooption." In the 1890s, Kaiser Wilhelm II even enlarged the program.

Reform came more slowly in France, whose syndicalist unions concentrated on massive general strikes instead of more effective businesslike unionism, whose socialists tended to be communists while on the soap box but often became comfortable bourgeois when elected to office, and whose working class was not as intensely urban as those of Germany or England. Reform was also very slow in the United States, where the lure of the frontier acted as an outlet for the mounting pressures of industrial hardship and slowed down any political action for social reform. The political structure of this country, with the power over urban conditions concentrated in the individual states rather than in the federal government, was then and still is an important obstacle to reform. The masses of immigrants that eagerly came to supply the muscle for American industry would get little governmental relief from the grinding conditions of the sweatshops until the beginning of the twentieth century. And, even then, the first legislation was less a beginning of social security than an outlawing of the worst excesses of exploitation, such as child labor, unsafe and unhealthy working conditions, impure food and drugs, and monopolies. Free public education, labor unions, and, above all, the remarkable social and geographic mobility of the American population must certainly take more of the credit for improving the welfare of the people than the central government's reform legislation.

The most important influence on the development of democratic-socialist and social-reform-minded parties was the Fabian Society, founded in 1884 in England. Named after Quintus Fabius Maximus Verrucosus (died 203 B.C.), the Roman general who managed to fight his enemies in every way except actual battle, the British Fabians were committed to the improvement of society by every tactic permissible within the legal limitations of the government and the ethical limitations of propriety. They lent active support to labor unions, public education, and the budding consumer cooperative movement and were effective political activists for social and economic reforms. Many intellectual reformers from the upper classes in England, with their penchant for hard work and sensible shoes, contributed a great deal of their energy, money, and imagination to the Fabians. At one time or another, the list included George Bernard Shaw, H. G. Wells, John Galsworthy, Bertrand Russell, R. H. Tawney, and Harold Laski.

Sidney and Beatrice Potter Webb (1859–1947 and 1858–1943) were the most brilliant of the many Fabian researchers. Their compelling and scientific writings for the Fabian cause did much to raise the *niveau* of socialist economics. In addition to writing forty-five books, numerous articles, pamphlets, and essays, the Webbs also published the *New Statesman*, an influential weekly, and founded the now-famous London School of Economics and Political Science. Their research methods were exceedingly thorough and painstaking. They ransacked old village records and union archives and attended innumerable working class meetings as observers; Beatrice Webb, who came from a wealthy family, learned tailoring and got a job as a "plain trouser hand" to observe the sweatshop more closely from within.

Never a political party themselves, the Fabians supported their causes through the liberal members of government and the Labour Party. Through their efforts, they saw the eventual success of social reform in Great Britain. It began with the humble, pre-Fabian efforts to reform public education, continued with the regulation of working conditions in mines and factories established during the terms of prime ministers Gladstone and Disraeli, and progressed with the implementation of social security measures and progressive taxes under the governments of Herbert Asquith and David Lloyd George. Today, their efforts have culminated in the strongly socialistic British economic system, with its nationalized industries and its cradle-to-the-grave social security. Its major reform work accomplished, the Fabian Society is today a research and publicity agency.

Many people in America feel that social reforms, rather than strengthening the free enterprise system and the market economy, as reformers claim, are part of a conspiracy, only slightly less wicked than communism, to undermine the cherished democratic way of life. To be sure, if the amount of government intervention that exists in the British economy were applied to the American economy, it would probably be repugnant to many Americans. But this is precisely the strength of the nonideological free enterprise system: it is flexible. Each country and each age have their own problems, preferences, and opportunities. It should be the prerogative of the people of each country to make whatever practical adjustments they want in their own economic systems, and only in this way can their economies yield the maximum amount of satisfaction for them. Of course, the citizenry must be both free to choose and aware of the economic choices that exist in each country, which means that the prime requisite for a free enterprise economy is a combination of political democracy and an enlightened populace, certainly not an undesirable combination under any circumstances. Freedom, the lack of coercion, the open flow of communication and opinion, without which enlightenment is impossible, these are the things that unite the nations of the so-called "free" world today. These are the things that make the traveler feel comfortably secure, whether he is arriving at the airport in Paris, London, New York, Stockholm, or Tokyo. And it is the *absence* of these things, not the communist nature of the economy, that would make him decidedly uncomfortable should he land at the Peking airport or the Tirana, Albania, airport.

The difference in the amount of socialism or social reform in the various free countries of the world is a matter of degree, *not* a matter of one country succumbing to the conspiratorial wave of socialism while the other is still breasting the flood. Every free enterprise economy is subject to some intervention. For example, the federal, state, and local governments in the United States account for 20 to 25 percent of the total national economic activity. The various government controls, regulations, licenses, and inspections touch practically all of the remaining private enterprise in one way or another. Interestingly enough, this represents a larger proportion of government activity in the economy, even though the United States considers itself capitalistic, than exists in such self-proclaimed socialist countries as Sweden or India. Even in the heyday of the English laissez faire, classical-liberal economy during the latter half of the nineteenth century, total economic permissiveness was proscribed by a combination of left-over feudal and mercantilist regulations, by local parish, village, and city ordinances, by tax laws, zoning laws, and by many other official and unofficial laws and customs. And Great Britain today, although certainly socialistic, should still be called a free enterprise system—or, as some prefer, a "mixed capitalistic enterprise system"[6]—because the vast majority of the economic decisions are made under conditions of free choice. Consumers decide what they want to buy; producers decide what they want to produce; young people are free to embark on the careers they choose; and families can move whenever or wherever they want. It is up to the British people, just as it is up to any free and sovereign people, to make sure that their economic policies don't infringe on their personal rights and freedoms and, if they do infringe, to make sure that the results are worth it. Above all else, this requires a free and vigilant people.

Perhaps one of the main reasons for the common misunderstanding about the nature of socialism and capitalism is the use of "left" or "right" to describe an economic system. According to these descriptive terms, communism would be the furthest left, then would come socialism, then capitalism, and finally, on the far right, fascism. As shown in Figure 9, *top*, this left-right continuum is divided somewhere between socialism and capitalism, with all the command economies (those economies in which some central authority makes the major economic decisions) on the left, and all the market economies (free choice economies) on the right. This arrangement is unappealing to both the free enterprise capitalists and the socialists, and for the same reason: they are both placed in juxtaposition to an economic system that violates the freedoms on which their own systems are based.

A preferable arrangement is shown in Figure 9, *bottom*. Here the economic systems above the equatorial division are basically free enterprise systems, some with more government regulation,

---

[6] "Capitalism" is usually taken to mean the private ownership of business, which is an important aspect of free enterprise but isn't all there is to it.

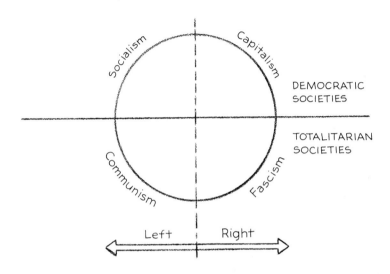

Figure 9. The scheme of isms.

some with less. Below the equator are the systems that are not free, communism because it claims to be a dictatorship of the proletariat, fascism because it is simply a dictatorship. Of course, fascists and communists consider each other an anathema, but it is a moot question whether it makes much difference to the ordinary citizen in these countries whether his working orders come from the central planning committee of some communist "democracy" or whether they come from the official elite of a fascistic regime.

The left-right distinction still applies in Figure 9, *bottom*. The societies on the left, socialism and communism, are largely concerned with matters of economic progress, such as economic growth and the distribution of income. In fact, theoretically, these material concerns are their raison d'être, although, in reality, nationalism and other motives are strong influences.

On the right are capitalism and fascism, systems which, for

very different reasons, are based relatively less on economic considerations. As we shall see, fascism is often a perverse recipe, consisting of national frustration, jingoist attitudes, a dash of persecution complex, some myth, a bit of crusading spirit, and a large dab of pride, all beaten to a froth by a charismatic leader who embodies in his image the identity of the nation. The economic policy of some fascistic governments is almost as regimented as communist economic policy; yet the purpose of the policy is to further the fascist "vision," which usually has something to do with national honor and military power. Neither are the more benign dictatorships, the ones that don't quite qualify as full-blown fascist states, much concerned with matters of economic progress. These governments, often found in the world's underdeveloped countries, expend most of their efforts in staying in power and suppressing the real or imagined revolutions that threaten them.

Capitalist systems are found in societies that have something like "life, liberty, and the pursuit of happiness" as their main focus. While they often do have a government economic policy, these policies are not intended to be coercive, and the emphasis of the society is on such things as individual freedom, civil rights, and justice. Both above and below the equator in Figure 9, *bottom*, the division between left and right is very indistinct. The equatorial division, however, is critical.

To be perfectly objective, no one ism should be considered more natural than any other. If the record of history is taken as the criterion, then any system involving command from a central authority would seem the most natural because, through the ages, some form of theocracy, aristocracy, monarchy, or oligarchy has been the most prevalent system. Yet, for most Westerners in the free world today, nothing less than a democracy would seem right. It is largely a matter of the age, the geographic area, and the customs and traditions of the people. Ultimately, the economics of some isms do make more sense than others. We have already seen how the Marxist economics of communism is unrealistic and eventually becomes impractical. We will also see that the economic programs of fascism, which developed after World War I, were conceived out of the traumatic fantasies that these countries suffered after that war. But even the democratic and essentially free enterprise systems of capitalism and socialism, reasonable and logical as they seem to us today, must never be taken for granted as naturally, inalienably right. They are creations of society, just as all the other isms are, and must be constantly tended, cultivated, and adjusted by society.

Thus, free enterprise grew with the help of the adjustments the social reformers demanded, and the system continued to function. The stresses and strains of rapid industrialization, while still very much in evidence, became less of a threat to the very existence of free enterprise itself. Actually, the reforms of the late 1800s were very small and mild compared with some of the much larger reconstructions of free enterprise that took place in the twentieth century. But the fact that reforms were possible at all, indeed, that the system prospered with these adjustments, is very significant. It shows that the free enterprise system is an adaptive and pragmatic approach to dealing with the economic needs of society rather than a rigid ideological system. Reforms could be made from within the system without resorting to overthrowing it; without this flexibility, free enterprise might not have survived the first phases of industrialization.

CHAPTER 7

The Arrival of Modern Economies and Economics

The outstanding victory of free enterprise was not in the campaign for adjustments and reforms but in the progress of industrialization itself. By the late 1800s, the Industrial Revolution was rolling along faster than ever and reaching into most of the areas of Western Europe and North America. Railroads were running deeper into the fertile plains of the American Midwest and the Russian steppes, bringing back agricultural produce to the rapidly growing markets of the industrial cities and bringing fierce competition to the smaller local farmers. In the United States, railroad mileage increased from 94,665 miles in 1876 to 379,508 miles in 1913, or almost 7700 miles each year. It was the age of colonialism. No continent remained untouched by the European powers, and the millenia-old separation of the several races of humanity, which had each developed their own cultures and their own histories in isolation, was over. From this point on, the history of the world was once again a single story. As if to symbolize this regained unity, world trade tripled from the 1870s to just before World War I.

Capital accumulation in industrial enterprises mushroomed as larger and larger quantities of new investments were channeled into use by the efficient new financial institutions. Technological advances brought about whole new industries, such as the electrical industry, many new branches of the chemical industry, metallurgical industries, textiles, and communications. Mass production, the key to twentieth century manufacturing, was beginning. Petroleum, which had been a nuisance to farmers as it oozed out of the ground or, even worse, was sold as a health elixir in medicine shows, was purposely pumped from the earth for the first time in 1859 in Pennsylvania by "Colonel" E. J. Drake. His Eastern financial backers developed an industry that extracted middle weight distillates, called kerosene, which became the main lighting oil. Perhaps most important of all was the development of the new steels, especially the new high carbon, chromium, and tungsten steels, without which the wheels of all of the other industries would have had to turn much more slowly. Figure 10 gives an indication of how the wheels of industry accelerated in the United States from 1860 to 1914.

The American frontier opened up anew to adventuresome farmers. As they pushed further west into more arid land, the Homestead Act gave them more and more land per family, from 160 acres in 1862 to 640 acres in 1916. Fencing off the range lands, now possible because of the cheap, new, barbed wire, made scientific cattle breeding possible. The discovery of nitrogen, potash, and phosphates as the basic plant foods began the chemical fertilizer industry, which increased its sales 900 percent between 1879 and 1919. Higher education for the masses through land grant colleges instilled a very practical American-type "know-how" into essentially unacademic and even anti-intellectual rural minds.

The surging growth created enormous amounts of new income and new wealth. Average per capita real income (money income corrected for price variations) in the United States

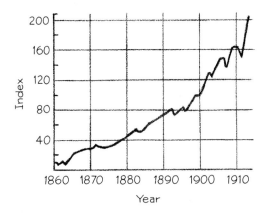

Figure 10. Index of manufacturing output, 1860–1914 (1899 = 100). (Edwin Frickey index from *Historical Statistics of the United States, Colonial Times to 1957*, U.S. Bureau of the Census, Washington, D.C., 1960, p. 409.)

doubled from about 1870 to just before World War I. However, in all the growing economies much of the new income remained in the hands of the capitalists, small and large scale, who owned and operated the industries. For example, in Great Britain real wages per worker increased only about 20 percent from 1876 to 1914. The money wages of the working class in the United States increased by about 80 percent, from about 12 cents an hour to about 22 cents an hour, from 1880 to just before World War I. But over the same period, consumer prices paid by workers increased by about 50 percent so that the purchasing power of the wages, that is, the real wages, increased only by about 40 percent. Certainly these increases in purchasing power meant a definite improvement in the lives of the wage earners, but the recurring booms and depressions of the business cycle that had become a characteristic of industrialized market economies (as can be seen in the irregular upward movement of the index of manufacturing output in Figure 10) made the flow of income irregular and undependable.

Furthermore, it is hard to gauge with indexes how well off the working people were and how much their increased income improved their lives. Even if one checks the best price indexes, he will find that they ignore many of the factors that make life pleasant or miserable, and when comparing different periods of history or different economies, the difficulties are even greater. Is an average Englishman today really worse off than an American, as the various measures of material standards of living seem to indicate? Do the Asian peasants, African tribesmen, or Latin American peons, who often support a family on less than one-tenth of the real income of the average American family, really enjoy life only one-tenth as much and have only one-tenth as much food, clothing, and shelter as the average American family? Obviously not. But, as any observant tourist can verify, there are some real differences in the standards of living around the world. Exactly what the differences are and how much they differ are more complicated questions. In the period roughly from 1870 to 1913, it is safe to say that the total, real, national incomes of the industrializing economies increased rapidly, wages improved moderately, but urban living and working conditions, under which increasing proportions of the population had to live, remained poor.

A NEW DYNAMIC

While the quality of life for the working classes didn't change very much, the quality of life for the rich classes certainly did. To be sure, many of the rich lived the caviar-and-champagne life that they had always had. But a great deal of the new wealth was spent not only on yachts, estates, orgies, and safaris, but also on new steel mills, railroads, factories, grain elevators, and shops that, in sum, were the substance of the industrial expansion. This new eagerness to invest their wealth in economic activity seems to have been an entirely new kind of motive for the wealthy. Throughout the ages, the profit motive led men to invest their wealth in trading and manufacturing ventures that promised them a good return. But the extraordinary proportion of the investment in this period of industrialization and the intensity with which the business ventures were (and still are) managed seemed to indicate a stimulus more potent than just the profit motive. The economy became subject to a new and even strong dynamic force, and many theorists offered their explanations for it.

Max Weber (1864–1920), an eminent German sociologist-economist-philosopher, tried to explain this new source of economic energy by theorizing that much of the spirit of modern capitalism grew out of a Protestant Ethic, a Calvinist asceticism, which required men to be completely devoted to their vocation or business, as if it were their religious calling. According to this ethic, capitalists were supposed to bring enthusiasm, inventiveness, and total commitment to their jobs because these traits would prove their genuine faith. In this sense, the conduct of a capitalist in his business was as important to his salvation as the conduct of a minister in his pulpit was to his. Income became a measure of the businessman himself; it became an indication of how virtuously he lived and whether or not God smiled upon him. Of course, the income was not to be consumed in a profligate or even indulgent way. The righteous capitalist lived frugally, saved his income, and invested it in his business. It made little difference what business the capitalist pursued, whether he was a tradesman, a steel magnate, a stock speculator, or a dealer in junk. If he was an honest, hard-working, "heads-up," successful operator, devoted to his business, he could assume the mantle of righteousness.

How different this Protestant Ethic philosophy is from the historically more prevalent lack of respect usually felt for businessmen! Traditionally, whether in the Greco-Roman Age or in medieval times, land ownership, the clergy, government, and the military were the only careers with status. The relatively high esteem enjoyed by the businessmen of the High Middle Ages was a short holiday out of the long millenia during which they were suspiciously regarded as chiselers, parasites, and outsiders. But Max Weber's Protestant Ethic didn't explain this new economic energy entirely. For instance, it isn't completely convincing that the sequence wasn't the reverse: that capitalism brought on the Protestant Ethic. It doesn't explain the dynamic economic energy also put forth by the Catholic areas of Western

Europe, nor does it take into account the cumulative effect of the new discoveries in both geography and technology.

Thorstein Veblen (1857–1929), founder of the American institutionalist school of economics, which explained economic behavior as being largely determined by the psychological customs of our society, saw the new dynamic as the age-old predatory motive dressed in a modern costume. And he cast a jaundiced eye on it all. Through the ages, he argued, predatory exploiters have descended on peacefully productive people, plundering, raping, and generally satisfying themselves at the expense of these humble and hard-working groups. It started with the nomadic tribes sweeping down on settled prehistoric villages— the hunters and meat eaters vicitimizing the grain-eating farmers. It continued with the legionnaires forcing tribute from peaceful barbarians and with the feudal aristocracy exploiting the labors of their serfs. In the industrial system, said Veblen, open military coercion was no longer possible, but the predators could still squeeze the goods out of the peacefully productive folk by using the large industrial enterprises as their instruments. The entrepreneurs were not in the business of making textiles, home appliances, railroads, or sausages; they were in the business of making profits. Good workmanship, the quality of the products, honesty in business practices, and humane working conditions were of interest only to the peaceful, productive working class. They interested the entrepreneurs not a whit, or, if so, then only to the extent that these qualities might affect profits. And, just as the nomad warriors, the legionnaires, and the feudal lords prided themselves on their toughness, courage, and military prowess, so the new predators prided themselves on their competitive toughness, their business courage, and their high profits.

Through the ages, these predators used an ostentatious display of their leisure to serve notice to all members of their society that they were, in fact, predators and not workers. From this fact, Veblen got the title of his most important and most popular book, *The Theory of the Leisure Class*, first published in 1899. In witty and biting prose, Veblen satirized an industrial society whose leisure class shows off its prowess by "conspicuous consumption," a term still popular today. Perhaps, Veblen's most compelling example was the form of consumption that was the most visible and the most useless, that performed by women. By making this normally productive sex as leisure-bound as possible, society lends emphasis to its message. The upper class Chinese bound their women's feet, making them more or less incapable of any work that had to be done while standing or walking. Veblen found that just about the same situation existed for women of capitalist society stuffed in their corsets, which are, "in economic theory, substantially a mutilation, undergone for the purpose of lowering the subject's vitality and rendering her permanently and obviously unfit for work."[1] So, Veblen argued, the industrial economy has been made to serve the predators, who use it to make profits—only incidentally turning out products—and who sought thereby to aggrandize their status among their peers through a vulgar display of leisure. This unhappy situation is what makes the industrial economy run.

Again, we may be skeptical. Theories about the causes of man's behavior always seem to leave something to be desired. But whatever the explanations offered, it seems clear that with the coming of industrialism, economic behavior was scrutinized more closely than ever before. At the same time the ethical direction of the society was more and more strongly influenced by the practices of the entrepeneurs. The church, established traditions, and even military power seemed to be receding in importance as determinants of society, and in their places the economy emerged as the prime mover. It is important, therefore, that we try to understand the motives of those persons who began to make the most influential economic decisions. "The customer is always right" became a favorite motto of stores and businesses, and sophisticated market research about the whims and fancies of the affluent consumer has itself become a big business today. But, in the long run, consumers are relatively passive when it comes to making the big decisions that establish

---

[1] Thorstein Veblen, *The Theory of the Leisure Class* (Mentor Books, New York, 1953), p. 121.

the limits and methods of production in an economy. It is the leaders of the productive enterprises who articulate the decisions that actually determine the form of the economic system. It is to this leadership that we must look now in our search for the economic dynamic.

THE ENTREPRENEUR

What moved the economy from the mildly profit-seeking, slowly developing, pre-industrial stage to the burgeoning industrial system that it has become was its chief decision maker, the entrepreneur. According to Joseph A. Schumpeter (1883–1950), an Austro-American economist who taught at Harvard University after 1932 and whose analysis of the entrepreneurial function is generally considered definitive,

> the function of entrepreneurs is to reform or revolutionize the pattern of production by exploiting an invention or, more generally, an untried technological possibility for producing a new commodity or producing an old one in a new way, by opening up a new source of supply of materials or a new outlet for products, by reorganizing an industry and so on.
>
> To act with confidence beyond the range of familiar beacons and to overcome that resistance requires aptitudes that are present in only a small fraction of the population and that define the entrepreneurial type as well as the entrepreneurial function. This function does not essentially consist in either inventing anything or otherwise creating the conditions which the enterprise exploits. It consists in getting things done.[2]

Thus, the entrepreneur is the focal point at which the dynamic forces, whatever they are, materialize into action for economic progress. The enterepreneur doesn't really respond primarily to

---

[2] Joseph A. Schumpeter, *Capitalism, Socialism, and Democracy*, 3rd ed. (Harper & Brothers, New York, 1954), p. 132.

the profit motive; it is the capitalist-investor who receives the profits, and the two—entrepreneur and investor—are often not one and the same person. Neither does the entrepreneur seek power; the business wields the power, and again management and entrepreneur are not necessarily one. Nor do Veblenesque social status or Weberian Protestant righteousness seem to be the main motives of the entrepreneur. Rather, he seems to be an adventurer, a pioneer, an artist sculpting in economic clay. It is unlikely that any one person is an entrepreneur very often or very long. One can imagine that soon after a successful innovation, the managerial or the capitalist personality takes over.

Is the dynamic force that sustains the industrialized economic system then a will-o'-the-wisp? Is it an irrational spirit rather than a businesslike calculation? Many economists avoid the question and simply assume that for all economic behavior, decisions are made in a rather mechanical dollars-and-cents way. They postulate the existence of an "economic man," who rationally and objectively computes all the tangible pros and cons of an economic problem and makes a decision that will maximize profits. As we shall see, this imaginary construct is the dynamic implicitly assumed for almost all of the economic theories written from the late 1800s to the present. But not even the economists themselves are completely satisfied with it. They are the first to emphasize its presumptive nature, but they continue to use it because without economic man most of their theories would be invalidated.

Recently, some attention has been given to the suggestion that economic man doesn't seek to maximize profits, that he seeks merely to satisfy the profit motive. According to this point of view, the main effort of business management is to operate on the safe side of their break-even point—where revenues exceed costs—rather than to try to wring every last drop of profits out of the business venture. But the problem with this otherwise quite plausible idea is precisely the problem inherent in giving up the premise of rational economic man: if business merely "satisfices," what are the motives that are substituted in place of the total maximization effort? Could it be that non-dollars-and-cents motives, such as status, power, comfort, or others, could be instrumental in economic behavior, and, if so, how can these motives be accounted for in economic theory? The rising spector of an economically irrational and immeasurable theory makes most economists scurry back to the safety of their economic man.

Dante (1265–1321) seems to have understood the basic motive for human behavior.

> For in every action what is primarily intended by the doer, whether he acts from natural necessity or out of free will, is the disclosure of his own image. Hence it comes about that every doer, in so far as he does, takes delight in doing; since everything that is desires its own being, and since in action the being of the doer is somehow intensified, delight necessarily follows. . . . Thus, nothing acts unless (by acting) it makes patent its latent self.[3]

And this applies to economic behavior and decision making as well as to behavior in general. Throughout time, there have been a variety of activities that were particularly satisfying as means of identifying one's own image. One could discover new lands, pioneer into the frontier, lead armies of legionnaires, go on a holy crusade, be a powerful aristocrat, be an artist, become a priest or even a Robin Hood or a Rasputin. With the coming of industrialization, economic behavior was lifted out of the category of humdrum necessity and raised to the status of high adventure. As much or more personal satisfaction could be found by striving to be an entrepreneur—a captain of industry—as could be found in most of the other careers of life. The industrial economy began to attract many persons with the dynamic need to project their personal image or make a name for themselves, who would have been drawn into other professions at other times and in other places.

---

[3] Quoted in Hannah Arendt, *The Human Condition* (University of Chicago Press, Chicago, 1958), p. 175.

THE FLOWERING OF MARGINALIST ECONOMIC THEORY

The new kind of economy required a new kind of theory. The old classical economic theories seemed no longer to apply. Malthusian population theory and Ricardo's iron law of wages predicted the eventual coming of a rather dismal stationary subsistence economy. Classical labor theory of value led straight to Marx's forecast of a violent revolution of the suppressed masses. Rent theory seemed to point clearly to the injustices of a wealthy and large land ownership.

In the eyes of the energetic business leaders of the new industrial economy, all these theories must have appeared heroically irrelevant. As far as they were concerned, the main economic problems were: how to make profits, how to meet competition, and how to accumulate wealth. Social problems, except as they were dealt with through the gradual reforms, were essentially ignored. Economic health through good and profitable business would cure most ills, and such ills as remained must be natural— otherwise they would have been cured by the open market economy, right? Or, at least, this was the prevailing point of view. Although the rapidly growing, rapidly changing industrial economy was a very recent and a very radical departure from tradition for them, most business leaders blithely accepted it as a completely inevitable and natural system.

For the first time in history, the supply of commodities began to be abundant. Not that the mass of working class people became affluent, but the tone and sequence of the economy changed, from producing just the simple necessities of life and manufacturing these directly for the final consumer, to producing many kinds of commodities that had never existed before and manufacturing goods for inventory to be mass-marketed. Whereas once the shoemaker or the tailor made his wares for a particular customer, after measurements were taken and fittings arranged, now these products, in many styles and varieties, began to be manufactured in volume as "ready to wear" for the eventual customer, who would select his choice from the stock of finished products. Whereas once economic production concerned itself with food, shelter, clothing, and a few limited tools of production, the modern technology of the ongoing industrial revolution introduced many new consumer products—foods, such as ice cream, clothes, such as cotton knit underwear, and housewares, such as kerosene lamps—and a vast new array of producers' goods needed for the sophisticated techniques of production. Of course, the new commodities were produced commercially on a large scale, but even many of the old standbys that had usually been homemade—children's clothes, pies, and laundry soap—began to be commercially produced. Not only was commercial production more efficient, but the disintegrated industrial family was no longer the effective production unit of home commodities it had once been when it was a larger kinship group.

The abundance of production, the flood of consumer commodities and producer goods, meant that markets acquired an unprecedented importance, and we must understand that the industrial system is also a market system. More labor than ever before was performed for wages, and families bought more goods and services to satisfy their needs than ever before. The productive process—from raw materials to finished consumer commodity—was longer than ever, which meant that markets for the sale of raw materials, semifinished goods, and wholesale commodities, and, finally, retail markets for the finished product had to be developed.

These markets tied the whole productive process together. Figure 11 illustrates this process. It shows how money and real goods and productive services flow circularly through the economy from the people to the productive enterprises and back again. And it views the economy from a new perspective. Unlike the physiocrats' economic table (Table 2), mother earth is forgotten here. All the relations of the economy to the physical environment are ignored. Only the relationships among people in terms of the money and commodities exchanged are considered.

In the inside, counterclockwise circle of Figure 11 we see that the people supply the enterprises (which include all commercial businesses and farms) with the productive energy (labor, man-

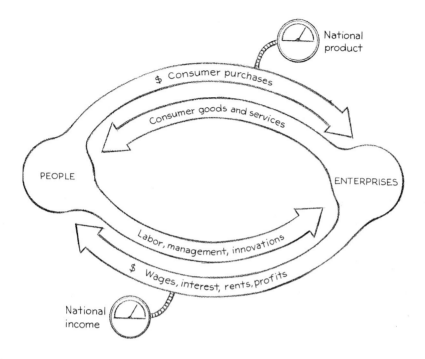

Figure 11. The circular flow of the market economy.

agement, innovations) to produce the goods and services. In turn, the enterprises supply the people with the goods and services for their consumption. The inside circle in this figure, then, deals with *real* economic quantities. The outside, clockwise circle is the *money flow* that mirrors exactly the inner flow of real economic quantities. Measuring the flow of money in purchases of finished products for a year gives the annual Net National Product, or simply National Product. Measuring it for a year in wages, interest, rents, and profits gives the National Income. Since the money flow is a closed circuit, these two measurements are essentially the same. The people get paid for their productive services, and, in turn, they pay for consumer goods. Whether we look at the inside circle or the outside circle, the people and the enterprises are in a symbiotic relationship with each other. They sustain each other organically, both in terms of the counterclockwise flow of real economic goods and services and in terms of the clockwise flow of money.

With the growth of markets in this new kind of economy, the old labor theory of value was no longer adequate. This simple theory didn't explain the short-run fluctuations in prices; nor did it explain the differences in prices among the growing variety of new commodities. In this new world of abundant production, something more than the cost of labor and other factors of production determined prices, even in the long run. Faced with the rising heat of competition, many businessmen must have wondered if the production process actually had any control over prices at all. But if production costs didn't determine price, what did?

Marginal Utility

W. Stanley Jevons (1835–1882), an Englishman, was sure he had the answer. On the first page of his book, *The Theory of Political Economy*, he asserted that "value depends entirely upon utility." Jevons insisted that the ultimate end of economic activity was the Benthamite avoidance of pains and procurement of pleasures and that the utility of economic commodities for this purpose is what gave them value, nothing else. The supply of labor and the costs of production were irrelevant except as they set limits beyond which commodities could not be produced, given the level of utility they provided. What actually determined the value—and simultaneously the price—of an economic good was not how hard or easy it was to make, but how useful it was. Furthermore, the goods themselves had no inherent value. They "contained" no quantity of labor hours or other costs of production, as the classical economists had believed. "The ore lying in the mine, the diamond escaping the eye of the searcher, the wheat lying unreaped, the fruit ungathered for want of customers, have no utility at all."[4] For Jevons, the proper

---

[4] W. Stanley Jevons, *The Theory of Political Economy*, 5th ed. (Kelley and Millman, New York, 1957), p. 43.

focus of economics was on the relationship between commodities and human requirements. The commodities themselves took on economic meaning only in such a relationship, and to focus economics on an accounting of labor hours spent in production, as Mill and Ricardo had done, was unthinkable.

Jevons did not enumerate the various pleasures and pains that were supposed to determine the ultimate ends of economic activity, as Bentham had tried to do, but he theorized that their importance would be revealed by the prices people would be willing to pay for the goods that had utility toward these ends. Indeed, total pleasure, or the total utility needed to achieve total pleasure, had no place in Jevons' theory. Instead, price was determined not by total pleasure or total utility but by *marginal utility*, the utility of the unit just purchased or about to be purchased, the marginal unit of a commodity. For example, the price paid for a pair of shoes isn't determined by the usefulness of shoes in general to the consumer but by the usefulness of that one pair of shoes to the consumer at the time of purchase. Human nature being what it is, the marginal utility would tend to decrease as more and more of the commodity was being used, as Bentham had already discovered. Thus, the more a person consumed of one kind of a commodity, the more sated with it he'd become, the less utility he would derive from each additional unit of that commodity, and the less he would be willing to pay for it. Figure 12 shows that diminishing marginal utility is to the consumer what diminishing marginal returns, as shown in Figure 7, *bottom*, is to the producer.

This symmetry between production and consumption theory is very appealing to many economists who have developed a sense for the austere aesthetic of economic theory. Such niceties do make theory more engaging and, perhaps, easier to teach, but, we must warn that they never constitute a proof of a theory. Rightly or wrongly, economists have often been accused of preferring the aesthetic qualities to realism in their theories.

As in the case of marginal productivity, modern economists have postulated that there may be an initial stage of increasing marginal utility, where the consumption of a commodity whets the appetite for more, a kind of economic *hors d'oeuvre* theory.

198

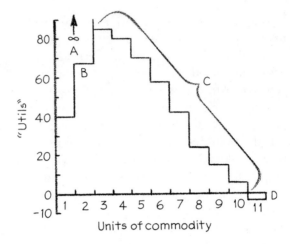

Figure 12. Diminishing marginal utility.
A: immeasurable utility for the first units of a
commodity that is essential to life; B: increasing
marginal utility of commodities that have an
"appetite-whetting" phase; C: diminishing marginal
utility; D: negative marginal utility if the eleventh
unit is consumed by mistake or under coercion.
("Utils" are an arbitrary index of the level of utility.)

(See the ice cream example on page 131.) For commodities
essential to life, however, the first few units would be infinitely
useful, and there could be no stage then of increasing marginal
utility.

The theory of diminishing marginal utility also explains how
people adjust the quantities of the various commodities they
buy to one another. For example, given a fixed budget, the
customer will choose quantities of commodities from among all
his alternatives in such a way that, in the end, he could not
increase the sum of the marginal utilities from all of the different
kinds of commodities he bought by substituting more of one
commodity for less of another. In other words, the ratios between
the marginal utilities and the prices of all of the different kinds
of commodities available to the consumer have to be equal, as
shown in Table 4, which shows the hypothetical levels of utility

derived from successive quantities of commodities purchased by a housewife doing some shopping for her family in a neighborhood grocery store. She needs to buy only apples, butter, brown sugar, and raisins because her pantry is well stocked and new quantities of any other goods have little utility for her that day. She also wants to limit her expenditures to 4 dollars. She puts apples in her market basket until she has "enough," that is, until the utility derived from the last (marginal) apple in ratio to the price of apples is equal to the ratios between marginal utility and price for each portion of butter, sugar, and raisins that she has put into her market basket in the same way. As it

Table 4. Equalizing marginal utility/price ratios

Commodity	Utility of each successive unit of the commodity									Price
	1	2	3	4	5	6	7	8	9	
Apples, per piece	30	40	34	30	26	24	22	20	–	10¢
Butter, per pound	180	–	–	–	–	–	–	–	–	90¢
Brown sugar, per pound box	60	50	–	–	–	–	–	–	–	25¢
Raisins, per pound box	114	108	99	90	–	–	–	–	–	45¢

turns out, in this rather arbitrary example, when she buys 8 apples, one pound of butter, 2 (pound) boxes of brown sugar, and 4 (pound) boxes of raisins, the ratios of all the marginal utilities to their respective prices are equal, in the same order: 20/10, 180/90, 50/25, and 90/45. If she had more than 4 dollars, she could have bought more of each of these items and perhaps some other items too, and the ratio of marginal utilities to prices would have decreased. If she had only $1.75 to spend, she would have bought only 6 apples—giving a marginal utility to price ratio of 24/10—no butter, one box of brown sugar—giving a ratio of 60/25—and 2 boxes of raisins—giving a ratio of 108/45.

Again the ratios are equal, but with less money to spend, the marginal utilities remain higher and the ratios are higher.[5]

All this is a microcosmic example used for illustration. In fact, the housewife's entire family budget is allocated for all the items that the family buys in the same way, and when all the ratios of the marginal utilities to their respective prices are equal to one another, no improvement by spending more on one kind of item and less on another is possible, and the family has optimized its consumer expenditure. Of course, since prices, utility preferences, and the budget are always changing, the effort to optimize tends to be forever ongoing.

Jevons' theory was not greeted with enthusiasm by his contemporary classical economists in England, who were unhappy about his efforts to overturn the economics of Ricardo and Mill. Like every other human endeavor, science must also endure long lags while vested interests fitfully hold on to the old before they will begrudgingly give way to the new. Nonetheless, his book, *The Theory of Political Economy*, first published in 1871, went rapidly through several printings.

Even more important than Jevons' theory per se in ending the reign of classical economics was the fact that other economists, working independently of him, began constructing similar theories based on marginal utility. Antoine Augustin Cournot (1801–1877), J. H. von Thünen (1783–1850), and H. H. Gossen (1810–1858), the first a Frenchman and the last two Germans, had preceded Jevons by several decades with their own theories of marginal utility, but the time had not been ripe for their ideas. Léon Walras (1834–1910), a Swiss, and Karl Menger (1840–1921), an Austrian, were contemporary with Jevons, and when they also independently developed theories of marginal utility, the tide began to turn. The supremacy of the English

---

[5] In this example, the ratios can be made to come out equal with a 4 dollar budget or a $1.75 budget, among others. But clearly, the step-by-step diminution of marginal utility with successive units of the commodities means that there will be many instances when it will be impossible to get the ratios exactly equal. Some economists only half jokingly speculate that this is one reason why we always seem to need just a little bit 'more money—to even up our ratios.

classical school (which may have seemed supreme only to Englishmen anyway) was now at an end. Economics became once more a European science, with its best work being written in French and German, as well as English.

What tied the new theories of all these economists together was their emphasis on the marginal—the most recently added or subtracted—unit rather than the total quantity. This was true no matter what quantity they were considering: the cost of production, the output of a commodity, the utility, and so on. The largest part of the total quantity, they argued, is water over the dam, or, to use a slightly reengineered metaphor, you can't cross a bridge until you come to it. Decisions are always made about the unit to be added or subtracted, however large or small it may be, and not about the entire history of the particular undertaking, unless, of course, the marginal unit is also the first and only unit. And what these economists were after was a better understanding and a more valid analysis of economic behavior, specifically, economic decision making. In fact, some marginalist economists saw a whole philosophy of human behavior in their new marginal analysis. That may have been excessive, but they did succeed in reemphasizing the human content of economic science, an aspect that tended to be sorely neglected by the increasingly arid catallactics[6] of the classical school.

SUPPLY AND DEMAND AND ALFRED MARSHALL

Still, the enthusiasm of these marginalist economists did not establish their new theories firmly in the body of accepted economic science. It remained for another great synthesizer, Alfred Marshall (1842–1924), to perform this function. Along with Adam Smith, David Ricardo, John Stuart Mill, and Karl Marx, Alfred Marshall was one of the world's great economists. He was the son of a cashier of the Bank of England, a rather tyran-

---

[6] Economics as a science of the prices and quantities of commodity exchanges.

nical father, who was the author of a tract entitled *Man's Rights and Woman's Duties*. He forbade young Alfred to play chess and banned mathematics from his son's education because he thought it was irrelevant to the ministry, the career he had picked out for him. He also decided that his son should study at Oxford. In the end, Alfred rejected the ministry and studied mathematics and physics devotedly at Cambridge. But he wasn't a rebel; in fact, his main quality was caution, veneration for his intellectual predecessors, and avoidance of controversy. He was a sensitive soul, and his interest in economics began to awaken out of a desire to do some good for ordinary people, whose well-being did, indeed, leave much to be desired. By 1867, after just a year or so of lecturing in molecular physics, he began to develop his system of economics. Within a short time he was teaching economics and held the chair in political economy at Cambridge until his retirement in 1908.

The first edition of Marshall's major work, *Principles of Economics*, did not appear until 1890, much to the consternation of those, like Jevons, who had heard of his genius but had no access to him personally. For the cautious Marshall, however, oral communication was safer than committing any potentially controversial ideas indelibly to paper. And from his position at Cambridge, the oral tradition was quite effective. Common gossip at the time had it that half the economics professorships in Great Britain were held by former students of the great man. It seems strange to us today, when every science is almost suffocated under an unending deluge of scholarly publications, that a whole school of economics could be founded on ideas expounded in the classroom alone. Still, when it finally came out, his *Principles* was the most complete and thorough exposition the science of economics had had to that time. The range of Marshall's contributions was so large that they touched almost every major aspect of the science; but, above all, he established the acceptability of marginal analysis beyond question.

Typically Marshallian, the way he achieved this acceptability was by reaffirming the importance of the classical economists' concern with supply. Labor and costs of production were ultimately more important determinants of economic and social

structures than consumers' desires and demands: "while wants
are the rulers of life among the lower animals, it is to the changes
in the forms of efforts and activities that we must turn when in
search for the keynotes of the history of mankind."[7] In Marshall's
reasonable and craftsmanlike hands, marginal analysis became
a very powerful tool. With it he developed a battery of other
tools, which have been used by economists ever since, including
supply and demand curves and their elasticities, which will be
dealt with below. This was Marshall's main contribution. He
designed the tools that economists of all "schools" and perspectives could use. In this way, his synthesis of the science was independent of his own ideological slant, and his analytical tools
could survive the life expectancy of his or any other particular
point of view.

Underlying the entire body of marginal analysis is the idea
of equilibrium, that is, the idea that something is "solved" when
it balances out. Ultimately, equilibrium of the entire economy
is created by the forces of production and consumption, culminating in the arbitration of the open market. It is no mere
coincidence that marginal analysis led economists naturally to
mathematics, especially the calculus, and seems to have led
quite a few mathematicians naturally to economics. The greater
precision possible through this mathematization is not the least
of the contributions of marginal analysis to economic science.

The establishment of equilibrium for both production and
consumption begins with the utility considerations of the individual members of the economy. For consumers, the utility of
commodities is a positive value for which they are willing to
pay money. Of course, each consumer has his own idea of how
much money he is willing to pay for how many goods, depending on his personal preferences, on how much he bought recently, and on his financial condition. But for every consumer,
what begins as a diminishing marginal utility schedule, as shown
in Figure 12, becomes an individual demand curve, with the
consumer putting his money where his mouth is, so to speak.

---

[7] Alfred Marshall, *Principles of Economics*, 8th ed. (Macmillan, New York, 1952), p. 85.

The lower the price, the more the consumer is willing to buy. This is called the Law of Demand. All that remains, then, to arrive at the aggregate market demand curve (which is the kind of demand curve we will need to solve the market equation for the price and total quantity of the commodity sold) is to add together all the individual quantities that the individual consumers would like to buy at each price level, which is shown in Figure 13.

Here, for simplicity's sake, only three hypothetical individual consumers are considered to form the total aggregate market demand for some hypothetical commodity. The three individual demand curves are shown on the left side of the equation; the aggregate demand is shown on the right. Notice that the vertical price axis, P, is the same for all diagrams, but that the horizontal axis, Q, showing the quantity of the commodity demanded (limited to some convenient time period like a month or a year) changes its scale in the aggregate demand diagram to accommodate the larger quantities.

For producers (laborers, management, investors, landlords, agents, suppliers, etc.), the utility of their productive efforts is negative, unless they get paid for their trouble. These payments constitute the costs of production for the business firm. A quick glance at the production function in Figure 7, which shows how inputs of labor produce outputs of coconuts, shows that the relationship between inputs and outputs is not a constant one-to-one ratio over all the different output rates. Given the fixed

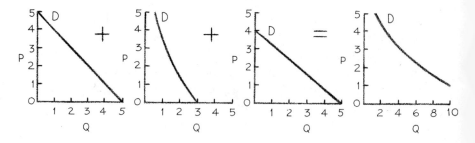

Figure 13. The aggregation of individual demands (P = price, Q = quantity, D = demand).

physical proportions of any production operation, there is bound to be some middling speed at which the operation is most efficient, as any gasoline-economizing motorist knows. Therefore, the costs of production form an interesting variable relationship with the level of output, and the efficiency of production and the amount of profits earned have a lot to do with the careful choice of the most efficient production speed. Assuming that each firm has found its most profitable production level (to be explained in the section The Theory of the Firm, below), an aggregate or market supply curve can be constructed that will show the relationship between the price and the quantity supplied. If the price is low, only the most efficient (that is, low-cost) firms can profitably carry on production; then the quantity supplied will be low. As the price rises, more and more firms can 'enter into production, and those already producing can increase their output level by enlarging their plants or even by running inefficiently fast for a while; then the aggregate quantity supplied increases.

Thus, the market supply, as shown by curve S in Figure 14, has the opposite slope from the market demand curve. And with demand and supply reacting in opposite directions in response to variations in price, there can be only one price that both the demanders and the suppliers will agree on for any given quantity of merchandise. If such a price is possible at all (and, by the way, there are an infinite number of impossible markets that a wild imagination could think of: nuclear submarines for sports fishermen, filet mignon for school lunch, and so on), it will be shown at the intersection of the market demand and supply curves, where the quantity demanded will equal the quantity supplied (E in Figure 14). Should the price be temporarily too high, the quantity supplied will exceed the quantity demanded; stores and warehouses will begin to experience an uncomfortable glut of unsold goods; and the price will soon have to come down. Should the price be too low, exactly the reverse will happen. Stores and warehouses will begin to look disconcertingly empty as the eager customers snatch the bargains off the shelves faster than they can be replenished. Price increases will be the natural adjustment. Without any regulation or control from central

206

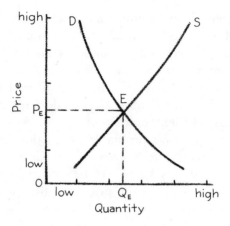

Figure 14. Economic equilibrium through supply and demand. Where the aggregate market demand and supply curves intersect, E, they agree on a price and on the quantity of the commodity exchanged over some convenient time span, like a month or a year. Thus, the market is cleared: at this price, all the goods supplied for sale are demanded for purchase. The equilibrium price and quantity are labeled P_E and Q_E, respectively.

authorities, the market forces will tend toward an equilibrium in which the price is adjusted so that the market is "cleared"— everything offered for sale is bought.

Thus, the controversy between the theory of value based on the labor cost of production and the utility theory of value is laid to rest. In Marshall's own words, "We might as reasonably dispute whether it is the upper or the under blade of a pair of scissors that cuts a piece of paper, as whether value is governed by utility or cost of production."[8]

Part of the beauty of this marginalist-Marshallian analysis is that all of the variations that can take place in the economic

---

[8] *Ibid.*, p. 348.

process between initial production and final consumption focus their effects on the market equilibrium of aggregate supply and demand. This structural simplicity has become so appealing to many economists that they often speak of the "Law of Supply and Demand." Hundreds of different economic situations can be depicted by making adjustments in these curves, drawing them more horizontal or steeper, shifting them around in the graph, or giving them kinks and jumps. For example, should cigarette smokers ever take the threat of lung cancer seriously, cigarettes would have less utility than before, and people would be markedly less eager to buy them. This situation would be illustrated by shifting the market demand curve leftward, showing that at every price level, a smaller quantity of cigarettes would be purchased. If the market supply of cigarettes is unaffected by the cancer scare, which would presumably be the case (unless tobacco farmers and cigarette producers anticipated the declining demand and produced less), the intersection of the new market demand curve and the supply curve would show a smaller quantity bought (and sold) and a lower equilibrium price. New inventions, sudden scarcities, real changes in the national income—because of changes in productivity and the purchasing power of money—a different kind of advertising, additional legal restrictions, changes in taxes and subsidies, natural catastrophes like earthquakes, or just a cheaper throwaway bottle, will be reflected by a change in one or both of these curves and will establish a new equilibrium price and quantity.

Surprisingly, in spite of all the enthusiasm for them, supply and demand curves don't really exist. They are imaginary constructs; that is, they are models of an hypothesized reality. Sometimes, however, imaginary constructs, which, by the way, are used in all the sciences, end up being accurate premonitions of reality. The novelist C. P. Snow wrote about the British physicist, Ernest Rutherford, who made an imaginary construct of the atom out of tennis balls, sealing wax, and strings in order to show how he thought atoms behaved. According to Snow, when Rutherford finally split the atom in 1919, he began to see that it really consisted of parts that looked like his strings and tennis balls.[9] Neither supply nor demand curves can be extracted very well out of the actual records of prices and quantities in the various markets. What the curves try to show is what *would* happen to the quantities supplied and demanded *if* the prices varied and *if* all other things remained constant. Of course, "all other things" hardly ever remain constant, not even for a day, and all the surveys, market research, and sociological studies cannot change supply and demand curves from imaginary constructs into real situations.

ELASTICITY

Elasticity of Demand

Still, many businesses, governments, and even consumer groups are intensely interested in knowing what these imaginary curves might look like. For instance, a vending machine operator will want to know what will happen to his sales of candy if he increases the price from a dime to fifteen cents. It would be marvelous for him if people bought nearly as much as before, in spite of the 50 percent price increase. But the price change would be an invitation to bankruptcy if so many people stopped buying from his machines that he would lose most of his sales. What he really wants to know is, what is the relationship between the price and the quantity demanded shown by the market demand curve in the ten and fifteen cents range? Or, more succinctly in Marshallian language, what is the *elasticity of the demand*?

Similarly, a government will want to know the elasticity of demand before imposing a sales tax on a particular kind of merchandise. The tax would be self-defeating if it cut the quantity demanded so much that little or no tax revenue could be collected (unless, as in the case of cigarettes, the object is just that, to cut the quantity demanded). The uses of elasticity analysis are many and diverse. In the end, this is probably the most useful aspect of the supply and demand concept.

---

[9] C. P. Snow, *Variety of Men* (Charles Scribner's Sons, New York, 1967).

A simple way of calculating the elasticity of the demand curve is to compare the relative change in quantity demanded to the relative change in price, for which the following formula[10] is useful:

$$\text{Elasticity} = - \frac{\text{percentage change in quantity demanded}}{\text{percentage change in price}}$$

This ratio could turn out to be anything from zero to infinity. The degrees of demand elasticity are usually distinguished as shown in Figure 15. Generally speaking, for a demand curve situated near the center of a graph whose axes are marked off in reasonably similar proportions, perfect inelasticity would mean a straight, vertical "curve." Perfect elasticity would produce a straight, horizontal curve, and the in-between degrees would produce increased steepness of the curves' slopes as they become less elastic.

If the mathematical formula for the demand curve is known and expressed as a functional (f) relationship between the price, P, and the quantity demanded, Q, at each price level, as

$$Q = f(P)$$

then the elasticity at any single point along the demand curve may be calculated by using the formula

$$\text{Elasticity} = - \frac{P}{Q} \cdot \frac{\partial Q}{\partial P}$$

The use of the derivative $\partial Q / \partial P$ implies that the slope of the curve, that is, the ratio between the change in Q and the change in P, can be expressed for any point on the demand curve. The minus sign is needed again to make the elasticity term for the negatively sloped demand curve come out positive.[11]

---

[10] The reason for the minus is that demand curves have a negative slope (down from left to right).

[11] The calculus follows the formula for elasticity at the top of this page which becomes

$$E = - \frac{\Delta Q}{Q} \div \frac{\Delta P}{P} = - \frac{P}{Q} \cdot \frac{\Delta Q}{\Delta P} \rightarrow - \frac{P}{Q} \cdot \frac{\partial Q}{\partial P}$$

Figure 15. Degrees of demand elasticity (P = price, Q = quantity, D = demand).*

ELASTICITY RATIO, E	DEMAND CURVE	DEGREE OF ELASTICITY	EFFECT OF A CHANGE IN PRICE ON THE TOTAL AMOUNT OF MONEY SPENT ON THE COMMODITY**
E = 0	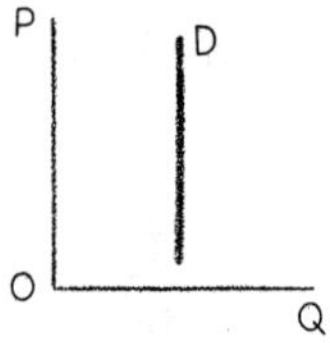	Perfectly inelastic	Directly proportional to the change in price
0 < E < 1	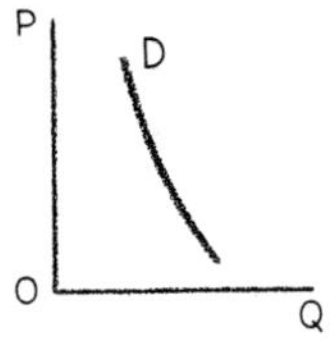	Relatively inelastic	An increase, with a price increase; a decrease, with a price decrease
E = 1	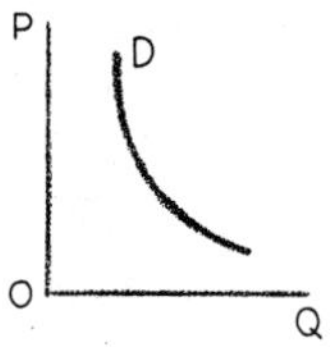	Unitary elasticity	No effect; the total amount of money spent will remain constant
1 < E < ∞	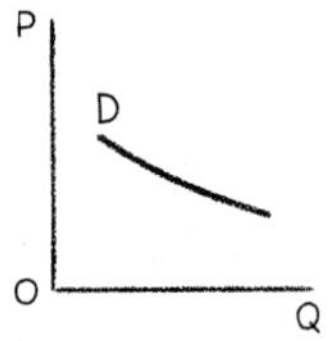	Relatively elastic	A decrease, with a price increase; an increase, with a price decrease
E = ∞	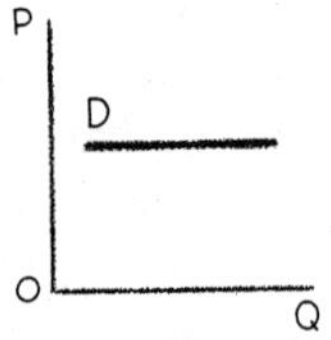	Perfectly elastic	Above a given price level, no money will be spent; at that price level and below, all the available supply will be bought

* The second, third, and fourth graphs assume that the scales of the two axes are constant and equal to one another and that the demand curve is well centered in the diagram.

** Assuming that the necessary supply is available at that price.

What makes the elasticity of demand either high or low is the degree of necessity or even stubbornness with which the consumer demands the commodity. For example, the elasticity of demand for food in general is very low because it is an absolute necessity in the long run and is rather important even in the short run. Regardless of the price, people will have to buy some minimum amount of food until all their money has been exhausted. But for any one particular kind of food, pork chops, for example, the demand elasticity will be high. Should the price of pork chops increase relative to other prices, people will choose hamburger meat or chicken instead. And should the price decrease relative to other prices, pork chops will be served for dinner more often than before. In other words, a high degree of substitutability will mean a high demand elasticity; a low degree of substitutability will mean a low demand elasticity.

Ironically, some commodities have an inelastic demand, in spite of their being quite unnecessary. This seems to be true of heavily advertised items, items that have a low unit price, habit-forming goods, and many "impulse purchase" articles. Their marginal utility/price ratio seems to be controlled by external influences, or it is so small that it remains below the consumer's decision making threshold—he never really thinks about the purchases. Or their low demand elasticity is due to mild addiction, as in the case of cigarettes and liquor, or hard addiction, as with chronic alcoholism and heroin consumption. A common joke is that the world's best market is for something that lends itself to advertising, sells for less than a dollar, costs less than a dime to make, and is legal though habit-forming. Watch the commercials on television, and you will see many examples of such products.

Elasticity of Supply

Elasticity of supply curves are only a little less useful than elasticity of demand curves. The formulas for calculating them are the same as those for calculating the elasticity of demand, except that the minus sign is unnecessary since the slope of the supply curve is positive. Assuming the demanders go along with it, an increase in price would always bring an increase in total revenue because the supply curve is positively sloped and both price and quantity increase together.

The different supply elasticities are useful in showing the effects of the passage of time in making adjustments to price changes. Alfred Marshall distinguished three time periods that caused three different degrees of supply elasticity (see Figure 16). In the *momentary* period, that is, the present instant with no passage of time, a change in price can bring about no change in quantity supplied because the production process, which is always subject to a certain amount of inertia, cannot respond instantly. The supply elasticity would be zero, perfectly inelastic, and the supply curve would be a straight vertical line at the quantity immediately available. Of course, "momentary" can mean different things in different industries. Marshall points out that once the boats have returned to harbor in the evening, the daily catch of fish is fixed, and no fluctuations in price will change the supply. In this case, "momentary" means about twenty-four hours. For a farmer, whose fields have been plowed, fertilized, seeded, and weeded by early summer, the quantity supplied is essentially out of his hands until early the next spring, when he again decides how much of each crop to plant. Except for the vagaries of weather and crop disease, his quantity supplied is thus fixed by early summer, and his momentary time period may be considered nine months long. No changes in price after that date can really affect his supply, unless he tries some last minute stunts. Again his individual supply elasticity will be zero, his curve straight up and down. At any one time, the actual market price will always be determined by market demand and the momentary market supply.

Another degree of supply elasticity is affected by a slightly longer period of time, called a *short-run* period. Here the supplier can adjust the quantity he supplies to changes in the price, but only within the limitations of his existing plant or productive capacity. If the price increases, the producer can run his machines faster or do whatever he has to do to increase output, as long as these changes don't lessen efficiency too much; but he does not have enough time to buy new machines, add more acres, or enlarge his plant in any way. Conversely, if the price decreases, he can slow down output; but he cannot dismantle

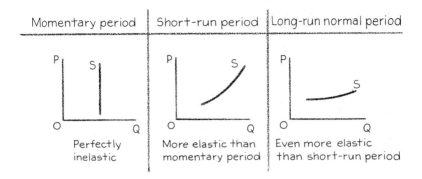

Figure 16. Degrees of supply elasticity.

his factory or sell his farm in that short a time. The supply elasticity could be anything larger than zero, depending on the physical characteristics of the production process, but it is not likely to be very elastic, and the supply curve will slope upward to the right more or less steeply.

In the *long-run* period, all adjustments are possible. More productive capacity can be added, new ground can be broken, new firms can enter the industry. Or factories and farms can be sold off, and businessmen can leave to seek their fortunes in Brazil. The market supply curve will be even more horizontal and even more elastic than is possible in the short-run period. The price determined by the intersection of the long-run market supply curve and the market demand curve Marshall called the *normal* price because it is supposed to show the ultimate outcome after all the adjustments in price and quantity have been made. That the actual market price at any one time is the result of the momentary, perfectly inelastic supply curve intersecting an equally tenuous market demand curve does not deter economists from insisting that prices are always tending toward the long-run normal price. If new situations didn't constantly intervene, a smooth and final adjustment process could flow from the momentary, through the short-run, and to the normal price. If this were accomplished in every market in the economy, something like a stationary state would be achieved.

However, though it be an imaginary construct, the long-run normal supply curve is a very convenient analytical tool. When juxtaposed on a graph with the market demand curve, as in Figure 17, it can be used for a variety of different analyses. For instance, suppose a new technological breakthrough makes a particular product much less expensive to produce than before; perhaps, a new, much smaller, more powerful, and cheaper automobile engine is invented. This will cause the long-run supply curve, S_1 (drawn as a straight line for convenience), to shift down the distance from X to Z to S_2. But who will benefit? Will the automobile manufacturers be able to sell more cars at the same price? Or will the customers be able to buy the same number of cars at a lower price? It depends on the comparative elasticities of the particular demand and supply curves. As shown in Figure 17, *left*, when the market demand curve is more elastic than the supply curve, the consumers benefit from only a small reduction in price, from X to Y, while the producers experience a relatively larger increase in sales, from M to N. When the relative elasticities are reversed and the same X-Z shift is experienced by a supply curve that is more elastic than the demand curve, as in Figure 17, *right*, the consumers benefit from a substantial drop in price, from X to Y, but the producers have only a relatively smaller increase in sales, from M to N.

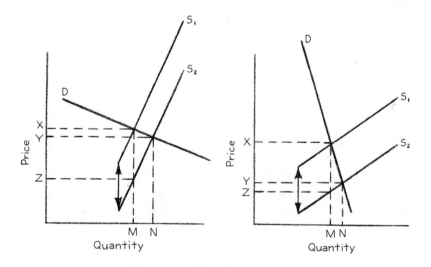

Figure 17. Supply and demand elasticities.

The same figure can be used to analyze the effects of a tax. Suppose a tax equivalent to X-Z is placed on the sales of automobiles. S_2 is now the before-tax market supply and S_1 the after-tax supply. Who bears the brunt of the tax? In Figure 17, *left*, while the consumers make do with N to M fewer cars, they don't experience much increase in price (even with the tax included), just Y to X. The producers, however, not only sell fewer cars, but, as if to add insult to injury, they get much less money for them (the government gets the tax), Y to Z. In Figure 17, *right*, the relative elasticities between demander and supplier are reversed, and the demand curve is less elastic than the supply curve. The consumers experience a large Y to X increase in price. The producers lose only N to M sales, and the price they receive after the tax drops only Y to Z. Again, it is a matter of relative elasticities. The party to the exchange with the least elastic function in the market will have the weakest bargaining position and will bear the major burden of the incidence of the tax.

All of this is accomplished with the long-run normal market demand and supply curves. These curves, because they are supposed to show the consumers at their most sophisticated and the producers at their most efficient, should produce the lowest market prices and the largest quantities sold that the industry is capable of. This is the basic virtue claimed by the free enterprise market economy. We have seen that the demand curve that most accurately expresses the consumers' desire to exchange money for goods results from careful consumers individually weighing all prices and marginal utilities and making the best decisions possible within their budgets. But how do the individual businessmen find their firm's most efficient level of production? And how does this result in the long-run normal supply?

THE THEORY OF THE FIRM

Businessmen make all their decisions by trying to answer their most basic question, namely, "Will it pay?" Whether the business is big or small, whether the decision involves a simple or a complicated issue, it always boils down to the same question. The farmer thinking of buying a new plow and the president of General Motors considering the development of a new line of automobiles must both try to answer the question. For an established enterprise that is trying to maximize profits, the most common question is, "Are we running at the most efficient output level?" Or, putting it more concretely, "Would it pay to expand production by a few units per week?" "Would a cutback in our output rate help our profits?" Clearly these are questions about what to do on the margin. They ask if the production speed should be changed a few notches one way or the other, not whether a business enterprise is worthwhile at all, although that too can be a marginal decision at times.

Part of the answer to "will it pay?" depends a great deal on the price of the commodity produced. If the price received is high, additions to the production process may pay for themselves. But if the price is low, simply staying in business at all may be a cliffhanger. The other part of the answer depends on how much the contemplated marginal change will cost. We have already seen that production is most efficient at some middle output level, when increasing the output by a few units per week would not cost much at this "cruising speed." But adding the same number of units to the output when the business is already roaring along at close to top speed may be very costly. At the other end of the scale, when the business is operating at a very slow speed, efficiency is also very low. Any contemplated marginal changes would cost a great deal at that end too, except that successive additions to the output level would become cheaper as the more efficient cruising speed of operations is approached.

How is the firm's most efficient and most profitable production level found? Simple! Any business opportunity that looks like it will pay for itself is eagerly grasped. What this means is that the production level will be increased until it doesn't pay to increase it any longer, and the optimum is found. This situation is illustrated in Figure 18. Curve MC is the marginal cost per unit of output. The price received for the commodity is the straight horizontal line, P. (For the moment, let's assume that the price is given.) After initial losses, every production increase

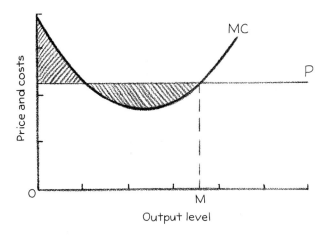

Figure 18. Optimum position of the firm.

pays for itself up to output level M because the price exceeds the marginal cost. (Although the marginal cost is higher than the price in the beginning, a perspicacious businessman will have seen that it would soon become a well-paying proposition to expand production.) But beyond output level M, it is clear that marginal cost is rising rapidly higher than the price. If the businessman had not expanded all the way to M, he wouldn't have squeezed every last drop of profits from his business opportunity; yet any step beyond M costs him more than he gains. So M remains the optimum output level, and the distance from zero to M signifies the optimum quantity of production per week (or any suitable time period) for that firm.

Adding together all the distances from zero to M from all of the firms producing the same commodity gives us the total quantity supplied at that price. Repeating the same process at a number of different price levels would indicate the long-run normal supply curve. At the lower price levels, fewer firms would stay in business, and the total quantity supplied to the market would be smaller. But the costs for these fewer firms may also be lower because they will all be buying smaller quantities of their factors of production and may be able to get them at lower prices. (Like everything else, factors of production also have supply curves sloping up from left to right most of the time.)

Conversely, at higher price levels, more firms will enter the industry, the firms already in the industry will increase their output levels, and the total quantity supplied will grow. Since larger quantities of the factors of production must be bought, costs of production will also be higher.

Marshall recognized that larger output levels per firm may introduce more efficient mass production techniques. These *economies of scale* (to use the professional term) would actually lower the commodity price rather than raise it as output levels are increased. He also recognized that when more firms entered the industry, certain external economies[12] may appear that would have the same effect. According to Marshall, however, these adjustments will have run their full course in the long run, and eventually the firm's cost behavior will be as originally described: the marginal cost will first decrease and then increase as the output level is increased.

The short run is very important, however. In this time period the especially clever or hard-working entrepreneur can make above-normal profits by taking advantage of an opportunity that other firms have not recognized. Perhaps he has a new commodity, a new production process, or any other advantageous innovation. When the other firms have caught on to his innovation (which they will do eventually), they will increase the market supply of the new product so much that its price will be driven down and the cost of the factors of production will be driven up. The extra profits that were a gold mine for the first entrepreneur dry up when all the firms get into the act. Still, those short-lived extra profits spur on the ambitious, who constantly seek new and better ways to run their businesses, and thus provide a spur to the market economy. In recognition of this benefit to the economy, society has helped the innovator to prolong his short-run profits by granting him legal patents and copyrights that give him exclusive rights over the innovation for

---

[12] External economies are windfall benefits for all firms, such as those that come from being in a growing industry. For example, the building of a special railroad line to the factory neighborhood to take advantage of the new business there will benefit all the firms but will not cost them anything.

a specified number of years—in the United States, up to seventeen years for patents and twenty-eight years for copyrights.

To visualize how the extra profits of the short run disappear in the long run, another kind of cost curve must be introduced; this is curve AC in Figure 19, the average cost. By its height above the horizontal axis, it shows the average unit cost at each output level; that is, at any one output level, average cost equals the total cost divided by the number of units produced at that output level. More than any other cost curve, the average cost curve clearly shows the most efficient cruising speed of the firm. Average cost is very high at low output levels where the engines of production are idling wastefully; then it dips down to its lowest point when the operation is at its most efficient; and finally, as output levels increase further and the inefficiencies of excess speed creep in, the average cost rises. It is no accident that the marginal cost curve and the average cost curve intersect at the lowest point, M, of the latter. It is an easily explained mathematical necessity. As long as the marginal cost—the cost of each added unit of production as the output level is increased—is lower than the average cost for all units combined, the average will be drawn down. When marginal costs are higher than average, they will pull the average up.

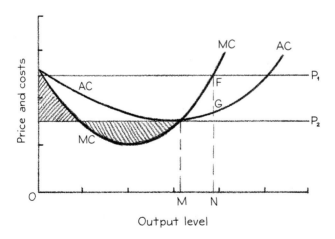

Figure 19. Optimum position of firms in the long run.

Thus, the intersection can only be at one point on the average cost curve, namely, the lowest point.

Now let's look at our clever entrepreneur who somehow found an opportunity to make excess profits. In Figure 19 this is shown by P_1. It would pay him to increase his output level to N, where MC intersects this price line. At this level, he is receiving a price per unit that is higher than the average cost per unit by an amount indicated by the distance F-G. Multiplying this per unit extra profit, F-G, by the number of units produced each week or month, zero to N, will give the total extra profit the businessman makes each week (or any suitable time period). But now comes the catch. His envious competitors are quick to take notice of his clever profit-making innovation, and when they join in on this good thing, they help to increase the total market supply and inadvertently drive the price down, as shown by P_2. (As explained above, they also push up cost, but this situation is too cumbersome to draw in the figure.) Now it pays our businessman to produce only up to level M again, and his excess profits have disappeared. Of course he is still earning "normal profits," which are often considered to be about a 6 percent return on the capital invested in the firm. These normal profits are considered a cost (and are included in the average cost curve) because they are the amount that must be paid for the capital invested in the firm, whether the capital belongs to the businessman himself or was borrowed. Should the price be driven down even lower than P_2, the firms will be suffering losses and may eventually even drop out of business. As they do, the shrinking market supply will push the price up again. In the long run, P_2 will prevail.

All this interaction means that the well-adjusted, long-run normal market provides the consumer with commodities at a price equal to the lowest possible cost. In the short run, if this is not the case, then that is the price society must pay for dynamic change and growth. Under perfectly competitive conditions, this theory of the firm applies throughout the entire economy, from producers of energy, raw materials, and agricultural goods to producers of finished goods for the consumer. With the general population driven by a desire to maximize their marginal utilities as consumers and to maximize their compensation for the disutility of their productive labors, and with business managers and entrepreneurs seeking to maximize their profits, the market is the superb arbiter that assigns each person and each business his just reward. To the most productive goes the biggest income. It is all very automatic and very rational.

But it is not completely convincing. There is something too perfect and glossy about it, and a look at the assumptions that underlie this marginalist system will reveal the cracks in the foundation. These early marginalists assumed, some explicitly, some implicitly, that a market always consisted of large numbers of buyers and sellers. How large, exactly, is hard to pinpoint, but the markets would be at least large enough that any one demander or supplier could have no significant impact on the aggregate market demand or supply all by himself. Therefore, he would have to accept the market price as given, and no amount of effort on his part, not even advertising, could improve the situation. Furthermore, it was assumed that in any one market, all of the commodities would be essentially homogeneous, that is, there would be markets for different grades of potatoes, markets for different kinds of steel, markets for a variety of textiles, but there would be no need to distinguish specific grades or varieties according to individual producers. Brand names were not needed.

Another assumption was that any businessman could get in or out of a market with ease. Artificial restrictions on entry to certain kinds of businesses, like licenses, initiation fees, or monopolists' techniques for the exclusion of competitors, were disdained by the early marginalists as bad sportsmanship in business. The natural restrictions on entry, like the prohibitive cost of setting up a modern steel mill or oil refinery, were largely ignored in their theory. And throughout their analysis, the marginalists assumed that everyone would know what everyone else was doing; perfect communication would assure that gaps in the economic equilibrium could exist only in the short run.

Of course, in the late 1800s when marginalist theory was being developed, these assumptions may not have appeared as unrealistic as they do today. Businesses were smaller; products were more homogeneous; special product design, advertising, brand names, and trade restrictions did not play the important roles that they do today in the economy. The Industrial Revolution was well under way, but the hunger for the basics, food, textiles, simple metals, and fuels, was still there in spite of the new abundance of goods being produced. In these circumstances, all our contemporary efforts to titillate the already satiated consumer were unnecessary. The factors of production were simpler too. Relatively much more unskilled and, therefore, homogeneous labor was used. Management techniques were hardly sophisticated by today's standards. Industries were already becoming technical, but nothing at all existed like the "brain industries" of today, such as the computer, electronics, and pharmaceutical industries.

Yet, as these modern complications become increasingly and rapidly important in the industrial economies, many marginalist economists refused to recognize them. Blithely they ignored the macroeconomic concerns, that is, the concerns that deal with the whole economy in the aggregate, such as the business cycle, economic growth and development, inflation, monopoly power, poverty, and inadequate social welfare. In their opinion, these were all to be taken care of by the microeconomics of individual decisions made by producers and consumers working in an open market. If there were problems, these economists reasoned, they were expected as the result of competition and free enterprise. To this day, there are economists who stick by the old marginalist verities and, like Bible-thumping fundamentalists, see the modern conditions as sinful aberrations of the ideal assumed by their analyses.

THE THEORY OF CAPITAL

Some marginalists, however, did try to expand and improve the analysis so that it would fit reality better. The Austrian economist Eugen Von Böhm-Bawerk (1851–1914) is noted for his careful analysis of the role of time in the production process. Among all the sciences, perhaps only physics is as concerned with the time dimension as is economics, and, in both physics and economics, time complicates all relationships. For example, if two economic commodities have exactly the same value but one is available now while the other is available a year from now, then the present value of the two commodities isn't exactly equal after all. The value of the second commodity is discounted (a certain percentage is deducted from its evaluation) because of the year-long wait for its appearance. Waiting for something is a disutility, even if no risk is involved—although it often is involved. If a person is asked to abstain voluntarily from present enjoyment of a commodity while someone else borrows it for a year, the abstainer must be reimbursed the year's discount of the commodity's value when it is returned at the end of the year (in addition to whatever other depreciation may have occurred). The rate of this reimbursement for wating is called the *interest rate,* and it is expressed as a percentage of the face value (the original value) of the commodity. The commodity that is most commonly lent at interest is money, and abstinence from the consumption of the things money can buy is called *saving.*

Abstinence from consumption, because it is counter to human nature, is a disutility, but it is offset by some very powerful rewards besides the interest it earns when it produces loanable funds. If the output from production is reinvested in the production process rather than consumed, it will usually cause the next production batch to be larger. If this next output quantity is again invested in the production process, the next production generation will be still larger. This is called the theory of roundabout production. Of course, it is assumed that the output reinvested is in a suitable form, such as machines and intermediate goods, and not in the form of consumer commodities. When several batches of output have been suitably reinvested in the production process, a very much larger output of consumer goods can be produced with just the normal, original amount of productive effort.

In 1889, Böhm-Bawerk illustrated the process of roundabout production with concentric circles, each numbered for the year in which the output was produced. Every year the same production effort is made (the center circle), but when the output is not consumed but rather suitably reinvested, it grows and pushes out one ring at a time with each reinvestment. As shown in Figure 20, by the fifth year the annual production effort pushes forth a prodigious outside circle, which may now be in the form of consumer goods.

In modern terminology, the effectiveness of this roundabout production is called the *productivity of capital*. At first, when a new investment presents a fresh and dynamic opportunity, the rate of this productivity of capital is higher than the interest rate, and it pays businessmen to borrow money to invest in the "roundaboutness" of their production as well as to reinvest their own unconsumed incomes. But even capital is subject to the law of diminishing returns, and in a stationary state the rate of productivity of capital for all business opportunities could drop as low as the interest rate; then lending would stop. It would no longer pay to increase the roundaboutness of production beyond this point, and all the output may be taken in the form of consumer commodities.

Thus, the disutility of waiting is what makes interest payments necessary; the productivity of capital is what makes paying interest possible. And as long as new business opportunities keep the productivity of capital above the interest rate, it will pay to make new investments.

One of Böhm-Bawerk's purposes in developing this analysis was to refute Marx's belief that capitalists made no contribution to the production of value and that capital was merely an accumulation of labor hours. With increased industrialization, it was becoming quite obvious that capital was one of the positive factors of production, along with natural resources, human efforts, the body of knowledge and technology, and so on. Today, most economists recognize the existence and productivity of all these diverse factors and, for convenience, lump them together in a kind of holy trinity called Land, Labor, and Capital. Throughout history, there have always been different interpretations of the ultimate source of material value. Greco-Roman societies were suspicious of the entrepreneur; the medieval Christian church damned interest and, indirectly, capital; the physiocrats credited mother earth with original productivity and no one else; and the classical economists and Marxists, in

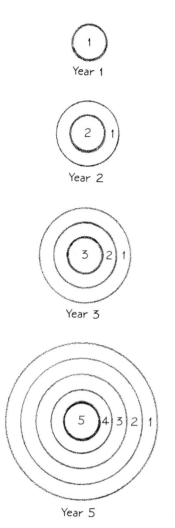

Year 1

Year 2

Year 3

Year 5

Figure 20. Böhm-Bawerk's roundabout production. The output from year 1 is squeezed out by the output of year 2. Then the output from both years 1 and 2 is squeezed further out by the output of year 3. These intermediate goods (output of years 1 and 2) will grow and ripen over a five-year period until the output from year 1 has ripened into consumer goods and may be nibbled away. (Adapted from Eugen Von Böhm-Bawerk, *Kapital und Kapitalzins,* 4th ed., Gustav Fischer, Jena, 1921, vol. 2, p. 143.)

the best humanist tradition of their day, gave all the credit to man himself. Even now too much talk of productivity of capital evokes sneers from those who wonder if this theory is nothing more than an apology for the rich. Unlike the natural sciences, the theories of the social sciences must try to be in tune with contemporary social beliefs as well as objectively accurate in order to be acceptable. (Or do the natural sciences suffer this necessity too?)

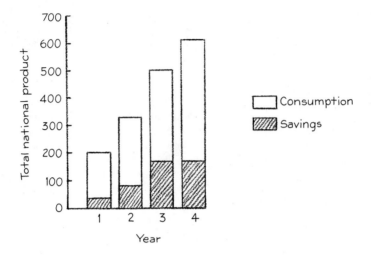

Figure 21. Growth of the national product.

Applying the theory of roundabout production to the economy as a whole, instead of to a single firm, gives a good explanation of the process of total economic growth. Beginning with year one in Figure 21, if a small part of the annual national product can be saved and invested, the next year's production will be a little larger and next year's saving will be a little easier. The process of economic growth proceeds geometrically year after year until it becomes possible, even necessary, to slow it down to a manageable rate by increasing the volume of annual consumption. This turn of events, increased consumption relative to saving, is the ultimate purpose of economic growth.

THE THEORY OF MONOPOLY IN COMPETITION

Along with Marshall's momentary, short-run, and long-run periods, Böhm-Bawerk's careful analysis of time in relationship to capital, interest, and production lent a much more realistic sense of dynamism to economic theory. Another effort at realism was the updating of the theory of the firm. As we have seen, the original marginalist assumptions of large numbers of buyers and sellers, homogeneous products, freedom of entry into the market, and perfect communication were becoming glaringly irrelevant. In 1933, two economists published a more realistic theory of the firm independently of one another and on either side of the Atlantic. One was Harvard professor Edward H. Chamberlin (1890–1967), who wrote *The Theory of Monopolistic Competition*; the other was Cambridge professor Joan Robinson, who wrote *The Economics of Imperfect Competition*.

As their titles imply, both books tackled the analysis of business behavior when the idealistic assumptions of the original marginalists were dropped. The original "perfect" competition was now allowed to be imperfected; the firms no longer needed to be small in relationship to the total market; the commodities could be differentiated from one another by product design, advertising, and brand names, and it was assumed that each firm could somehow have an influence on price. The model for the monopolistic or imperfect competitor, then, is not a wheat farm or a two-man coal mine, but rather an automobile company, a supermarket chain, the town's only jewelry store, or even the shoe shine boy who works one particular city block all to himself. In other words, any competitor that is unique by virtue of some product, service, geographic location, or whatever distinction—any competitor that isn't interchangeable with all the others in his market—is, in some large or small way, a monopolistic competitor. Certainly the vast majority of modern businesses fits into this category.

Figure 22 illustrates the firm in monopolistic competition. Since each firm can influence the price—primarily by the quantity supplied—the price line (AR, average revenue) slopes downward from left to right (it is drawn as a straight line here for convenience). In fact, in dealing with the average revenue curve, the supplier is facing his own private demand curve, the demand curve for his own product. When he expands production, he finds that he must lower his price to sell all of his products. And, in doing so, he not only lowers the price on the newly added units of output, but he normally has to lower it on his entire production. Expanded output, therefore, hurts the sup-

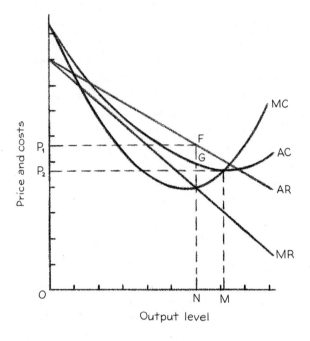

Figure 22. The firm in monopolistic competition.

plier in two ways: the extra output sells at a lower price, but, even worse, unless he can insulate the market somehow for the extra output, the original output per week or month also sells at the lower price. However, this double liability imposed by the marginal output is not shown by the average revenue curve. Instead, the marginal revenue curve, MR, serves this purpose. The height of this curve above the horizontal axis shows the increase in the total revenue received when output is expanded by a marginal unit. Because this marginal revenue curve shows the "retroactiveness" of the price decreases, it falls more rapidly than the average revenue curve. Of course, the mathematical relationship between the marginal revenue and average revenue follows the same rules as the relationship between the marginal cost and average cost explained on pp. 219–220.

The monopolistic competitor may act differently from Marshall's perfect competitor by advertising his products, designing them so that they are distinguishable from similar products, marketing them in preferable areas, building customer loyalty, and so on. But he is slipped precisely out of the same mold as the perfect competitor when it comes to maximizing profits. The monopolistic competitor also wants to find his optimum level of output. As always, his marginal cost curve tells only one-half of the story, and its intersection with the average revenue curve is no longer a critical point because the AR slopes and indicates different prices at different output levels. Instead, it pays the monopolistic competitor to expand his output level until the marginal cost exactly equals the *marginal* revenue. Beyond this point, an expansion would incur more extra costs than it would earn extra revenues. Before this point is reached, an expansion would incur more extra revenues than extra costs. Thus, the optimum level of production for the firm is when MC equals MR, at point N. The price will be at point P_1. At this output level and price, the firm will be earning its maximum possible profits, including extra profits—usually called *monopoly profits*. These monopoly profits are equal to the distance F-G per unit, because the price is higher than the average cost, and they total F-G times the distance from zero to N in each accounting time period. They are not necessarily temporary but may continue through the long run. When they do, monopoly profits are acknowledged as the social cost to be paid for a monopolistic market structure.[13]

In many businesses, such as gasoline stations, corner grocery stores, privately owned motels, and small dress shops, this monopoly profit tempts so many small businessmen into the market that it becomes overcrowded. These businesses can crop up around every crossroad like mushrooms after a spring rain. Then, the price line, AR, is pushed down, and the monopoly profits disappear. In other industries, where the suppliers are fewer in number, more sophisticated, and able to coordinate their policies overtly or covertly, and where freedom of entry

---

[13] The structure of a market is usually defined by the kind of competition that prevails in the market, such as perfect competition, monopolistic competition, oligopoly, or monopoly.

into the industry is naturally or artificially restricted, the market supply and demand may be so manipulated that the extra monopoly profits become very large. Public utilities, petroleum refining, steel, cement, business machines, and many other big industries have been accused of such manipulation. The root cause of monopoly profits, however, is always to be found in the market structure, the fact that modern businesses naturally tend to form monopolistically competitive markets. The businessmen may not be unethical in their profiteering or antisocial or even greedy; they are maximizing profits in the same way that all other rational businessmen operate, although at times their fervor may seem excessive. Certainly, to accuse them all personally of malice is to pursue the symptoms and to ignore the pathology of the disease.

Competition for the customer's dollar, even in those industries called oligopolies where the producers are large and few in number, can be vigorous. Economists sometimes regard this competition as a kind of game and have developed a game theory based on the work done by the mathematician John Von Neumann and the economist Oskar Morgenstern during World War II.[14] In abbreviated form, this theory explains how two competing "players" each choose their best possible strategies among the available alternatives. For example, suppose two competing airlines are trying to maximize passenger loading on their London to New York run. Let's assume that the fare is fixed by an international convention and that the airlines' various competitive strategies all cost the same. Let's also assume that the total number of passengers is constant so that what one airline gains the other loses; this is called a zero sum game. The airlines try to tempt passengers to their planes by one of four different strategies: they can advertise, they can give free drinks to the passengers, they can show movies in the cabin, or they can do nothing. (Assume that doing nothing somehow costs the same as the other three strategies.) Of course, neither airline knows what strategy the other will choose. The numbers in bold-

---

[14] John Von Neumann and Oskar Morgenstern, *Theory of Games and Economic Behavior*, 2nd ed. (Princeton University Press, Princeton, N.J., 1953).

face given in the payoff matrix in Table 5 show the number of passengers gained monthly by Jet Airlines. The numbers in italics show the monthly gains made by Stream Airlines.

Table 5. A zero sum payoff matrix

		STREAM AIRLINES			
		Advertise	Free drinks	Show movies	Do nothing
JET AIRLINES	Advertise	0	*1500*	*1000*	**1000**
	Free drinks	**1000**	*1000*	*500*	**2000**
	Show movies	**1500**	**500**	**1000**	**3000**
	Do nothing	*2000*	*3000*	*2000*	**1000**

A quick glance at this given payoff matrix clearly shows that, no matter what strategy Stream Airlines chooses, Jet Airlines' best strategy is to show movies. With this strategy, at worst it will still gain 500 passengers, and that is the best of the worst outcomes of any of its four strategies. Stream Airlines' best or "dominant" strategy is to give free drinks to its passengers. With this strategy, at worst it will lose 500 passengers to Jet, but it could lose much more with any of the other strategies. (That the intersection of these two dominant strategies involves Streams losing 500 passengers to Jet every month is unfortunate for Stream Airlines and should induce it to look for other more clever strategies, in which case the traveler probably stands to gain.)

Seen from the standpoint of either airline, the intersection of these dominant strategies is a "minimax" solution, which means that the minimum possible outcome of either airline's own strategy is at a maximum at the same time that the maximum possible outcome of the rival airline's strategy is at a minimum. Both airlines will want to stick with their chosen strategies, and the minimax solution is stable and predictable. Of course, most realistic payoff matrices don't afford the ready-made minimax solution given in Table 5, but with the application of probability and other mathematic techniques, various different games lend themselves to a meaningful analysis and a minimax solution along these lines. How realistic this games theory is, with its given payoff matrices, its limited number of players, and its other restrictive assumptions, is questionable. It is being applied in other contexts, such as the military analysis of national security and international relationships. Many economists think games theory may continue to develop into one of the best ways of analyzing conflict and competition among the large industrial units in the advanced economies of the world today.

The underlying social cost of oligopolistically and monopolistically competitive markets is that the quantity sold by each firm is less than it would be under perfect competition. If we look at Figure 22 again, we can see that the perfect competition optimum, zero to M, is at the output level where average cost is at its lowest and the price is P_2. At the monopolistic competition optimum, zero to N, the firm has given up some of its efficiency in exchange for the higher price and the monopoly profits. Some economists argue that this is a price well worth paying for the diverse product designs possible with such competition. Others argue that, in fact, more is sold in the aggregate market because the advertising possible with such competition awakens a latent demand. Still others argue that the comparison of monopolistically and perfectly competitive firms on the same diagram is spurious. For example, a huge, mass production, highly technical, and sophisticated automobile firm couldn't be a perfect competitor under any circumstances, regardless of public preferences.

At any rate, the word "monopoly" always has an unpleasant ring to the public's ear, no matter what form it takes. The rapid industrialization that swept through the United States after the Civil War left many citizens uneasy about the growing size and power of business firms. By the end of the 1800s, this uneasiness had grown to a full-blown public uproar about the monopolies that were exploiting the nation. Then, the issue wasn't about abstractions like optimum output levels, marginal cost, or average revenue curves. They were concrete cases of farmers being charged outrageous rates by the railroads, of the American Sugar Refining Company controlling the price of 98 percent of all the sugar sold in the country, of the Standard Oil Company jockeying to build a giant empire that would exclude all competition. Everywhere companies were trying to escape the normal forces of market competition by forming combinations of various types, presumably on the old maxim, "If you can't beat 'em, join 'em!" In the United States and in Europe, companies joined together by forming pools, cartels, trusts, holding companies, and mergers, a monopolist's nomenclature for denoting various degrees of combination from a simple gentlemen's agreement to a centralization of financial power to a complete union of firms.

The monopolies used all the legal and illegal means at their disposal to gouge the public for profit. They bankrupted competitors, kept their own subsidiaries in line with threats of violence, lobbied for tariffs to protect themselves against foreign competition, intimidated state legislatures, bought state and federal congressmen, and cheated on contracts. Public morality was incensed, and organized opposition to these excesses began to form. Disadvantaged small businessmen, consumers and workers, and farmers, all representing substantial voting power, were in active opposition to the combinations. The Granger movement effectively opposed railroad exploitation in the Midwest, and in several states farmer-labor parties became powerful. By 1890, seventeen predominantly agricultural states had passed antimonopoly laws, and in that year the federal Sherman Antitrust Act was passed. The Sherman Act was used successfully against railroad combinations in 1897, but ironically the first use of the act was against labor unions in the famous U.S. vs. Debs case that went all the way to the Supreme Court in 1894. Monopolists continued with immunity until 1911, when the Sherman Act was effectively used to break up the combinations formed by Standard Oil, American Tobacco, and Du Pont, among others. The end of the most blatant antisocial monopolies seemed in sight. Since that time, the U.S. Department of Justice's antitrust division has been occasionally more, occasionally less, active, and American business has generally tried to steer clear of an open and unabashed display of collusion, price fixing, and the monopolistic restraint of trade.

Still, the "crime" of the monopolist is hard to incorporate into our body of morality. It is not mentioned in the Ten Commandments, and the everyday social ethic has little to say about it either. When, after World War II, several officials of General Electric, Westinghouse, and other firms were actually jailed for their price-fixing tactics, these otherwise upstanding community leaders, church members, directors of the Community Chest and the local Boy Scout troop could hardly believe that they were considered criminals. One such convicted businessman hanged himself in his jail cell, probably not because the three-year sentence he had received was too much to bear but because of his broken social status. It does seem a rather moot distinction to litigate against those businessmen who fix prices by combinations and to praise those who do the same (if a little less directly) through advertising, lobbying, and other acceptable efforts to control the market. That one should be a sin while the other is part of "American business know-how" is inconsistent and will require some better solution.

CHAPTER 8

The End of Liberalism

In spite of monopolies, the grueling conditions of urban life, the rapacious abuse of the countryside by burgeoning industries, and unequal standards of living, capitalism permitted the economy to expand rapidly throughout the Western world during the nineteenth century. Historians speak of this period as the *Pax Britannica*, a peaceful standoff between the major Western powers, with the British navy providing the critical balance. It lasted from the end of the Napoleonic Wars in 1815 to the outbreak of World War I in 1914. During this hundred years' peace, Europe and the United States blossomed as the richest, most powerful, and most dynamic civilization the world had ever known. Every corner of the globe was touched by this new force in some way. Western navies visited every harbor; trading posts were established in the far reaches of all the world's continents; and new ideas and influences disturbed the less advanced soci-

eties of Africa and threatened the stability of the ancient civilizations in Asia. By the late 1800s, it certainly seemed as though
the Western world was achieving some kind of practical utopia,
a realist's Garden of Eden, where science and industry were
working together to take the drudgery out of work, to spread
democracy and eliminate oppression, and to establish a high
material standard of living with freedom from hunger and want.
Classical liberal and marginalist economics seemed to be working, and every aspect of society, rationalism, freedom, and openness seemed to set the tone for success. Perhaps liberalism had
found the ultimate truth, the "right way" for mankind.

But somehow bad seeds had begun to grow in this "garden."
Perhaps liberalism carried its own seeds of self-destruction; perhaps it was just age-old human nature reasserting itself. Side by
side with liberalism, new intellectual currents were beginning to
undercut its foundations. Darwin's theory of evolution seemed to
show that man was just another beast after all, admittedly a
smart one, but one certainly not capable of the enlightened behavior and pure heart that liberalism had postulated. Freudian
psychology was exposing the dark, irrational recesses of the
mind. By the turn of the century, the arts had embarked on a
perverse and bizarre course, which they are still struggling with
today; a new-found affinity for a tough and preferably gory
"realism" colored much of the creative work in unpleasant hues.
Ideas of violence and struggle seemed to exert a new magnetism.
Already by the middle of the 1800s, Marx had preached revolution and Schopenhauer had written that the blind will to survive was the ruling truth of the universe. Later in the century,
Nietzsche glorified power and courage as against reason, and
the Social Darwinists, led by Herbert Spencer, justified the
emergence of rich and powerful industrialists as a natural result
of the survival of the fittest. Jacob Burckhardt lamented that
democracy would mire civilization in mediocrity, and Oswald
Spengler saw salvation in an anti-intellectual "triumph of
blood," where people would think in terms of their race. Anti-
semitism became more vocal, even though the preceding century
had been a period of the most successful Jewish integration into
Western society.

And at the end of the one hundred years of peace, the world was outfitted with the largest standing armies it had ever seen, backed by even more reservists. In this age of liberalism, military conscription had become compulsory in all the countries of the great powers. International trade turned into imperialism, as the trading outposts were transformed into mines and plantations, and native tribesmen were metamorphosed into regimented laborers. From 1870 to 1900, Africa and Southern Asia, which had been commercially dominated but not ruled outright by the Europeans, were partitioned among the great powers and turned into colonies, dependencies, and protectorates. Combinations of all sorts polluted the freedom of the domestic market; local tariffs were raised ever higher in order to restrict the international market. Paradoxically, almost everyone seemed to agree that peace, freedom, democracy, capitalism—all the aspects of liberalism—were the best choices for humanity; yet everyone seemed to be holding his breath, waiting for all hell to break loose.

THE GREAT WAR

It did, on June 28, 1914, when the Austrian Hapsburg Archduke Francis Ferdinand was assassinated by a young Serbian nationalist on the streets of Sarajevo. The assassination itself seems too small an event to have set off a world war, but the repercussions from it entangled the complex alliances of the Western nations into a hopeless snarl. The balance of power, on which the Pax Britannica had been based, had degenerated into several mutual defense pacts that with the slightest conflict could, and did, engage practically all the Western nations. Although war was "in the air" by this time anyway, the burden of much of the guilt lies with the often arrogant and stupid diplomacy that failed to untangle the situation before it was too late.

In the end, when German defeat was imminent, the very Kaiser, aristocrats, and members of the German military officers' caste who had done so much to cause the war unloaded the whole mess on a hurriedly contrived civilian government, which was destined never to govern effectively. The Czarist government had already been overthrown in Russia. The lands of Hungary, Austria, Bulgaria, and Turkey were also about to come under new management. Meanwhile, the victorious Allies, instead of building a new basis for world peace, tried to extract booty from the vanquished powers by insisting on a series of ruinous reparation payments.

Although it can hardly be estimated in monetary terms, one economic historian guesses that the material destruction and wartime expenditures cost a total of about 600,000,000,000 dollars to all sides, or twelve times the annual national income of the United States, then around 50 billion dollars.[1] Of the 65 million men mobilized during the war, 9 million were killed, 5 million more were reported missing, 7 million were permanently disabled, and 15 million were seriously wounded. Factories, railroads, farms, all industry lay exhausted and depleted after the war years, during which maintenance, replacement, and modernization were postponed. National currencies were devalued by inflationary war financing, whereby governments used large amounts of newly created money to buy war materials from the economy, after which the money circulated around vainly trying to find civilian goods to be exchanged for in wartime economies that had less than normal supplies of such goods. Governments borrowed too much money from their central banks (which could use the securities as reserve assets on which to base credit expansions) rather than from private individuals, who would have had to restrict their expenditures by the amount of securities they had bought. (See the discussion on the effects of this practice, p. 96.) And, of course, it seems to be politically impossible to raise taxes high enough to finance a war, even though they would be noninflationary. Money in circulation in Germany increased by five times during the war. Eventually inflating prices spiraled the currency out of existence.

Also destroyed were the many small and large international trade arrangements that had been so useful in making Western

---

[1] Shepard B. Clough, *European Economic History: The Economic Development of Western Civilization*, 2nd ed. (McGraw-Hill, New York, 1968), p. 431.

capitalism operate smoothly, efficiently, and internationally during the previous one hundred years. With inflation and the burden of the enormous war debts in both victorious and vanquished nations, the currencies no longer enjoyed international confidence. For example, the French franc, which was worth about 20 United States cents in 1914, was bringing only 0.389 cents in 1926, a fluctuation that would make any long-term trading arrangements impossible. Besides, many of the traditional industrial patterns had been broken by the necessities of war production, and they could not be reestablished as they had been before the war because the exhaustion of industries and resources from the intense war effort forced them now to seek new patterns. The so-called "workshop" nations of the world lost many of their traditional markets to newcomers who had been able to fill the vacuum during the war. United States manufacturing production, which had risen by about 25 percent during the war, and Japanese production, which had risen by about 75 percent at the same time, easily replaced English, French, and German production. In 1921, British exports were half of what they had been in 1913. The high tariffs, left over from before the war, were compounded by the addition of new tariff boundaries resulting from the new states that were being created out of the crumbling old empires.

But every experience has its lessons, and war is no exception. World War I taught all nations the importance of economic as well as military strength. The days when armies could engage one another in formation on the battlefield while civilians went on with business (almost) as usual, even to the point of maintaining trade between the belligerent nations, were gone forever. War's influence was total now. The Allies drew a choking blockade around the Central Powers, closing off as much as possible the life flow of both sea and land shipping to Germany and Austria. The Germans countered with submarine attacks on British shipping in the English Channel, which were very effective at first, sinking about two million tons of shipping in the three months of February, March, and April, 1917, alone, and causing Britain's food reserve to sink to a panic level of only six weeks. Meanwhile, in Germany, 1917 became known as the

Rübenjahr, the turnip year, because turnips were the only staple food for the people, as the shortages eliminated just about everything else. With two-thirds of their imports blocked, the Germans had to turn quickly to developing substitutes, and their renowned chemists came up with many inventions, including synthetic rubber, even margarine.

In the end, the overpowering economic resources of the Allies were decisive. Huge convoys of merchant shipping guarded by warships broke the German submarine blockade. The British Empire provided materials from around the world. And when the United States at last entered the war on April 6, 1917, the scales tipped against the Central Powers. After the last big German push to the Marne in the summer of 1918, a cease-fire was arranged on November 11. Although the American army had fought for only four months and although out of every 100 artillery shells, the French fired 51, the British 43, and the Americans only 6, the overwhelming weight of the American economy's ability to produce manpower and matériel was the handwriting on the wall. On the day of the armistice, two million American soldiers were in France, and another million were on their way.

Like psychologists who learn about the normal mind by studying the abnormal mind, economists learned a great deal by working with the crazed wartime economy. In previous wars, the only economic planning that had been necessary was the logistics of armies and navies themselves. In this war, the entire economy had to be mobilized for the war effort. Not just government finances, but the entire flow of money through the economy had to be regulated as precisely as possible in order to control inflation and to keep the wheels of industry turning. Manpower, raw materials, and foodstuffs had to be allocated to their most strategic uses, for which central economic planning became a necessity.

The first such central planning was established in Germany by Walter Rathenau, director of the German public utilities company A.E.G. and founder of the *Kriegsrohstoffabteilung*, the War Raw Materials Department. This department established production priorities for the major industries, worked at increasing the output of scarce supplies, and subsidized research in synthetic substitutes for unavailable raw materials. Other countries soon followed suit with their own planning departments, which were solely governmental or also included trade associations and employee representation. In all nations, the universal draft was made more selective, sparing men with special skills and in priority occupations so that they could contribute more to the war effort by producing at home. Women and previously unemployed groups, the aged and the young, were encouraged to work in strategic industries. Food was rationed and prices regulated. The Allies even planned some aspects of their economies internationally, especially through the Inter-Allied Wheat Executive, established in 1916, and the Allied Maritime Transport Council, set up in 1917. A deluge of new taxes also tended to shape the economy into a fighting instrument as well as to raise the much-needed government revenue. The excess profits tax was aimed at war profiteers; the luxury tax tried to impose austerity; taxes on goods in short supply were a form of rationing; and many of the standard taxes, such as the income tax and turnover tax, were increased or instituted for the first time.

The central planning of the economies of these nations was a great social experiment, although it was probably not seen in that light at the time. It was the first time that modern industrial economies, which had always been more or less free enterprise economies, were steered on a prescribed course by the instruments of government. Not only were the economies managed; the people themselves were manipulated, and their thoughts were controlled by new methods of propaganda. Frightened and frustrated as they were by a brutal, seemingly never-ending war that they did not understand, the people were taught that the enemy was criminal and evil. Freedom of expression and freedom of the press were severely limited, and any sign of doubt or questioning was considered almost treasonous. The flames of hatred and intolerance were fanned until, at the end of the war, mutual mistrust among the nations became a serious impediment to a lasting peace. And the social sciences got their first bittersweet taste of being used as an instrument of power. None of these lessons was lost on the totalitarian regimes to come.

The several peace treaties that were signed in the various suburbs of Paris, after which they were named, were to put a bright, new face on Europe. It was hoped that the world would now settle down to peace and prosperity. President Woodrow Wilson, who was hailed throughout Europe as the savior of democracy and justice, tried to impose his famous Fourteen Points on the treaties. These points constituted a reaffirmation of the best liberalist philosophy and championed the old virtures of democracy, freedom, and openness in national and international affairs and in economic and political life. But the other Allies did not share Wilson's vision. The Treaty of Versailles with Germany seemed to be written in a punitive spirit, especially to the Germans, and the reparation payments from Germany that it provided for were to become economically unfeasible. The many new nations created by this peace: Finland, Estonia, Latvia, Lithuania, Poland, Czechoslovakia, Yugoslavia, and the small, separate states of Austria and Hungary, created as many problems as they solved. The League of Nations, Wilson's brainchild, was a great improvement over the international anarchy that would have prevailed without it. Yet it was viewed by many nations as an instrument to maintain British and French power, and, ironically, the United States never joined. Ultimately, all the efforts to insure peace failed, and Europe came to grief again within two decades.

THE HOPEFUL TWENTIES

Still, the twenties gave hope to optimists. The almost feudal structure of the economies in the Eastern European countries was modernized; some steps were taken toward political democracy; land reform resulted in redistribution and transferring ownership to the tenants who did the farming. These last reforms were feasible in those nations where the old German aristocracy had owned the land and could now be conveniently deposed; but it was less successful in Poland and Hungary where native landlords would have had to be dispossessed.

Less reason for hope was the weakening agricultural price structure. Desperate shortages of foodstuffs during the war had pushed farm prices very high, but now the abundance of peace-time production made the prices drop again. Agriculture throughout the Western world was beginning its long drive to mechanization, new hybrids, new fertilizers, and improved methods, which only added to the abundance and the low price levels. And these new developments often forced the farmer deep into debt for the new machines. Many agricultural areas suffered dislocations caused by a gradual shift in demand from the old staples of wheat, corn, rye, and cotton, to fruits, vegetables, dairy products, meat, and rayon—the artificial fiber that began to substitute the chemist for the farmer. This shift was brought about by the higher standards of living, improved methods of food shipping and processing, consumer enthusiasm for vitamins and new foods, and the new industrial technology. Since all of these factors tended to push the farmer off his farm and pull him into the city, there was another large exodus from the land during the 1920s. Still, both agricultural production and agricultural prices, while decreasing relative to the rest of the economy, increased by about one-third during this period.

In industrial production, on the other hand, the picture was almost pure bliss to behold. There had been a postwar depression in 1921, but by 1925 prewar output levels had been regained or exceeded. By 1929 world trade was actually twice its 1913 level, which wouldn't have been a bad growth rate, even without a crippling war. New technology and affluence were creating new products, methods of production, and industries.

The main attraction for the American consumer was the automobile. Millions of Model T Fords had already been sold, but when the new Model A was first displayed in 1927, with its stylish new shape and its glistening new pyroxylin paint colors, it rivaled, to some, the Lindbergh flight and the Sacco-Vanzetti execution as the sensation of the year. The automobile was weaving a new fabric for the American way of life. What the railroads had done for the Industrial Revolution, the automobile was now doing for a social revolution that created an unprecedentedly mobile civilization. The automobile gave geographic freedom to the average person, a freedom that can supersede all others in a country with as much space as the United States. It initiated a chain reaction of social developments, including the growth of suburbs, which were made possible by automobile commuting. Supermarkets, too, sprang up because the car allowed shoppers to buy in larger quantities and to travel farther than the corner grocery store. Buying in larger quantities spurred the production of refrigerators, and the larger mobility made telephones more important than ever. Almost every niche of the economy and society, from the roadside fruit stand to the petroleum industry, from the church supper to resort hotels, was profoundly affected by the automobile, that agent of air pollution with which the American public became so infatuated.

The number of automobiles in the United States grew from 6,771,000 in 1919 to 23,121,000 in 1929. The first public radio broadcast in the United States was in the fall of 1920. The sales of radios totaled $60,000,000 in 1922 and continued to grow, reaching $842,548,000 by 1929. Cigarettes, cosmetics, vacuum cleaners, gramophones, chain stores, department stores, no-holds-barred advertising, and thousands of new movie houses made the twenties indeed "roaring." Mass production techniques were honed ever finer. Business machines became extensively used; continuous rolling mills were introduced to steelmaking; and there was a movement to standardize parts. If the depressed textile industries or a struggling agriculture left some lagging doubts in the minds of Americans, the advice of the times was to "concentrate on the doughnut, not the hole."

By the mid-twenties, even the prospects of Germany looked promising. The reparation payments had caused monetary catastrophe earlier in the decade. The European Allies had insisted on these payments because, among other reasons, they intended to use them to repay the American loans made during the war. Since the Americans wouldn't cancel the loans, neither would the other Allies give up the indemnification due them from Germany. When the financially pressed social democratic government of Germany, called the Weimar Republic, was unable to meet these payments, French and Belgian troops were sent to occupy the Ruhr Valley, the industrial heartland of Germany. In response, German workers went on strike, and the Weimar government began a disastrous deficit financing to obtain the relief funds to sustain the workers. In 1914, four German marks had equaled one United States dollar. By 1921, it was 62.6 to one; by October 30, 1923, it was an incredible 62,000,000,000 to one. At that rate, the purchasing power of all German savings accounts, mortgage debts, and other monetary funds was completely wiped out. Talk of continued reparation payments and the repayment of American war debts dwindled. The Germans established a new currency, based on a variety of different kinds of reserves, that held stable at about four marks to the United States dollar. And the economy's course was set for a trip up the garden path to recovery.

In spite of these adjustments, the economic dislocations of the World War had merely been papered over. The war-matériel-producing industries were still grossly overexpanded; satisfactory patterns of international trade had not been established; tariffs still encumbered world commerce; and currency exchange rates tended to be unnatural, distorting the international flow of goods. But the public could not comprehend these underlying frailties. The 1920s became a decade of wildly speculative business ventures. It seemed that everyone wanted to try his hand at being a financial wizard and to make a killing in one or another of the big booms that swept across the economic landscape like a Kansas twister. In the United States, thousands of ordinary working class householders bought Florida real estate lots sight unseen. That these may have been dismal plots of unusable swamp or tidal flats didn't concern them; their only intention was to resell quickly at a profit. An even more tempting boom existed in the stock market. Indeed, fortunes could be made quickly there. The Dow-Jones index of industrial stock price averages soared upward from 99.18 on October 14, 1925, to 381.17 on September 3, 1929, almost quadrupling itself in less than four years.

Although industry seemed healthy enough, in 1927 industrial production did not advance, and the boom that was going on seemed unrealistic. The Federal Reserve system initiated new monetary policies that would restrain banks from lending money to customers for investments in the stock market. Beginning in 1928, the Federal Reserve system began raising the discount rates—the interest rates at which member banks borrowed the reserve money they need from Federal Reserve banks. The idea behind higher discount rates was to discourage member banks from expanding their loans and investments to the point where they would run short of reserves. The Federal Reserve system also began selling government securities from its own stockpile to private individuals, banks, and firms to absorb investment funds. It hoped that with less money and credit available, there would be less speculation, and the stock market boom would ease off. Instead, businesses themselves, which were already operating at less than full capacity, felt the pinch of these policies first. As production and profits declined and unemployment increased, the stock market boom was less realistic than ever.

THE GREAT CRISIS OF CAPITALISM

Optimistically, still in the spirit of the twenties, the Friday morning, October 25, 1929, New York *Times* headline read, "WORST STOCK CRASH STEMMED BY BANKS." The day before, "Black Thursday," the bubble had burst. Over twelve million shares of stock had been traded in a panic on the floor of the New York Stock Exchange, but a consortium of banks led by J. P. Morgan and Company had turned the crash around with calm public statements of confidence. By the following Tuesday, this confidence had been used up. Regardless of the efforts of banks to shore up stock prices by large, well-publicized purchases, the market tumbled out of control as over sixteen million shares were dumped on the New York Exchange. In a few hours, fortunes were destroyed, the Great Depression had begun, and industrial capitalism began its most severe ordeal.

However, the stock market is not the economy. A stock market crash by itself would not necessarily cause the nationwide hardship, the unemployment, the financial losses, and the destruction of carefully built businesses and farms that were the brutal results of the Great Depression. In fact, there were thousands of Americans who themselves had never "played the market" and who now watched in sweet gratification as their get-rich-quick cousins came in for a tumble. But the weak foundations of the 1920s boom, which had been so conveniently papered over, soon showed their dangerous cracks. Banks began to fail, as those who had invested in already overexpanded industries and in speculative investments could not pay back their loans. Businesses postponed all expansions in their plants and equipment to wait for more secure economic conditions, and workers, who would have found jobs in these expansions, became unemployed. With increasing unemployment, disposable income began to decline, and aggregate consumption expenditures declined almost as fast. The result was that sales of all goods—including the star performers of the twenties, the automobiles, electrical appliances, and the other glamorous commodites—declined. With lower sales, profits turned to losses, wages were cut, more layoffs became necessary, incomes declined further, and sales went down another notch.

Nor was there any relief to be found in the international economy. The other major industrial nations were suffering the same hardships as the United States. Their banks, too, were failing; their workers were being laid off; and their businesses were losing money. Tariffs, which were already high, were raised even higher to guard against foreign competition and the "dumping" of foreign goods, with the result that international trade and all the economic activity associated with it fell to about a third of its former level by 1933. Optimists clung to straws, predicting that "prosperity is just around the corner," but, in fact, the same spiral that had boosted the economy to its dizzy heights in the twenties was now operating in reverse. All the people—workers, farmers, businessmen—expected conditions to get worse and made decisions on that basis. It was a case of a self-fulfilling prophecy.

The misery of the Great Depression is difficult to measure in economic statistics. During the major downswing, which lasted from 1929 to 1933, the annual Gross National Product (G.N.P.)[2]

---

[2] Gross National Product is the most commonly used measure of the economy's performance. It is essentially the sum of all the consumer goods and services and all the new investments made in one year. Net National Product or, simply, National Product is the same measure adjusted for the depreciation of capital that has taken place during the year.

in the United States shrank from 104.1 billion dollars to 56.0 billion dollars, and the other measures of economic health and activity shrank similarly. Table 6 gives the annual figures for some of the key measures.

Table 6. Depression statistics (billions of dollars)*

Year	G.N.P.	Consumption	Savings as a percentage of disposable income*	Domestic investment	Corporate profits before taxes	Price index*	Percentage unemployed*	Exports	Imports
1929	104.1	79.0	5.1	16.2	9.6	100	3	7.0	6.3
1930	91.1	71.0	4.6	10.3	3.3	96	9	5.4	4.8
1931	76.3	61.3	3.9	5.5	−0.8	86	16	3.6	3.4
1932	58.5	49.3	−1.2	0.9	−3.0	78	24	2.5	2.3
1933	56.0	46.4	−1.3	1.4	0.2	77	25	2.4	2.3

Source: U.S. Income and Output, and 1962 Supplement, Economic Indicators (Government Printing Office, Washington, D.C., 1960 and 1962).
* Except for percentage and index columns.

Perhaps, the increase in unemployment from 3 to 25 percent tells the most directly human aspect of the story. Even a stolid imagination can envision the number of home mortgages fore-closed, automobiles and appliances repossessed, and college educations stopped in mid-course that such figures indicate. But hidden behind the unemployment figure lies the story of careers wasted, not only because of outright unemployment, but also because electrical engineers were forced to work as dish-washers and independent businessmen hired out as sales clerks. All the statistics of the depression give only mute evidence of the family tragedies or the army of hobos, which increased by more than ten times during these years, of bread lines, of hunger riots and raids on grocery stores, of desperation, suicides, and star-vation.

Political Repercussions

Ironically, the poverty seemed to exist in the midst of plenty. The country's fields were as fertile as ever, but because of declining prices, farmers were going broke. The factories had not been destroyed by war or catastrophe, and the machines that had run so smoothly in the 1920s could still operate as well in the 1930s. But the factories stood idle and the machines were still. Something had happened to the force that made all these things come to life; something had happened to the markets, to credit, and to business expectations. The ordinary people were very confused by these events, and it seemed that the time would have been ripe for a revolution. Seeing that the depression hurt mainly the little people, leaving most of the rich and powerful still in full command of the (admittedly) depressed industry, some people argued that, indeed, only a revolution could install a new structure which would get the economy going again.

The Communist Party was successful in recruiting many hundreds of followers, who saw the system they advocated as a solution to the malfunctioning free enterprise system, but it was far short of the thousands and millions that would have made a revolution possible. The Stalin purges of the late thirties and the U.S.S.R.'s mutual nonaggression pact with Germany disaffected many communist supporters, enough to kill the budding movement in the United States. Anyway, to the vast majority of people the communist promises seemed as empty as the capitalist ones. Instead, there was a tendency to gravitate toward powerful personalities who seemed to give hope of reforms, positive plans of action, and a reaffirmation of unity and purpose, not only because of the economic depression but also because of the general political unrest that accompanied it. This kind of emotional appeal had brought Benito Mussolini to power in Italy in 1922. It brought Adolf Hitler to power in Germany in 1933, and Francisco Franco to power in Spain in 1936. Although democracy survived in the United States, Americans were not immune to fascist temptations, and Louisiana Governor and then Senator Huey Long, who initiated sweeping social reforms at the cost of democratic procedure, Catholic radio priest Father

Charles E. Coughlin, and rabble-rouser Gerald L. K. Smith
were among those who built notorious careers on an appeal
that had very much in common with fascistic principles and
methods.

In the Presidential election year of 1932, the Great Depression
was already three years old and close to its worst stage. It was
obviously a time for change, and legions of distressed and dis-
heartened American citizens trooped to the polls and swept
the Democrat, Franklin Delano Roosevelt, into office, establishing an enthusiastic and vigorous new leadership that promised to give the country a "New Deal." With Roosevelt, a new
era of American politics began that still evokes great admiration
from some and causes hackles to rise on others. From this time
on, the federal government clearly assumed responsibility for
the welfare of the people. Liberalism took on a new meaning.
It no longer referred to the laissez faire economics of the classical
liberals; rather it was the label applied to those who advocated
government reforms and programs to improve the social welfare
of the masses. The liberals now were the interventionists, political
activists, the people with concern for the masses, and the old
classical liberals—those who had fought the mercantilists for
over one hundred years—were now the new tories, the conservatives, and even the reactionaries.

The New Deal was nothing if not active. In quick succession,
dozens of new governmental agencies were formed that came to
be known by their initials, the so-called alphabet agencies. Every
nook and cranny of the economy came into some aspect of the
program's activities. Banks were temporarily closed and then
reopened under strong supervision. The dollar was taken off the
gold standard domestically and devalued in international exchange in order to make American exports, especially agricultural products, more competitive abroad. The Securities and
Exchange Commission (SEC) was established to police the stock
markets and to prevent some of the dealings that were responsible
for the unwarranted speculative boom. The Federal Deposit
Insurance Corporation (FDIC) was formed to insure savings
and commercial accounts in banks; the Reconstruction Finance
Corporation (RFC) made government loans to depression-
injured businesses; and the Farm Credit Administration (FCA)

did the same for farmers. Unemployment was tackled by the Civilian Conservation Corps (CCC), the Public Works Administration (PWA), and the Works Progress Administration (WPA), which tried to give employment to all those who needed it.

Federal money was also given to the states for their own construction projects on schools and roads. The Tennessee Valley Authority (TVA) became a world-famous pilot project for the government planning of flood control, regional economic development, and cheap electricity—all in one fell swoop. The Social Security Act and the Fair Labor Standards Act dealt with public welfare. The Wagner Act gave unions, especially the newer industrial unions, their best climate for growth. Farmers were subsidized to restrict their acreage in cultivation and even to destroy some of their crops, in an effort to drive up agricultural prices. Home owners were given aid; relief agencies for the destitute were established; and the tax structure was overhauled to make the income taxes more progressive—to "soak the rich," as the critics said. In all this rush of programs and projects, the focus was always on the welfare of the poor, the working man, the farmer. For these efforts, Roosevelt won the undying allegiance of millions of working class Americans, who elected him to the Presidency three times more. The first years of the New Deal stand out as being perhaps, the most active, the most vigorous, the most electrifying years of any administration in United States history.

THE KEYNESIAN REVOLUTION

There was no political revolution in the United States caused by the depression, but economists speak of their own private Keynesian revolution in economic theory. The New Deal had embarked on its radical new course without any theoretical structure to guide it or to give it intellectual justification. With a scatter shot of programs, the economy was tackled in a pragmatic and improvisational way. Although Roosevelt surrounded himself with a "brain trust" of intellectuals, largely drawn from leading universities, economists had little scientific technology to offer. The classical liberal economists and the marginalists had simply not dealt with the problems of depressions to any great extent. The former had concerned themselves with the welfare of the aggregate economy, exemplified in the title of Adam Smith's book, and their perspective was that of a pre-industrial economy. The marginalists thought that the economy could create the best of all possible worlds simply by being left alone; the market would take care of everything. Say's Law, which states that the process of production creates the income with which everything that is produced will be bought, was supposed to work immutably. Any short-run imbalances would be quickly corrected by appropriate adjustments in prices.

Furthermore, the influences of money, credit, and monetary policies had been ignored. A crude "quantity of money" theory, which seems to have been generally accepted, equated the price level with the quantity of money. It stated that, other things remaining constant (which, of course, they never do), the more money there is, the higher prices will be. Or, restating the theory, if all the buyers in an economy have $100 and the sellers have ten commodities, the average price will be $10. If the buyers had only $10, the average price would be $1. The prominent American economist Irving Fisher (1867–1947) allowed other things not to remain constant and rewrote the theory as an equation that has come to be known as the Fisher Identity (identity, because the two sides of the equation are not only equal; they are identical):

$$MV \equiv PQ$$

where M is the quantity of all money (currency and demand deposits), V is the velocity with which that money is spent (expressed as an annual turnover rate), P is the general price level, and Q is the quantity of all goods sold in a year. The more sophisticated Fisher Identity still takes into account the quantity of money theory, but the effects of changes in production are reflected in Q, and the effects of banking policy and the eagerness of people to hold money (the so-called liquidity preference) are reflected in V.

Of course, the realities of economic fluctuations have been recognized for a long time, and since the Bible story of Joseph's explaining the Pharaoh's dreams as a forecast of seven fat and seven lean years, there has even been a written business cycle theory of one kind or another. In 1917, John Maurice Clark (1884–1963), an American economist, developed the "accelerator principle" to explain how a small change in demand for consumer products can set off a much larger change in demand for producers' goods, that is, for industrial plant and equipment—capital. The principle is based on the characteristic of modern industrial production that an investment in machines and other capital equipment several times greater than the annual output is required to produce that annual output.

In the hypothetical example for a machine manufacturer shown in Table 7, the stock of machines is worth $400, four times the annual output of consumer goods, $100. Each year 10 percent of the machines wear out, and the annual replacement for this depreciation is $40 worth of machines. Suppose, after two years of business as usual, annual sales suddenly increase by 10 percent. The stock of machines will have to grow to a value of $440, meaning that the annual production of machines will have to double from $40 to $80 per year ($40 for new stock plus $40 for replacement). Thus, a 10 percent increase in consumer demand accelerates to a 100 percent increase in the demand for producers' goods.

Table 7. Operation of the accelerator principle

YEAR	CONSUMER DEMAND	STOCK OF MACHINES	DEMAND FOR MACHINES
1	$100	$400	$40
2	100	400	40
3	110	440	80
4	120	480	84
5	120	480	48

Even conservatively estimated, considering all the new income created in the machine industry, year 4 may again show a $10 increase in consumer demand, necessitating a $40 increase

254   The End of Liberalism

in the stock of machines and an annual demand for $84 worth of machines ($40 for new stock plus $44 for replacement). But, should the consumer demand merely level off in year 5 at the new high rate of $120 per year, then no new machines need to be added to the stock, and only replacements will be needed to maintain the stock of $480 worth of machines. The annual demand for machines will now drop to $48. Workers in the machine industry may have to be laid off, incomes will go down, consumer demand may weaken, and a progressive shrinkage of the economy may set in. The accelerator can dive as well as climb.

When enough industries are expanding or contracting at once, a great deal of economic instability can be attributed to the accelerator principle. But, by itself, it didn't suffice to explain the unemployment and the severity of the Great Depression, and economists couldn't understand what was happening during the early 1930s. Why wasn't Say's Law functioning? Why couldn't businesses sell their goods? Why couldn't workers sell their labor? What effect did bank failures and the drying up of credit have on the economy? Perhaps, if only prices and wages would fall far enough, everything would straighten out again. But wages weren't falling fast enough, and businesses were cutting their operating costs by shrinking output and laying off workers, instead of maintaining full output and full employment at lower wages. Prices, too, were falling, but still the unsold goods were mounting in the warehouses. Maybe the economy had a built-in ratchet effect that allowed the Fisher Identity to function upward, as money and the other variables increased, but wouldn't allow it to function downward. Such price and wage decreases that did take place, instead of reestablishing a healthy, full employment economy, merely darkened the cloud of gloom that hung over businessmen and workers alike. Hope of better times seemed further away than ever.

In 1936 the Great Depression was almost seven years old. It had touched bottom in the early thirties, but, instead of swinging upward again, business conditions dragged along with only a slight improvement. The energetic policies of the New Deal seemed to have had a mild success for a few years, but the depression still dominated the landscape. In this year, *The General Theory of Employment, Interest, and Money* was published, and the world of economic theory and analysis was thunderstruck. Here was a new approach that seemed to comprehend the forces of the depression, and, more, it provided a prescription for its cure. Here was a book on economic theory that scrapped the marginalists' microeconomic perspective—which focused on the individual firm and the individual consumer—and replaced it with a sweeping macroeconomic analysis, which dealt directly with the problems of nations. Instead of profits, costs, and prices, the primary focus was on aggregate employment, the supply of money, and the rate of national investment. Here, at last, was a theoretical system that was relevant to the 1930s, to the Great Depression, and to the policies of desperate governments.

John Maynard Keynes (1883–1946), the author of this book, was born to the intellectual life. His father, John Neville Keynes, was a Cambridge logician and political economist, and his mother was, among other things, a justice of the peace, an alderwoman, and the mayor of Cambridge, England. John Maynard always traveled in the very best of educated and artistically creative circles. At Cambridge, where Marshall was his mentor in economics, he belonged to the elite and simply named "Society" club. Later, he was a member of the extraordinary "Bloomsbury group," the nerve center of English literature and philosophy, which counted Leonard and Virginia Woolf, Lytton Strachey, and Clive Bell among its most active members at the time.

His interests and achievements ranged far and wide across the culture of his day. He was a brilliant conversationalist. He was intensely interested in the theater and married a famous Russian ballerina, Lydia Lopokova. He made a fortune of half a million pounds by dealing in foreign currency exchanges, and he published learned articles on both mathematics and economics. He took increasingly powerful administrative positions with the British government, participated in the Paris peace conferences after World War I, was made a Baron in 1942, and helped establish the International Monetary Fund and the World Bank at the end of World War II.

This economist lived the life that the highest stratum of the intellectual bourgeoisie aspire to in their fondest dreams, a life of adventure and excitement, of mental as well as financial achievement, of cultivation and high style, and a life of power and recognition. It is said of him that when he died, his only regret was that he hadn't drunk perhaps still a little more champagne.

Central to Keynesian economic theory is the not unfamiliar idea of equilibrium; that is, when producers intend to produce annually exactly as much as purchasers intend to buy annually, the economy is then in equilibrium. Or, put another way, when the annual national income, Y (to be created in the production process), is used entirely for the annual aggregate expenditures on finished consumption and investment goods, C + I (ignoring government expenditures, for the moment), equilibrium will prevail: $Y = C + I$.

So far, this sounds like Say's Law: the production process begets the income with which the aggregate product is purchased. But there is an important difference. Indeed, Y always equals C + I *after the event*—when the year is over and consumers and producers have made the necessary and sometimes painful adjustments in their consumption, investment, inventories, and so on. The important Keynesian point is that *intended* Y does not always equal *intended* C + I. Keynesian equilibrium would only exist when the aggregate producers' production plans coincided with the aggregate expenditure plans of consumers and investors. And although a Keynesian equilibrium doesn't require it, this equilibrium should preferably be at a level where the national resources, especially labor, are fully employed. In a sense, then, Keynesian economics is an analysis of the determinants of intentions.

The biggest single component of the aggregate expenditure is, of course, consumption. Keynes emphasized that as income increases, consumption also increases, but at a lower rate. For example, suppose a family whose annual income is $10,000 usually spends $9000 and saves $1000. Its average propensity to consume, then, is 90 percent. Should the head of the household get a new job where his income increases by $2000 per year, the family's annual consumption expenditures are likely to increase by only $1500 while savings are increased proportionately more, by $500. Thus, the propensity to consume the

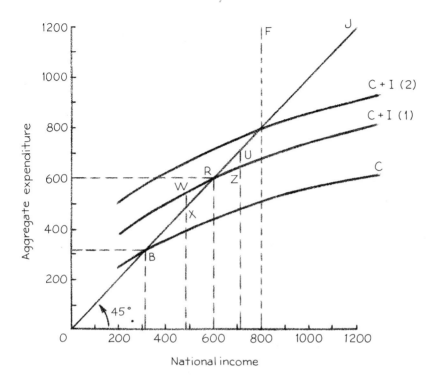

Figure 23. The Keynesian equilibrium: Y = C + I (billions of dollars).

additional marginal income is 75 percent and is lower than the original average propensity to consume of 90 percent. In other words, in the jargon of economics, the marginal propensity to consume is less than the average propensity to consume. The reason is partially the inertia of spending habits, which usually prevent people, both as individuals and in the aggregate, from making immediate adjustments in their standard of living when confronted with a change in income (potentially tragic when the income change is downward). Also, richer people need to spend a lesser proportion of their income to live well. It seems that even consumption, taken as a whole, follows the law of diminishing returns.

This behavior of consumption expenditures at different income levels is shown for the aggregate economy by the "consumption function," C, in Figure 23. It illustrates the decreasing urgency of consumption as the national income is increased. The 45-degree angled line, J, is drawn on the graph as a helping line. Broken lines drawn perpendicular to the graph's axes from any point along this diagonal will mark off equal lengths on the axes and, thus, indicate an equality between aggregate expenditure and national income. Where the consumption function C crosses the diagonal line J, in this case at point B, expenditure and income are equal, and they are both about 310 billion dollars on the graph. At less than 310 billion dollars national income, consumption exceeds income; at more than 310 billion dollars national income, income exceeds consumption. Of course, consumption can only exceed income when there is a stockpile of savings that can be withdrawn for this purpose.

What the Keynesian consumption function shows is that only one level of production exists that will satisfy the aggregate effective demand for consumer goods. Unlike the erroneous implication of Say's Law that any level of production can generate an income adequate to purchase that production output, the diminishing returns determinants of consumption introduced with the Keynesian consumption function show that the coincidence of intended production and consumption occurs only at one unique level of national income, which must lie along the 45-degree helping line, J.

Actually, the whole economy is not in equilibrium at this level because we have omitted investment expenditures so far in our analysis. Investment also varies out of proportion with the level of production and national income. As national income grows, a greater (although not necessarily proportionately greater) amount of investment is induced simply because a larger economy requires a larger capital stock and presents more opportunities for investment.

In Figure 23, the investment function, curve C + I (1), is layered on top of the consumption function, C. Although the tendency for induced investment counteracts the shallowness of the consumption function's slope, the two together, the C + I (1) function, retain almost the slope of the consumption function, and the necessity for a unique equilibrium point still pertains. As before, this equilibrium is indicated where the function intersects the diagonal, now at point R, giving a national income and aggregate expenditure level of 600 billion dollars. Again, this is the only national income at which intended production and intended aggregate demand will be equal.

Should the economy be producing a national income that is less than this equilibrium level, for example, at about 480 billion dollars, then the aggregate consumption and investment expenditures will be larger than aggregate production. C + I (1) will be above the diagonal J by an amount equivalent to the distance W-X. This excess aggregate demand may push prices up and will certainly draw down inventories of the consumption and investment goods, which will signal producers that business is better than they expected. They will expand their output levels until these signals stop coming in, that is, until equilibrium is reached at the 600 billion dollar national income level, point R. Conversely, should the economy be producing a national income that is larger than this equilibrium, for example, at about 720 billion dollars, then the aggregate consumption and investment expenditures will not suffice to buy up all the production of final goods. C + I (1) will be below the diagonal. There will be unsold goods equivalent to the distance U-Z. Inventories and warehouses will become uncomfortably glutted, and prices may be forced a little lower. These will be unmistakable signals to the producers, but they signal that the producers overestimated their markets and should now cut back their output levels, which they will do until the signals stop coming in, at the 600 billion dollar national income level R, where all final products are purchased.

So the Keynesian equilibrium, Y = C + I, is stable at its unique national income level, and aberrations from that level are self-correcting. But there is no guarantee that this stable equilibrium will be at a desirable national income level. The economic outlook—the expectations for future business conditions—will have a great influence on it. If the outlook is gloomy, consumers will restrict their expenditures to the daily necessities, postponing purchases of "hard goods," consumer durables such as automobiles, homes, furniture, and appliances, in an effort to avoid financial burdens that they may not be able to bear. Businessmen will put off investment expenditures until the outlook for sales seems more promising. Then, aggregate consumption and investment expenditures will be very low. Production will also have to be low, or unwanted stockpiles of unsold goods will accumulate. And the economy will find itself in a perfectly stable equilibrium at a low level of national income. Then, the C + I (1) function will intersect the diagonal J at a low point. To illustrate this in Figure 23, point R may be considered such a point if the dotted line F is considered the level of national income at which all the economy's resources would be fully employed. Under these circumstances with the equilibrium at R (600 billion dollars), many national resources, most obviously labor, will be unemployed.

If, because of some inflationary increase in the quantity of money together with a very optimistic business outlook, aggregate expenditures rose enough to push the C + I (1) function up to where it would intersect the diagonal J at a national income level above full employment, to the right of the dotted line F, the Keynesian equilibrium would still hold. However, since real production can't increase beyond F, the achievement of equilibrium would be purely through inflation, by increasing the prices of goods and increasing the money measures of expenditures and national income.

But Keynes's readers in the 1930s weren't very worried about inflation. The Great Depression was their overwhelming concern. And, at last, an economic theory was able to explain this unpleasant phenomenon to them. But if it was an accurate diagnosis of the depression, what was the cure? Again Keynes's theory seemed to make good sense, perhaps, because many of the New Deal policies had been doing all along what he now prescribed on the basis of his sophisticated and revolutionary new analysis. Essentially, the prescription was this: shift C + I upward, to C + I (2), so that the stable equilibrium would come closer to line F. In real terms that would mean: (1) keep prices and market demand up to make business conditions look rosy again; (2) encourage consumption expenditures by keeping wages high and employment full and by redistributing the income from the rich (who saved too much anyhow) to the poor, who would spend most or all of their incomes; (3) support agricultural prices; (4) support labor union activities and encourage wage increases; (5) keep employment full by encouraging investments for industrial expansion and new industries; and (6) facilitate investments by maintaining a low interest rate and making an abundant supply of credit available.

How much new expenditure would be needed to begin to shift the C + I function upward to a new full employment equilibrium at 800 billion dollars national income in Figure 23? Certainly not the full 200 billion dollars difference between the existing unemployment equilibrium at 600 billion dollars national income and the full employment equilibrium. Because the slope of the C + I function is so close to the slope of J, a small vertical shift of the C + I (1) function to C + I (2) produces a large horizontal movement at the point of intersection with J, which also means a large movement in the national income level, shown on the horizontal axis. Thus, a small increase in aggregate expenditure would result in a larger increase in national income, by a ratio that is called "the multiplier."

The multiplier is determined by the marginal propensity to consume, which is the behavioral characteristic lying behind the slope of the consumption function, as we have seen above. It can be explained arithmetically. An increased expenditure of, let's say, one million dollars will, of course, mean an immediate increase in personal and business income of the same one million dollars for those businesses and persons who make the sales. Naturally, this new income will not remain idle but will be spent. If all of it were spent and then respent again and again, the initial one million dollars of new investment could increase national income indefinitely. But it doesn't happen that way because some of the new marginal income is saved at each respending. If the amount of the saved marginal income is one-third, the amount respent will be two-thirds, and the total new income created by respending an original one million dollar expenditure again and again will be (in dollars):

$$1,000,000 + 666,666 + 444,444 + 296,296$$
$$+ 197,531 + \ldots = 3,000,000$$

Or, putting it another way:

$$1,000,000 + 1,000,000 \times \tfrac{2}{3} + 1,000,000 \times (\tfrac{2}{3})^2$$
$$+ 1,000,000 \times (\tfrac{2}{3})^3 + 1,000,000 \times (\tfrac{2}{3})^4 + \ldots$$
$$+ 1,000,000 \times (\tfrac{2}{3})^n = 1,000,000 \times \frac{1}{1 - \tfrac{2}{3}}$$
$$= 1,000,000 \times 3 = 3,000,000$$

The multiplier will be equal to three.

Thus, the multiplier, M, can be expressed as a formula in terms of the *marginal propensity to consume*, MPC:

$$M = \frac{1}{1 - MPC}$$

In the above case, where the MPC equals $\tfrac{2}{3}$, the multiplier will be three. If the MPC were to equal $\tfrac{9}{10}$, the multiplier would be ten. Obviously, the larger the MPC, the larger the multiplier, and the less additional aggregate expenditure is needed to start a large increase in equilibrium national income.

But now the question is, how do we get the multiplier multiplying? How is the first new consumption or investment expenditure implemented in a depression? What if, in spite of expansionary policies in the areas of money, taxation, labor, agriculture, etc., private consumers and businessmen don't take the hint? Keynes's answer: turn to the government.

Let the government undertake construction projects and other programs that will spend money and employ labor. To finance these projects, the government should simply run a deficit, borrowing money from financiers and banks, which certainly have it to lend but wouldn't lend it to private business enterprise. The new income thus created will prime the pump and get the economy moving again. Keynesian economists frequently layer an additional expenditure function, labeled G, on top of the C + I function, forming a total C + I + G function, to indicate the importance of this government spending technique.

New government spending would be the main instrument of this expansionary policy. The income tax should be rigorously restructured to make it more progressive, that is, to soak the rich and relieve the poor, thus encouraging a relatively larger consumption out of a given national income. Other instruments, also, like radical agricultural and labor policies, tariffs and subsidies, and outright relief payments to put money directly into the hands of those who will spend it ought to turn the trick. In fact, anything that created jobs and got money flowing could be used. Perhaps not too facetiously, Keynes suggested:

> If the Treasury were to fill old bottles with banknotes, bury them at suitable depths in disused coalmines which are then filled up to the surface with town rubbish, and leave it to private enterprise on well-tried principles of *laissez-faire* to dig the notes up again (the right to do so being obtained, of course, by tendering for leases of the note-bearing territory), there need be no more unemployment and, with the help of the repercussions, the real income of the community, and its capital wealth also, would probably become a good deal greater than it actually is. It would, indeed be more sensible to build houses and the like; but if there are political and practical difficulties in the way of this, the above would be better than nothing.[3]

But this is the kind of talk that made, and still makes, the economic conservatives see red. Roosevelt, his New Deal, and now these eggheaded new theories seemed bent on destroying established "economic morality." The unbalanced budget of the government's deficit financing, paying workers to do useless work or, worse, no work at all, taxing the rich proportionately more than the poor, interfering with private businesses and even creating government-operated businesses, imposing easy money and low interest rates in the face of an unfavorable business outlook, encouraging labor unions and subsidizing agriculture—all these practices seemed foolish, unfair, and even malicious to the conservatives. They warned that the "creeping socialism" of these policies would soon be the undoing of American capitalism. The

---

[3] John Maynard Keynes, *The General Theory of Employment, Interest, and Money* (Harcourt, Brace, New York, 1936), p. 129.

recession of 1937 and 1938, which reintroduced a downward trend and kept national income from even equaling the 1929 level at any time during the thirties, was often blamed on the antagonism of business to the New Deal and its willful obstruction of New Deal policies.

Keynesian economics does leave much to be desired. Even though consumption function analysis is the most important macroeconomic technique used today, its application seems to be more successful for expansionary national economic policies than for solving the problems of inflation and overfull employment. In any event, the "fine tuning" of the economy that was supposed to be the great achievement of the much-praised "New Economics" of the 1960s in the United States, purportedly the finest flowering of Keynesian economics, was irredeemably distorted by the gross expansionist requirements of the Indochina War. Under those conditions, severe inflation at the end of that decade and in the first years of the 1970s was certainly politically unavoidable.

Furthermore, Keynesian analysis is concerned primarily with the short run so that the many effects of technological change on employment and growth, the special problems of underdeveloped countries, and the effect of population growth, among other such long-run considerations, are given short shrift or ignored altogether. Keynes's rather cynical approval of wasteful and inefficient practices, as long as they resulted in higher employment and income, is also out of place in a world that must now be concerned with the conservation of scarce resources and the preservation of environmental quality. Nevertheless, the substantial improvement in national economic policy making, the extraordinary completeness and accessibility of our national income accounts and statistical series, and the great increase in macroeconomic sophistication owe much to Keynesian economics.

As it turned out, American capitalism was neither ruined nor the lingering depression undone by the theories or policies of Keynes or Roosevelt. Instead, an overpowering event of history suspended the normal functioning of American economy for a while and wiped out forever the last traces of the depression. That event was World War II.

THE ABNORMAL ECONOMICS OF WARFARE

In a very real sense, World War II was merely chapter two of World War I. The intervening twenty years of peace, although they looked promising for both capitalism and democracy at first, seemed to end in a fiasco. The Great Depression gave overwhelming evidence that the world's economic structure was diseased, and the collapse of democratic hopes in nation after nation appeared to indicate the same for democracy. Instead of solving problems, World War I, "the war to end all wars," created many new ones that festered like untended wounds until they broke out as the causes of another holocaust. The economic problems were distorted world trade, inadequacy of the gold standard as a monetary vehicle for maintaining this imbalanced world trade,[4] overexpanded industries, and rampant economic nationalism in the midst of the depression. All these problems certainly made it seem as though the great capitalist nations were trying to unload their surpluses and their problems in a murderous imperialist war, which was pretty much what Lenin had predicted. Yet, whereas most wars seem to have some more or less important economic causes (remember "No taxation without representation") and it might be argued that business interests fuel the flames of war for their own profits, most wars must also have other motives, especially irreconcilable cultural and political differences. And these latter causes, rather than economic ones, were mainly responsible for the Second World War.

That the forces for democracy were floundering during the 1930s in the Soviet Union, in Turkey, and in Chang Kai-shek's China caused little concern in the West, but that they were also being drowned in Western European countries—Italy in the twenties, Germany and Spain in the thirties—was unnerving. There was little that the democratic nations could or

---

[4] There was again an international liquidity crisis. World production of gold had not kept pace with world trade after the big nineteenth century gold rushes had spent themselves, first in California and Australia, then in the Klondike and South Africa. Currencies were forced to maintain their redeemability in gold on smaller and smaller fractional reserves of the metal.

would do about it. The memories of World War I were still fresh, and people were profoundly unwilling to go to war again, whether it was to prevent Hitler's takeover of the Saar in 1935, the Rhineland in 1936, Danzig in 1937, or Austria in 1938; or to prevent the establishment of Franco in Spain in 1936, Mussolini's blatant seizure of Ethiopia in 1935, or Japan's incursions into China in 1931 and 1937. However, when Hitler occupied all of Czechoslovakia in March of 1939, his salami-slicing tactics were going too far, and England and France abandoned their appeasement policies and began forming alliances. The Stalin-Hitler nonagression pact relieved German fears of a two-front war, and World War II began when 1.5 million German troops invaded Poland on September 1, 1939.

At first, most of the action was in Eastern Europe, and the Western European nations, still poorly prepared for war, hoped against hope that by some diplomatic miracle, the Nazi demon in the German soul might be soothed. But by 1940, Hitler's victorious armies swept through Western Europe with about as much ease as they did in the East, and it seemed that the end was very near.

It must have seemed that way to Hitler too, who had seen his plans for a quick, brilliant, and successful campaign, called a *Blitzkrieg*—lightning war—succeed on every front. He had only to finish off Britain in the West and relieve himself of his dubious ally, Russia, in the East, and the Third Reich could rule Europe for a thousand years. But, aided by the use of its newly invented radar, the desperately thin defenses of Britain held against the air war waged by Goering's Luftwaffe. In the same year that Germany attacked the Soviet Union, 1941, Hitler actually ordered cutbacks in war production because he felt victory to be within his grasp. But by 1942, his forces were suffering severe shortages of matériel, and the Blitzkrieg idea was lost forever somewhere in the endless territory of Russia. From this moment on, the war, like World War I, became one of economic productivity or, more accurately, of economic attrition between the Allies and the Axis powers. Again, as in World War I, the United States had given, at first, only half-hearted assistance to the Allies, but its isolationist timidity was sundered by the

Japanese attack on Pearl Harbor on December 7, 1941. Once again, the global sources of supply provided by the United States and the British Empire and their tenacious defense of the all-important sea routes turned the tide for the Allies. By 1943, Hitler was seriously overextended and was turned out of Africa and repulsed from Stalingrad.

Prodigious quantities of American supplies were flowing to the Allies in Europe by this time. Russia was supplied with American food, clothing, guns, trucks, machines, and airplanes via the Arctic Ocean and the Persian Gulf. American production of aircraft in 1943 had quadrupled over the 1939 level, and the production of merchant ships had increased almost 60 percent. Italy was invaded. German cities were bombed, not by the original pinpoint method, by which airplanes would fly during the daylight hours and carefully bomb selected targets, but by saturation bombing, by which hundreds of airplanes, flying in the cover of night, would saturate an entire area with patterned droppings of thousands of bombs, certainly destroying the selected targets and also everything else for miles around. More than anything else, this Allied bombing technique illustrates the economic nature of the war. Only enormous productivity could create such an air force; only a war waged directly against the enemy's industries and transportation could justify its use. In the United States, the Strategic Air Command, which carried out these bombing raids, soon outranked the Tactical Air Command, which consisted of fighter planes and carried out air support for military maneuvers. The days of the flying Red Baron were over. The days of push-button war and super-bombers had begun.

On April 30, 1945, Hitler's days were also over. He committed suicide in his bunker as Russian troops were entering Berlin. A little over a week later, by May 8, 1945, the war in Europe was over. About three months later, on August 6, the world's first atomic bomb was exploded in the air over Hiroshima. It had been developed in the strictest secrecy in the United States, ironically, with substantial technological help from scientists who had fled to this country earlier to escape the onslaught of Nazi Germany. Another atomic bomb was dropped over Nagasaki on August 9, and the formal surrender of Japan was signed on September 2. World War II was over.

The Aftermath

The total cost of the war to all belligerents is estimated at about $3,000,000,000,000, five times as much as World War I. Probably over 35 million people, civilians and military, had been killed, and at least that many more people had been wounded. A good proportion of the entire human race had suffered, and a great deal of the accumulated wealth of civilization—its industries, cities, traditions, and culture—had been destroyed. Germany and Japan, especially, were a shambles. By contrast, the United States, which had contributed much to the war but had escaped unscathed on its home soil, was better off than ever. From 1939 to 1944, its real output increased by 70 percent. The output going to civilian consumption increased 50 percent, and that going to the war effort increased about 200 percent.

For the American economy, World War II was the biggest public works program imaginable. Not in their wildest dreams could the New Dealers have conjured up a make-work project as this one was. All of the depression's economic slack, the unemployment, the excess industrial capacity, the underemployed farmland, was taken up. At the same time that the armed forces increased from 370,000 men in 1939 to 11,410,000 in 1945, the civilian labor force decreased only by about 1½ million, from 55,320,000 to 53,860,000, because millions of previously unemployed Americans went to work for the first time.

In the same years, annual tax receipts, largely from the progressive income taxes, increased almost tenfold, from just under 5 billion dollars to over 44 billion dollars, and the national debt (the accumulated deficits of the federal government) increased from 40.5 billion dollars to about 258.7 billion dollars. In Keynesian terms, the $C + I + G$ function was shifted upward with a vengeance that would have been politically impossible in peace time. A new equilibrium was established at a level that not only put the previously unemployed back to work but drew millions into the wage-earning labor force that had never been there before. Americans, by the millions, earned money as they never had before, as shown by the change in per capita national income (national income divided by population) from 1929 to 1950.[5]

1929	1933	1940	1945	1950
$720	$320	$618	$1295	$1582

Of course, taxes and inflation ate up a lot of this money, and often the only thing to buy with the income was government war bonds since much of the consumer-goods-producing sector had switched to war production. But the feeling of economic health and vigor was unmistakable. All was forgotten of the depression's malaise in the exhilaration of this new-found economic strength.

The economies of the rest of the world were not in such good shape. The first problem most of them had to face, beyond the war destruction and exhaustion, was inflation. Every belligerent, including the United States, had expanded its money supply in order to finance the war and had tried to suppress the resulting price increases, as well as assure an equitable distribution of scarce commodities, by enforcing price control and rationing.

The technique of price control is simple enough. The government just prohibits prices above certain ceilings on those commodities that are in critically short supply and thus threaten large increases in price. For example, in Figure 24, it may be decreed that R is the desired price ceiling for a particular commodity, even though the natural price in the inflated economy would be at S, where the (money) demand and the supply curve intersect. Anyone buying or selling at a price above R would be dealing in a "black market" and, if caught, would be prosecuted under the law. However, at price R, a shortage between the quantity demanded and the quantity supplied, equivalent

---

[5] Adjusting these actual dollar personal income figures for the effects of inflation by dividing them by the Consumer Price Index for those years shows the change in real income more accurately. Using a C.P.I. base of 1947 to 1949 = 100, the adjusted per capita income figures were approximately:

1929	1933	1940	1945	1950
$973	$571	$1013	$1682	$1521

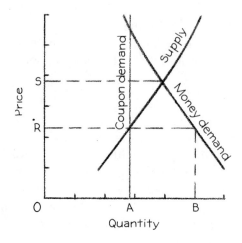

Figure 24. Price ceiling with rationing.

to the distance A-B, would develop. This could mean that only influential people or those who would wait in line the longest would be able to buy some of the scarce supply. A more equitable distribution system can be devised through rationing, which is typically a system of coupons distributed free of charge to consumers on the basis of some socially justifiable family allowance or other evidence of need. The coupons (chips, tokens, receipts, or whatever) are a secondary money system that must also be exchanged for the goods. Unlike regular money, however, these coupons are not inflated. Their quantity is strictly limited to that amount which will just "buy" the total quantity, A, of goods supplied at the price ceiling. Thus, price controls and rationing not only suppress inflation, but they also restrict the amount of commodities consumed by the civilian sector of the economy.

Foodstuffs were the main target of these policies, but clothing— especially shoes—gasoline and rent were also among those items that were rationed and/or price-controlled. For the American family during World War II, sugar, butter, and gasoline rationing seemed to have caused the biggest inconvenience.

In spite of these measures, prices still rose rapidly in all the countries. The table below give an indication of the inflation by showing the increases in the wholesale price indexes, based on 1938 = 100, in a few countries.[6]

Country	1945	1953
Italy	1950	5000
France	350	2500
United Kingdom	167	320
U.S.A.	136	220

The stringent police tactics of the Nazis had held German inflation in check rather well even though the Hitler regime multiplied the money supply rapidly during the war. At the same time, levels of production were kept as high as possible by government command. But when the war was over and the controls could no longer be rigorously enforced, no one would sell either his labor or his goods for the discredited Nazi currency. From 1945 through 1947, most of the economy couldn't function because it had no acceptable monetary vehicle. Primitive barter arrangements were often worked out for the exchange of basic food, clothing, and fuel, and, strangely enough, cigarettes became a kind of currency, a phenomenon that also occurs in prisoner of war camps and jails. In 1948, the occupation forces in Western Germany created a new German currency, which was distributed in exchange for the old money in a progressive way that redistributed the wealth, that is, those with only small amounts of the old currency were given a relatively better exchange rate than those with large amounts. Virtually the next day, markets began functioning again, and German recovery had begun.

Price control and rationing weren't the only ways governments interfered with their economies while they were warring. Taking a cue from Walter Rathenau's *Kriegsrohstoffabteilung* in Germany during the First World War, they established special

---

[6] *Statistical Yearbook 1956* (United Nations, New York, 1956).

agencies for economic planning. Natural resources, manpower, and investment capital were allocated to their most important uses, and imports and exports (such that existed during the war) were carefully controlled. Most of these controls were accomplished without resorting to outright coercion but rather by systems of selective subsidies, taxes, and other artificial inducements. But in Germany and the Soviet Union forced labor camps were used in a way that came close to slavery, and, of course, all the belligerents had a compulsory military draft. At any rate, it is only realistic to admit that much free enterprise was suspended in the noncommunist countries for the duration of the conflict.

And when the war was over, free enterprise did not resume as though nothing had happened. Indeed, classical liberalism had died with World War I and the Great Depression. Now, after the Second World War, the economies were in such disarray (except in the United States) that the necessity of some form of central planning was generally conceded in almost every country. The movement toward postwar economic planning was even felt in the United States, where, as early as 1943, the National Resources Planning Board published its *Security, Work, and Relief Policies*, which outlined a nine-point "Bill of Rights," including the right to work, the right to an adequate standard of living, and the right to security, rights which were presumably to be guaranteed by the government. This Bill of Rights never became policy, but the Employment Act of 1946 recognized the same sentiments, even though the legislation itself had been severely watered down in response to the active opposition raised against it by the National Association of Manufacturers and the Chamber of Commerce.

In Britain, France, and the Scandinavian countries, economic planning became part of the welfare-state-democratic-socialist governments that were being elected to office after the war. Along with government guarantees of full employment and welfare policies, these new postwar socialist governments nationalized many of the key industries of their economies on the principle that effective control was impossible without commandeering the "industrial heights." Thus, in Britain, the Bank of England

and the coal, gas, electricity, telephone, inland transport, and steel industries were nationalized; that is, they were bought from their private owners by the government. Similarly, in France, the Bank of France and the main commercial banks, the Renault company, Air France, and the coal, electricity, gas, and insurance industries were nationalized. In actual fact, the nationalization of these industries changed the economic picture very little. The company policies remained essentially the same; maximizing profits was still the goal; and the same management teams continued to sit in their same offices. As we have seen in the earlier section on ideologies (Chapter 6) and in Figure 9, democratic socialism and modern capitalism are hardly distinguishable. What is called "capitalism" in Germany may be called "augmented capitalism" in Japan and "socialism" in England. The pragmatic requirements of maintaining a viable economy seem to transcend ideological labeling.

By far, the most important postwar government program was undertaken by the United States government. However, this program was not initiated to augment its own economy but to help foreign economies. The program was foreign aid. After the Yalta and Potsdam conferences in 1945, it became apparent that Europe was dividing into two spheres of influence: the democratic, American-dominated West, and the communist, Russian-dominated East. This division, besides drawing the notorious "Iron Curtain" that started the Cold War and separated the world into two opposing military camps, also cut off industrial Western Europe from its natural economic counterpart, agricultural Eastern Europe. The economic recovery of the Western European nations would now, more than ever before, have to be based on an Atlantic international economy rather than on an international economy of the European heartland. The United States was amply equipped to carry out a program of foreign aid by supplying the necessary agricultural products. But the war-torn industries of Western Europe were still unable to get off the ground. They had been so devastated by the war that they were either unable to produce at all or were unable to compete with the efficient American industries that had been untouched by the war's destruction. The result was that the

274 The End of Liberalism

economies of Western Europe were not able to revive enough to pay for the enormous quantities of agricultural and industrial products that they needed for survival. Something more was needed.

In the other "camp," the Soviet Union was quite unconcerned about the recovery of the economies in its Eastern European sphere of influence and was bent on extracting reparations payments from them. But the United States, realizing that the fate of Europe depended on its economic recovery, took the unprecedented step of trying to help even those very nations it had defeated. It canceled its interallied war debts and made plans for the biggest and most successful international aid program the world has ever known.

CHAPTER *9*

Economies and Economics Just Yesterday and Today

RECOVERY, DEVELOPMENT, AND AMERICAN AID

From the end of the war in 1945 to the middle of 1947, American aid totaled eight billion dollars, over half going to the United Kingdom. On June 5, 1947, as part of his Harvard commencement address, General George C. Marshall, then Secretary of State, delivered his famous plan for economic aid that would feed another eleven billion dollars to the European countries from 1948 through 1951. On American insistence, the Organization for European Economic Cooperation (OEEC) was set up in Paris as a coordinating agency to distribute this Marshall Plan money to the various national economies. It was the first effective international planning organization, and in the course of its history it would give birth to an entire family of other instruments for international cooperation and control, beginning with the European Payments Union in 1950 and the European

Coal and Steel Community in 1952, and culminating in the Treaties of Rome in 1957, which created the European Atomic Energy Community and the European Economic Community, the last more popularly called the Common Market.

The Marshall Plan set the style for United States foreign aid. It was followed by President Truman's Point Four program of 1949 for the development of economically backward countries; the Mutual Security Act of 1951, which gave military assistance to friendly nations and, in the process, relieved their economies of the military burden; and many other larger and smaller aid programs. From 1945 through 1965, a total of 97,900,000,000 dollars was made available to foreign countries. To be sure, much of it was given away to buy security from communism, but much of it was also given away simply to help those countries that needed it, the war-damaged economies of Europe and the under-developed economies of the rest of the world. It was the first time in history that the victor helped its exhausted allies and vanquished enemies to their feet with such magnanimity.

Not all of the postwar aid came directly from the United States. In 1944, when it already appeared that the Allies would eventually overcome the Axis powers, a conference was held in Bretton Woods, New Hampshire, at which two new organizations for postwar recovery were created. These were the International Bank for Reconstruction and Development, called the World Bank, for short, and the International Monetary Fund. The first was to be an instrument for channeling long-term loans from largely private sources into war-torn industries and newly developing industries; the second was to make short-term loans from funds provided by the member countries to other member countries that, temporarily, had insufficient funds of internationally acceptable currency to meet their international debts. By the 1950s, the main purpose of the World Bank and all the other international economic development agencies had switched from the reconstruction of war-damaged industries in Europe to the new construction of the young economies of the vast undeveloped world of Asia, Africa, and Latin America. Both the International Monetary Fund and the World Bank sought to accumulate funds from many nations, but the United States was and still is the largest public and private contributor. The World Bank also sells bonds to obtain funds and secures its loans through the governments of the countries in which the loans are made. The International Monetary Fund lends only to those countries, numbering 115 in 1970, that have subscribed their quota of gold or currency to the fund. And when it makes loans, they are often accompanied by rigid conditions for economic reforms, which must be met, at the threat of excommunication from Fund membership. By mid-1970 the World Bank had loaned out over 14.5 billion dollars to 78 different nations, and the Fund had made short-term loans totaling about 20 billion dollars to over half its members.

Nor does this end the list of postwar organizations pledged to the health and growth of the international economy. To reduce tariffs and, thereby, stimulate world trade, the General Agreement on Tariffs and Trade, known simply as GATT, was established in 1948, and it has met with some success over the years, most recently in the "Kennedy round" of tariff-lowering agreements negotiated from 1964 through 1967, named after President Kennedy, who was the main instigator of the negotiations. The International Development Association and the International Finance Corporation, both offshoots of the World Bank, lend money on more flexible terms and for more specialized purposes than their parent organization. There are also several regional development banks, like the Inter-American Development Bank, the Asian Development Bank, and the Caribbean Development Bank, which concentrate on lending financial support to developing industries in their respective regions; these banks receive the bulk of their capital from the United States and Canada. The Food and Agriculture Organization and the World Health Organization work on encouraging improvements in the standard of living that can be derived from improved nutrition and health practices. With the exception of the regional development banks, all the above-mentioned organizations are affiliated in one way or another with the United Nations. But there are many other small and large, governmental and private organizations that work for economic development throughout the world, ranging from Russian aid for the gigantic Aswan Dam project in Egypt to the relatively few volunteer workers sent into the jungle by church groups.

As with the World Bank, the emphasis of all these agencies today is with the underdeveloped world because European recovery became an accomplished fact sooner than anyone could have guessed or hoped. The war's destruction had not touched the skills of the labor force, the technological knowledge, the entrepreneurial drive and managerial know-how, or the urban sophistication of the population. While it had destroyed the larger patterns of trade, it had not erased the intranational, regional, and urban patterns of trade and industrial location. Reconstruction, then, was often merely a matter of replacing the bombed-out or worn-out physical plant and equipment, which proved to be a much easier task than developing an industry from scratch in the virgin economic soil of undeveloped nations. And as plants and equipments were replaced, the newest and most advanced ones were installed. Some of the oldest cities of Europe, such as Frankfurt and Dusseldorf, became the most modern. In an ironic sense, it was better to have been completely destroyed than to have been only partially damaged because complete destruction allowed complete modernization. Germany was the chief recipient of this windfall. As shown in Table 8, by the early 1950s, all belligerents had regained or surpassed their prewar level of industrial production, and the next years saw very rapid growth.

Table 8. Index of industrial production (1953 = 100)

Country	1938	1948	1951	1958
France	72	77	99	142
Germany	77	40	85	150
Japan	79	36	77	168
United Kingdom	75	83	98	114
U.S.S.R.	30	45	80	170
U.S.A.*	34	76	89	109

Source: Statistical Yearbook 1959 (United Nations, New York, 1960).
* Manufacturing industries only.

Recovery was so unexpectedly phoenix-like that it was called an economic miracle, especially in Germany, where the popular term for it, "*Wirtschaftswunder*," became a permanent addition to the language. Still, for all its marvelous economic growth, Western Europe had lost the leadership position in Western civilization that it had enjoyed since the decline of Rome. In every aspect of life: art, music, literature, science and technology, fashion, travel, military and political influence, and especially in economic affairs, the United States was now the overwhelming presence. What began with lend-lease loans to the allies during the war and continued with the Marshall Plan seemed to culminate in chewing gum, Coca-Cola, and blue jeans, or, on a larger scale, in supermarkets, cars, and refrigerators. The French complained that "*Franglais*" was choking their beautiful language; the Germans despaired over the invasion of rock-and-roll; but to no avail. These were the trends of the future. Militarily, of course, Russia and the United States towered over everyone else. But even in growth rates, Russia's performance was equal to or better than that of the "miracle" countries of Western Europe, at least, according to the available measures. Ten years after the end of World War II, the one-two punch of the two world wars seemed to have had a telling effect on Europe, which, in spite of its recovery, was losing status in the world. Even its share of world trade, which had been about 50 percent before 1914, shrank to about 35 percent by 1950.

Perhaps even more than because of the wars, Europe was losing its political and economic potential by being fragmented into many separate nationalist economies. Almost two centuries before, Adam Smith had pointed out the benefits of large markets and free-flowing trade. Now, more than ever before, it was obvious that modern economic efficiency marched to the tune of huge mass markets, prodigious mass production, and phenomenal accumulations of capital. None of the European countries, taken individually, could compete with the behemoths, the United States and Russia. In 1947, three small states, Belgium, The Netherlands, and Luxembourg, united their economies in a rather thoroughgoing customs union ingeniously called Benelux. The OEEC of the Marshall Plan began plumping for this kind of cooperation in 1948, and, finally, in 1957, the

Treaties of Rome established the Common Market, an economic union of Benelux, West Germany, Italy, and France.

INTERNATIONAL TRADE AND PAYMENTS

The Common Market nations have substantially reduced tariffs and other artificial barriers to the free flow of goods, capital, and labor among them. Hardships caused by the adjustments to these new freedoms are ameliorated by a Readaptation Fund; administration of the Common Market is handled by a representative council; and a European Investment Bank and an Investment Fund, both set up to facilitate economic development, are also part of the scheme. The major sticking point in the 1960s and 1970s that has prevented total economic cooperation has been in agricultural policy. The member nations have been following independent farm price-support policies, and ironing these out is proving to be a rough political problem that may even result in some reemergent nationalism reminiscent of Charles de Gaulle. But the original motivating spirit for the Common Market included a strong drift of pan-European patriotism, especially on the part of its founding fathers, Jean Monnet and Robert Schuman, and this continues to be a force that may help the Common Market become the basis for something like a federated United States of Europe.

Unfortunately, the other side of the coin to every community of members is that a group of nonmembers must be excluded. The outsiders left by the Common Market are in a particularly precarious position because many of them had important economic ties to Common Market nations, which may no longer hold, and the Common Market nations are always tempted to ease the adjustment to their own free trade by raising the barriers to trade with the outside nations. In 1960, to protect themselves against these consequences, the "Outer Seven," Sweden, Norway, Denmark, Austria, Switzerland, Portugal, and Great Britain, joined in a European Free Trade Association, dedicated to lowering tariffs and other trade barriers among themselves. The United States, too, has worried about the exclusiveness of the "Inner Six" and has argued strongly for a broad free trade policy including all the Atlantic nations. The negotiations of Great Britain's entry into the Common Market have been largely a test of the Market's clannishness.

So international trade is having its successes as well as its troubles. The world is divided into two ideological blocs that won't exchange much with one another. Within one of these blocs the Common Market still has the potential for becoming an exclusive club. Tariffs and other impediments to international trade, such as quotas and discriminatory taxes, are not being lowered as rapidly as had been hoped after World War II. The leading exponent for lowering trade barriers has been the United States, functioning largely through GATT, but in light of the growing competition for America's own markets from foreign suppliers, especially Germany and Japan, it is questionable how long such enthusiastic leadership can be maintained; during the late 1960s and the beginning of the 1970s, the voices of protectionism have grown increasingly louder. America's expensive military entanglements, economic aid to underdeveloped countries, private investments in foreign industries, and the building of American plants abroad have only added to the problem, for since the late 1950s, the United States has been spending more money abroad than foreigners have spent in the United States.

This situation has resulted in a glut of American dollars held by foreigners. The foreigners invest these dollars in U.S. stocks, bonds, and government securities, and should such investments no longer seem profitable, they would be sold off, and the dollars would be sent crashing into the Federal Reserve Bank of New York for redemption in gold. This event would effectively deplete the U.S. gold stock and undermine the international faith in our currency. Purchases of gold have already eroded U.S. gold holdings from over 22 billion dollars worth in the late 1950s to about 10 billion dollars' worth in 1970, when liquid American assets held by foreigners and their central banks amounted to over 40 billion dollars. The mere knowledge that a total gold depletion could come to pass, however unlikely this might be, stands as a threat to the integrity of the dollar.

Part of the problem is that the currencies used all over the world for international trading purposes, mainly the U.S. dollar and the British pound, are burdened by having to support a growing amount of trade on a relatively constant amount of gold reserve. Especially in the 1960s and 1970s, this resulted in a "liquidity crisis," in which the shortage of gold was and is threatening to choke world trade. Under the auspices of the International Monetary Fund, a new kind of "paper gold," called SDR's (special drawing rights), was introduced in 1970, which serves somewhat the same kind of function internationally as government securities do when they are used as reserves along with gold by the Federal Reserve system. (See the Pyramid of Credit, Figure 3.) The SDR's are intended to be equivalent to gold in international trade and may be used in place of gold as a means of settling payments between countries. Their quantity is controlled by the International Monetary Fund. To make such an artificial device work requires a great deal of international cooperation and confidence. The heads of the major national central banks form a kind of elite club with regular meetings, usually in Geneva, and they serve as at least one building block in the foundation on which such international confidence can develop. Other foundation blocks may be the respectability of the Fund itself and, above all, the health and good prospects of the world economy and body politic.

International liquidity can be instantly increased by increasing the price of gold. The money value of the international gold stock would increase, thus serving the interests of greater international trade. However, countries with large stocks of gold would make a windfall profit at the expense of those with small or nonexistent gold stocks, and this is why such a simple expedient is not commonly employed. However, if an individual nation finds its burden of international payments too great, it can still unilaterally devalue its currency by increasing the price of gold as quoted in that currency, thus enabling it to wipe out a debt with a stroke of the devaluation pen. But only the smaller nations can get away with such tactics, and then only if their debts are in terms of their own currency—rather than in gold or in dollars or pounds. United States' international responsibility is deemed too large to allow nonnegotiated devaluation of the dollar by more than a few percent, at least since World War II. Besides, many nations would instantly match an American devaluation with a devaluation of their own to protect their gold supply, and thereby cancel much of the intended benefit for the United States.

THE "HAVE-NOT" NATIONS

The international trading problems of the majority of the nations of the world, the underdeveloped nations, are much more chronic than those of the countries we have been discussing. They have been relegated the task of supplying raw materials, sugar, coffee, cocoa, rubber, and bananas to the industrialized world. The markets for these products are not growing as rapidly as other markets, and their dependence on a single export leaves these countries in a bad bargaining position. Taking a cue from the Europeans, they have toyed with the idea of common markets, and trading blocs are at various early stages of development in Africa, South and Central America, and Asia. Perhaps such blocs will help relieve their economic dependence on the industrialized nations. But their problems are less the lowering of tariffs or the balance of payments among themselves than it is their own economic development.

After World War II, the economic development of these countries became the biggest single international economic issue in the world. Intercultural contact, which began with the Crusades on through the discoveries of new lands to the extension of trade to all corners of the world during Europe's Industrial Revolution, intensified even further with the colonialism of the late 1800s and reached flood proportions when the greatest international mix-masters, the two world wars, sundered forever the insulation between the world's peoples and continents.

All these historical developments, especially the Industrial Revolution, also intensified the economic differences among the various peoples. By the time World War II was over, the differences became unacceptable to that roughly two-thirds of the human race that found itself on the short end of the economic stick. The concern of the developed nations was hardly less great since they recognized in this inequality the potential for a great deal of trouble in the future. Ominous warnings of communist takeovers in these "have-not" nations added an ideological obsession to the normal economic and political concern. Part of the response of the developed nations of the world to the problems of undeveloped economies was to channel substantial amounts of financial, material, and technological aid to these countries, which accounted for a majority of the foreign economic aid distributed in the 1950s and 1960s by the United States. Of course, both sides of the world ideological split played this game, and Russia gave economic assistance to those countries not under its military domination in hopes of winning friends for communism—while the receiving nations played off both sides against each other.

The theoretical justification that both the United States and Russia give for the foreign aid is that they want to help the underdeveloped (a euphemism for "undeveloped") nations to raise their level of industrialization. The almost total lack of industrialization in these countries is caused by a vicious cycle of poverty, as shown in Figure 25. Somehow the cycle has to be broken, but this is a tall order. Ragnar Nurkse (1907–1959), the economist who first expressed this vicious cycle of poverty, put it in very human terms:

> a poor man may not have enough to eat; being under-nourished, his health may be weak; being physically weak, his working capacity may be low, which means that he is poor, which in turn means that he will not have enough to eat; and so on. A situation of this sort, applying to a country as a whole, can be summed up in the trite proposition: "a country is poor because it is poor."[1]

For such undeveloped economies to try to get out of the morass of their poverty on their own could be disastrous. People who are already undernourished, at the least, cannot put away money for investments! Any decrease in their standard of living, by trying to increase savings, for example, would probably result in a starvation level of consumption. At the same time, it would

---

[1] Ragnar Nurkse, *Some Aspects of Capital Accumulation in Underdeveloped Countries* (National Bank of Egypt, Cairo, 1952).

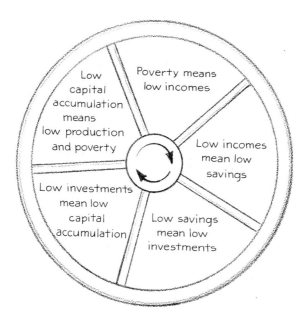

Figure 25. The vicious cycle of poverty and underdevelopment.

take much too long to accomplish and would not satisfy the impatient demand of the people to be admitted to the twentieth century. Foreign aid can come to the rescue by supplying the capital from outside. Industries built with foreign aid would raise incomes, which would allow a larger level of indigenous savings, which would mean more domestic investment and more industries. Thus, incomes would continue to be raised, and the vicious cycle will have been broken. The economy will now be on the road to development, and foreign aid will no longer be necessary. This simple theory explains the successful beginning of economic development in a few once undeveloped countries, such as Taiwan, South Korea, Israel, and Mexico. But in most cases, including those just mentioned, the process of economic development involves much more than merely relieving a chronic capital scarcity.

Many economists ignore the fact that much of the economic backwardness is due to a lack of economic resources. The first and foremost reason why the tribesmen of the North African deserts are so desperately poor is that their homeland has very few resources from which they can earn a living, unless, of course, there is oil underneath those endless stretches of barren sand. Likewise, the jungles of the Amazon or Congo rivers, so often claimed to be untapped treasure troves of economic wealth, have, in fact, yielded very little. Repeated explorations have discovered no invaluable mineral deposits, nor is the leached-out jungle soil very suitable for agriculture. In the monsoon areas of Asia, where population densities are very high, the apparent economic backwardness is not so much the result of a lack of resources as it is the result of the completely thorough utilization of all available resources, with no surplus left over on which to base growth. In that sense, perhaps, these rice-growing areas of Asia should not be called underdeveloped. They are already developed to the fullest extent possible within the limits of their economic capacity and are quite sophisticated in some ways. Both for the rice economies, with their low standards of living, and the underdeveloped economies, such lack of resource availability is often a major limitation to economic development.

But, since economic theorizing is largely the occupation of Western societies, where land inadequacies were seldom a restriction to economic growth, especially in the recent history of the Industrial Revolution, the main reason offered to explain this underdevelopment has been, not lack of resources, but capital insufficiencies, as in the vicious cycle of Figure 25. At any rate, this is one of the few factors about which nations can do something constructive. They cannot give more acreage to the peasants on Hainan Island, more rainfall to the tribesmen in the Sahara, or rich soils and coal mines to the rain-forest Indians of the Amazon. But they can arrange for more capital.

Economic aid to underdeveloped countries can also consist of technological aid. Certainly, one of the things that slowed down the Industrial Revolution in Western Europe and North America was the gradual way in which modern technology was discovered, and, just as certainly, one of the factors that helped the Soviet Union carry out its headlong rush into industrialization is that Western technology already existed. (This is a point the Russians hate to admit despite the fact that Karl Marx considered the development of technology one of capitalism's most positive contributions to posterity.) Thus, President Truman's Point Four program was designed to introduce modern technology to the underdeveloped countries. But there are drawbacks to technological aid since much of Western technology has different results when applied to underdeveloped economies. For example, the simple public health and sanitation measures, which are taken for granted in the developed nations, can lower the death rate drastically when introduced in underdeveloped countries, except that birth rates don't go down proportionately. As a result, those nations that can least afford huge increases in population are the very ones that are so burdened, and one wonders whether the improved public health and sanitation technology were not perhaps a diabolical joke.

Similarly, modern steel mills, petroleum refineries, and hydro-electric facilities can be built right in the middle of the population centers of underdeveloped economies and yet have almost no effect on them at all, except that some of the workers, who used to do the labor by hand that can now be done mechanically and electrically, become unemployed. Such modern instruments of economic production are often unable to employ very much of the local labor force, use any local managerial talent, or even sell their products locally. The inability of much of modern Western technology to make a dent on the traditional structures of these societies is not only an economic phenomenon; it can also be a military one. Billions of dollars' worth of the most sophisticated war equipment and hundreds of thousands of the world's best trained troops may have frustratingly little success against a peasant guerrilla army, as the American experience in Indochina has demonstrated.

Still, technological aid can be a help in economic development if the new technology is carefully tailored to the stage of economic development of the country in question and if it is matched with thoroughgoing efforts to educate the people to its proper use. The proper use of fertilizer, new kinds of seeds, basic business procedures, manufacturing technologies especially suited to small businesses, and so on have been successfully introduced in developing economies. One problem often encountered in this effort to educate the people and modernize procedures is a cultural resistance to such changes. Perhaps, this resistance can best be overcome by actual demonstrations of the new technologies, which will provide a high degree of credibility for the understandably suspicious laborers and peasants, and such demonstrations may even give them an opportunity to learn by doing. Aid personnel working in the underdeveloped countries themselves often argue that this method usually works much better than classroom lectures or other abstract teaching methods.

But cultural resistance to innovation and modernization may also be philosophical. When the philosophy of a country is one that disdains material wealth, economic progress, or even any concern at all about the standard of living in this earthly life, it is very difficult to overcome such resistance. However, while such outright denial of the present material world may be found among various Asian monks and priests, it is much less of a problem among the general population than it is often made out to be. Almost anyone in the world wants to live a little better and a little longer. What remains a problem is that most societies do not celebrate the virtues of individualism, such as innovation, competition, and entrepreneurial behavior, with the same conviction that the West does. Occasionally, when some programs of economic aid do not elicit the enthusiastic response that they would in the profit-motivated West, the foreign aid administrators are frustrated and wonder what's wrong with the people who are so reluctant to "take the ball and run with it." In fact, Westerners might learn something from the example of these societies. For instance, the nonentrepreneurial, face-saving, Confucian kind of behavior that is typical in many societies in monsoon Asia is an achievement that may, in the end, rank higher than mere industrialization. These societies have developed a highly refined and stable culture in the face of a very dense and massive population and have kept it intact for many hundreds of years.

If there is one biggest single impediment to economic development in most of the underdeveloped countries, it is the explosive population growth. We have seen how twentieth century technology has lowered the death rate while the birth rate remains high. The resulting increases in the numbers of people literally eat up all or most of whatever increases in total production these economies are capable of. In a significant number of such underdeveloped countries, it is questionable whether standards of living have gone up at all. In India, for example, while industrial production more than doubled in the two decades following the Second World War, the much more important agricultural production increased barely 10 percent. At the same time, the Indian population grew by well over 65 percent.

The point of attack in this problem is clearly lowering the birth rate. The inducement to family limitation that operated satisfactorily in Europe and North America long before the population was threatened with malnutrition or starvation, namely, the economic motive to restrict the number of children in order to secure a higher standard of living for the family, doesn't seem to operate in many underdeveloped countries. Often, because of the large kinship family structure—where nephews, cousins, and uncles just naturally move in—a couple, which might have been economically better off because they do have fewer children, is denied the economic fruits of their procreative restraint. Perhaps, any lack of restraint is primarily the result of religious and social customs that prize *machismo*, virility, fertility, and large numbers of offspring. Or, perhaps, in some countries the continued high birth rate results from government welfare allowances given to families on the basis of the number of dependent children they have, a twentieth century welfare measure superimposed on a pre-industrial society.

Whatever the cause, the high birth rates in underdeveloped economies are mainly the result of the lack of an articulated and active desire to limit the number of children, and merely introducing modern methods of birth control without introducing a motive for them is to little avail. The ease of the new methods of contraception, especially the intra-uterine device and the pill, give some hope, for where they have been introduced, some substantial decrease in the birth rates of both underdeveloped and developed countries has resulted.

Some Theories of Development

Whatever is introduced to the underdeveloped countries, whether it be grants of capital through foreign aid, the teaching of a new technology, or new birth control methods, it is generally assumed that the underdeveloped nations of the world need help from the developed ones if anything like an adequate rate of economic growth is to be achieved. Yet, some economists assume that economic growth is an autonomous process that is simply part and parcel of every nation's historical reality. Karl Marx theorized that economic development went through progressive stages, the last few of which were feudalism, capitalism, socialism under the dictatorship of the proletariat, and finally utopian communism. He believed that capitalist nations could look to socialist (communist) ones for an example of what their future would bring. Writing about a century later, W. W. Rostow of the Massachusetts Institute of Technology also described economic development as a series of progressive stages, in a book entitled *The Stages of Economic Growth*. Rostow distinguished five stages.

1. The traditional society, in which the people live more or less close to subsistence, their technology is pre-Newtonian, and their outlook is fatalistic in the long run, that is, they see no prospect for the permanent improvement of mankind's lot.

2. The preconditions for takeoff, in which new discoveries and technology, either created endogenously or introduced from outside, open up new opportunities and implant the hope for new and better things to come.

3. The takeoff, in which growth becomes self-sustaining, incomes are unequally distributed, and a high rate of saving by rich individuals or rich governments is possible, and investments rise from around 5 percent of the national income to about 10 percent, and economic development receives top priority by the society and its government.

4. The drive to maturity, in which investment increases from 10 to 20 percent of the national income, production increases substantially faster than the population, technology becomes highly sophisticated, and the economy is fully competitive internationally.

5. The age of mass consumption, in which high standards of living are enjoyed by the entire populace.

Rostow also speculated on a sixth stage, in which the consumers' materialist emphasis would be replaced by a greater interest in education, the arts, and the joys of having more children.

As the word implies, the most critical stage in Rostow's progression is the takeoff. His calculations show that Britain started its economic takeoff around 1785, France around 1820, the United States 1845, Germany 1850, Japan 1880, Russia 1890, and China, perhaps, around 1950.[2]

Gunnar Myrdal, the Swedish economist (born 1898), views the problem of economic development less historically and more pragmatically. He makes three main points.

1. The gap between the rich and poor nations is widening, not closing. Waiting for history to run its course would lead to global disaster.

2. Orthodox economic concerns with the growth of national production have obscured the important issue, which is that most of the undeveloped economies need a radically equalizing redistribution of their income and wealth. This needs to be done simply to raise the common people above grinding subsistence and to improve their labor efficiency. If such redistribution runs counter to the niceties of Western economic conventions, that merely proves the irrelevance of the conventions.

3. Rich nations must come to the assistance of the poor, and this assistance is best channeled to the undeveloped economies via carefully drawn central plans. This would lead to the establishment of much government intervention in these economies, of course, but that might be more conducive to rapid economic development than a laissez faire approach anyway, in view of the severe handicaps that overpopulation and stagnation impose on today's undeveloped economies.[3]

Myrdal's ideas do sound a little tougher and more realistic

---

[2] W. W. Rostow, *The Stages of Economic Growth, a Non-Communist Manifesto* (Cambridge University Press, Cambridge, 1960).

[3] Gunnar Myrdal, *Asian Drama: An Inquiry into the Poverty of Nations* (Pantheon, New York, 1968), 3 vols.

than most. However, they are probably still no match for the problem. The development of the undeveloped countries has not been a successful story. The gap between the rich and the poor nations continues to widen. The twenty or so developed nations produce and consume about 80 percent of the world's industrial production while half of the world's population is hungry.

Most people find it difficult to accept the fact that the future of these very troubled nations, such as India and the poorer states in Africa and Latin America, will very probably be a bleak existence of grim poverty, malnutrition, and even mass starvation. But it will be miraculous if all of these underdeveloped economies can pull out of their worsening population squeeze, their desperate poverty, their archaic social structure, and their hopelessness. The demands for foreign aid—of food to prevent famines, if nothing else—may go on for many decades.

INFLATION, STABILITY, AND GROWTH

Meanwhile, during the 1950s, the economic growth of the United States—on the extreme opposite end of the development scale from the underdeveloped countries—was not all what it was cracked up to be either. Fortunately, there was no immediate postwar recession, as some economists had feared. The vast unspent purchasing power accumulated during the war, when incomes were high but consumer goods lacking, had fueled an expansion instead. This same purchasing power also spawned a prodigious inflation. Production of peacetime goods could not keep up with demand. But the general outlook of the people, consumers and businessmen alike, was one of optimism and confidence. And the early fifties were further stimulated by the extra demands created by the Korean War. However, unemployment of a peculiarly chronic nature began to appear after that war, never dipping below a rate of 4 percent of the labor force during the rest of the decade.

This unemployment didn't seem to respond very well to good times and good business conditions. It was structural rather than cyclical, meaning that it was caused by some workers being made obsolete by new machines or losing their jobs because the industry moved out of town or even out of the region. People in poor rural areas, the old and the uneducated, and members of minority groups made up most of the unemployed. The fifties demanded and got a high level of mobility from its labor force. Americans moved around the country to fill better jobs and do a better business as they never had before. But those who could not move either geographically or socially or who had no opportunity for retraining were left out of the mainstream of American life.

To make matters worse, a series of short recessions seemed to come in ever more rapid intervals, the first interval being 45 months between the end of the 1949 recession and the beginning of the 1954 recession; the next one being 35 months later, the 1958 recession; and then only 25 months later, the recession beginning in February 1961. In spite of these recurring slumps, inflation plagued the economy incessantly. That all of the Western economies seemed to be experiencing an average of 2 percent increase in their price levels annually was small comfort because American inflation was especially severe in the export industries. In hopes of stemming the tide, the Eisenhower administration tried valiantly but unsuccessfully to balance the government's budget, and the Federal Reserve system, under the conservative leadership of William McChesney Martin, actually did succeed in expanding the nation's money supply less than the expansion of its Gross National Product.

Still prices continued their upward creep. Management blamed the unions, which kept demanding higher wages and fringe benefits and threatened strikes to press their demands. The unions blamed the inflation on management, which seemed to raise prices unconscionably soon after union wage demands gave them an excuse to do so. As this happened all over the whole economy, the increased prices canceled whatever gain in purchasing power the unions may have won for the workers. Somehow the competitive market didn't seem to work for reasonable price stability in the long run any more. Economists began to talk about "administered prices" rather than the open forces of supply and demand. Modern advertising and the skillful management of consumer demand seemed to give large firms the opportunity to increase prices whenever they thought it wouldn't hurt their public relations to do so. In other words, inflation, just like chronic unemployment, was a new structural characteristic of the American economy, much to the dismay of those who had hoped that standard monetary and fiscal policies could effect a cure. After a period of relative price stability through the middle 1960s, inflation again gripped the economy. As wars had done before, the Indochina War pushed government expenditures far above revenues, and the government had to borrow large amounts of money. The war did not have much popular support from the very start, and Congress was loath to raise taxes to finance it. The government and military leadership did not want to admit the extent of the country's involvement, which resulted in the Federal Reserve system's being unable to prepare the proper monetary framework for the extensive government borrowing. The quantity of money was increased to facilitate the government's borrowing, but it was increased as little as possible to prevent an inflation in the domestic economy.

The unfortunate results were skyrocketing interest rates, because of the tight money supply available to the domestic economy, and rapidly rising prices, because of the increase in the quantity of money spent in the war-plus-domestic economy. The high interest rates immediately became a heavy burden to small businesses, especially in the building trades, and were a major cause of increasing unemployment. Eventually even some of the nation's largest firms found the tight money to be a serious threat, as they had difficulty in borrowing the funds they regularly needed to continue operations.

The inflation caused by the Indochina War seems to have raised only a slightly different inflationary ogre: instead of the "administered prices" of the 1950s, there was the new "inflationary mentality"; that is, once inflation becomes normal, businesses and consumers expect price increases as a matter of course, and workers consider a year with less than a 5 percent wage increase to have been a step backward. In this state of affairs, a restrictive monetary and fiscal policy, involving high interest rates, low government expenditures, and high taxes, will cause unemployment and retard economic growth before it stabilizes prices. Meanwhile, the inflation is destroying the meager financial security of those whose incomes remain relatively fixed in dollar terms, such as pensioners, school teachers, and hospital orderlies, and it is eroding the competitiveness of American exports and the value of the U.S. dollar abroad.

Also disconcerting to Americans in the 1950s was the success the Russians were having. Their economic growth rates are generally conceded to have been around 6.8 percent per year from 1950 to 1958, slackening off to 4.6 percent into the sixties, all of which compared very favorably with the United States economic growth rate of about 3.2 percent per year. We must remember, however, that such comparisons can give a distorted picture. The Russians were starting off from a much lower level, and their concentration on heavy capital goods industries, such as steel, coal, and electric power, shows up better in statistics than the American growth industries, which were already those of a highly advanced economy, mainly the services, such as transportation, education, communication, medical care, and recreation. But Americans seem to believe religiously in statistics and just naturally expect to be first on any ranking system. Thus, when the Russians surprised the world with their Sputnik on October 4, 1957, it set off a nationwide soul-searching among appalled Americans about the state of American science, education, defense, and even physical fitness.

Meanwhile, all during the fifties the recovering Western European countries were being pinched less and less by the chronic shortage of U.S. dollars—dollars they had needed to buy the agricultural and industrial products they couldn't produce themselves. Not only were they becoming self-sufficient again, but they were even beginning to invade American markets with some success. The ubiquitous Volkswagen was the symbol of this new strength, and it seemed to infest the American countryside like a plague of some new kind of beetle. Many other products also found markets among the eager American consumers: clothing fashions, foods, and spirits; and the efficient new ship-yards and steel mills of Europe and Japan began to find markets for their products in the industries of the United States too. To be sure, the American economy continued to export more than was imported until the early 1970s, but taken together with the outflow of American dollars for foreign investments, economic and military assistance, and the soon-to-be-increased expenditures for the war in Vietnam, the commodity trade surplus could not outweigh the deficit outflow of dollars, and the dollar shortage abroad turned into a dollar glut (see the section on International Trade and Payments, p. 280).

CHAPTER 10

The New Dimensions
of Mature Economies

THE SOARING SIXTIES

The general dissatisfaction with this state of affairs came to a head in the Presidential election year of 1960. Both the Democratic candidate, John F. Kennedy, and the Republican, Nelson Rockefeller, stressed the need to increase the American economic growth rate, and the former's promise to "get America moving again" toward a "New Frontier" helped him win the election, although by a very narrow margin. In fact, the economy did start moving again; after the recession in early 1961, there came an eight-year economic boom that was the pride of the politicians, who, of course, took credit for it. The expansion was accomplished with basic Keynesian techniques; that is, tax rates were cut and government expenditures were increased. At the same time, government budget deficits did not increase as much as might be expected because the effect of the boom, with its greatly increased incomes, was to increase total tax revenues, even at the lower tax rates. Prices also remained about as stable as before, an average of 2 percent inflation a year, at least, until the Vietnam "police action" became a full-fledged war.

The policies that created the "soaring sixties" are a good case study of the dilemmas that face modern economics. For many of the major economic illnesses, reputable economic diagnoses are available that would suggest diametrically opposite cures. Here are just a few examples taken from the American experience during the 1960s.

1. Would the best cure for inflation be an expansive monetary policy that would encourage production and increase the circulation of goods, thus, increasing supply and lowering prices? Or would it be better to have a restrictive monetary policy that would shrink the quantity of money in circulation and, thus, via decreased demand, depress prices?

2. Would the best cure for government deficits be an increase in the tax rates to increase government revenues, or should tax rates be decreased to encourage consumption and investment, which would have an expansionary effect, and, thus, increase the tax revenues obtained from the larger national income?

3. Would the best cure for a deficit imbalance of trade be restrictive domestic policies so that fewer imports are bought, or an expansive policy so that industry can enlarge, invest in more equipment, and compete more successfully in the export market?

The traditional solution since World War II has been the "neoclassical synthesis," that combination of laissez faire and governmental intervention on which all industrialized "mixed economies" of the world are now based. According to this synthesis, Say's Law (all things produced will be purchased) and Fisher's Identity ($MV \equiv PQ$, allowing price movements to stimulate the necessary adjustments) will both work fine at full employment (often defined in the United States as 4 percent or less unemployment). Under full employment, a generally noninterventionist government will assure the most efficient and most rapidly growing economy. But should the economy find itself at substantially less than full employment, these classical theories won't work. Then expansionist government policies will be the only cure. Thus, the implementation of monetary policies, as described in the section on Banking, Money, and Gold in Chapter 4, and fiscal policies, as described in the section on the Keynesian Revolution in Chapter 8, depends on the state of the economy. With such flexibility, many of the dilemmas should be resolved.

Of course, they aren't completely resolved. The lethargic United States economy during the late 1950s (and again in the early 1970s) was characterized by unemployment on the one hand, which calls for Keynesian expansion, and inflation on the other, which calls for contraction or, at least, not more and bigger government expenditures. The neoclassical synthesis, by itself, is unable to attack such contradictory structural problems unless the various government projects that come under the heading of "Keynesian expansionist policies" also include sophisticated labor relocation and retraining projects, regulations of markets and advertising, and other government efforts to correct the structural inadequacies themselves. Many economists have just this in mind and would like government policies to emphasize such areas as civil rights and equalized economic opportunities, improved medical care (especially for the very young and the aged), increased public health and safety, aid to depressed areas, and increased education (especially adult education and retraining). This "welfare package," as it is sometimes called, would cost the taxpayers a lot of money, but it would be more than repaid, presumably, by the substantially increased rate of economic growth. Edward Denison of the Brookings Institution has estimated that American productivity would go up by 4 percent merely by eliminating all racial discrimination in the long run.[1] Similar gains in productivity may be expected from the elimination of discrimination against women.

---

[1] Edward F. Denison, *The Sources of Economic Growth in the United States* (Committee for Economic Development, New York, 1962), p. 198. The total long-run adjustments to full equality would take about a century, according to Denison's estimate.

Even in the simpler case, when business conditions are cyclically determined, the neoclassical synthesis does not resolve the dilemmas without a hitch because no one is exactly sure at what point to switch from activist government intervention to laissez faire. At one extreme are those who seem to feel that steady expansionist pressure from the government, like a one-a-day vitamin pill, helps the economy stay healthy. Their opinion, more than any other, prevailed during the 1960s, and their policies seem to have been rewarded with outstanding success and the approval of workers, consumers, and businessmen alike.

At the other extreme are those spearheaded by what is called the Chicago School—after Milton Friedman and other laissez faire libertarian economists at the University of Chicago—which believes that laissez faire is the best system practically all the time. They have great faith in the efficiency of the free market and advocate a government policy that is as economically neutral as possible. The Chicago School points out that many government programs have backfired or, at best, work lamely. Agricultural aid goes mainly to rich farmers, welfare sustains poverty, free state universities kill off private colleges, the Army Corps of Engineers builds a new canal only to ruin a delicate environmental balance, and so on. These "monetarists" argue that, contrary to the major Keynesian premise, the effect of fiscal policy, of taxes and government spending, on inflation or unemployment is essentially unpredictable and, therefore, useless. At a time when many people are beginning to feel increasingly threatened by an ever-growing government, by rising taxes, and by a disintegrating society, this point of view is gaining in popularity.

The Chicago School even disdains the standard active monetary policy of our central banks today. Friedman argues that a neutral, steady expansion of the money supply by perhaps 4 to 5 percent per year would be much better than the fluctuating manipulation practiced today. While the imperfect experimental laboratory conditions afforded by the real economy won't allow Friedman's point of view to be either proved or disproved, many economists, businessmen, and philosophers concerned with these matters are thinking seriously about it.

These economists would also like to see the competitive market assume many of the functions, including police and fire protection, the post office, and the conscription of young men for the armed services, that are traditionally assumed by federal, state, or local governments. Many of their ideas have great appeal, if not as sacred dogma, then, at least, as interesting suggestions, given the present circumstances. To cite just one example, during World War II, an all-out war against an obviously evil power, the military draft called virtually every man able to serve, and there were no massive injustices in the system of compulsory conscription. But, during the military actions of the 1960s, such as in the Dominican Republic and Vietnam, about which Americans are not in unanimous agreement, the draft had to become more selective, and, rightly or wrongly, a hue and cry about injustices arose. The solution to this situation, the Chicago School says, is a voluntary military service along laissez faire principles, in which military pay scales would be high enough to hire the adequate number of volunteers and which would probably result in a more equitable, just, and economically efficient military service.

It is an important question whether soldiers can be supplied better by the market than by compulsion. But in many cases, to make the markets function according to completely laissez faire principles would require an inordinate amount of government regulation and control to get rid of the forces that interfere with the free operation of the economy, such as monopolies, unions, and so on. Such regulation would, of course, tend to defeat the original intention. In any case, modern conditions of production and marketing seem to be taking the economy further away from the libertarian ideal, and political or ideological efforts to reverse this trend are unlikely to have much success. Still, there is substantial room for maneuvering between the conservative, noninterventionist approach and the Keynesian approach, whether the problem involves the cyclical application of the neoclassical synthesis or a solution of the structural problems. Economists can try to explain the cause and effect relationships in the economy and can try to predict accurately what the results of certain policies will be, but only a politically free and economically enlightened electorate can make the final judgment about how much to rely on the market and how much to involve the government. Realism and pragmatism should guide the electorate in this decision; ideological cant will only obscure the truth and pervert the desired outcome.

The healthy economic growth of the United States during the sixties was not only due to endogenous factors arising from within the economy itself, but it was also due to exogenous factors. One such factor was the detente that was reached with the Soviet Union, rather an uneasy one to be sure, but the prospect of the human race incinerating itself in a nuclear holocaust seemed less likely. Although profits can be made in war production, business thrives better on peace and security in the long run. Perhaps the "Pax ballistica" allowed us to have our cake and eat it too on this score. Another factor was the increasingly well-educated labor force, which represented an investment in human capital that was beginning to pay a handsome rate of return. As the figures for 1950 to 1969 show, the number of U.S. students enrolled in higher education per 100,000 inhabitants increased rapidly.[2]

1950	1955	1960	1965	1969
1508	1606	1983	2840	3643

Finally, scientific advances relating to both agriculture and industry also had a powerful effect on efficiency and output during the sixties. New herbicides, plastics, fibers, detergents, paints, jet engines, color television and transistors, lasers, metal-processing methods, and computers were among the many large and small advances that improved existing methods and products and created entirely new ones, all of which contributed to the healthy economic growth.

The Computer

Perhaps, the most important single advance was the development of computers. The computer is essentially a battery of electronic switches that will turn either on or off, yes or no, one or

---

[2] *Statistical Abstract of the United States 1970* (U.S. Bureau of the Census, Washington, D.C., 1970).

zero, in response to an input signal of some kind, and it will record the outcome on magnetic tape, printed paper, or some other medium. When the battery is properly arranged ("programmed" is the professional term), it can compute an enormous number of signals with almost instantaneous speed, with very little human labor involved, and with 100 percent accuracy. This makes it very useful for classifying, sorting, calculating, summarizing, recording, and communicating large quantities of data, mechanizing a process that would otherwise employ hundreds or even thousands of clerks full time. But, in addition to its ability to deal with large quantities, its speed has enabled mechanization to reach a level so dramatically elevated that it is graced with a new name: *automation*.

Before automation, man was the intermediary between the object being worked on and the tool doing the work. Prehistoric man guided his stone ax to hollow out his canoe, and today a power shovel operator does the same to dig the earth. Machines that run automatically, in the traditional sense, are automatic only in that the guidance has been reduced to occasional adjustments, sharpenings, repairs, or whatever the particular process requires. In an automated process, even this guidance is eliminated, as if a robot had taken over the job.

As so often happens with scientific discoveries, one of the first uses of the automated processes was for military purposes rather than for economic ones. The computer was used to hook up a radar system with anti-aircraft artillery to shoot down enemy planes. As illustrated in Figure 26, an approaching enemy airplane, 1, is picked up on radar, and its speed, altitude, and direction are computed. The computer instructs the cannon where to aim and when to fire, 2. If this first shot isn't successful, then the airplane is picked up again on radar in a second sensory event called feedback, its flight is recomputed, the cannon is instructed once again, and the airplane may be successfully shot down this time. If we ignore for the moment the subsidiary processes, like loading the artillery and keeping all the equipment in good repair, the anti-aircraft set-up could be considered a totally automated "closed-loop" system, and enemy airplanes could be shot down even while the soldiers are home on leave.

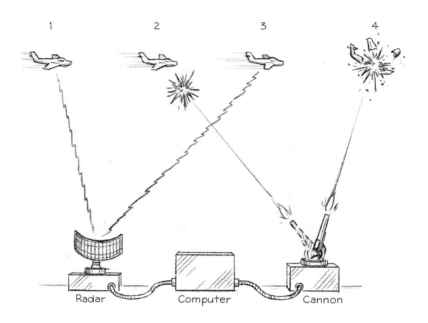

Figure 26. Automation: an anti-aircraft battery.

The army, however, was less interested in making it easy on its soldiers than in increasing the accuracy of the anti-aircraft artillery. Thus, automation, when it is properly set up, can perform tasks far beyond the capabilities of ordinary human beings.

In our (unfortunately) belligerent example in Figure 26, we can distinguish three levels of mechanization. First, the part of the process that packs the punch is the cannon and the explosive shell. Energy here is measured in thousands of foot pounds or in equivalent T.N.T. weights. Second, the servomechanisms, which move the gun around from one position to another and keep the radar screen revolving, require much less energy than the first part, probably measured in horsepower or watts of electricity. Most complex modern machines use these two levels of energy input, whether they are jet planes—which have enormously powerful engines to drive the planes forward as well as hydraulic servomechanisms for operating the wing flaps and many other accessories—or automobiles—which have big gasoline engines for forward motion as well as power brakes, power steering, and an automatically controlled transmission.

The third level of mechanization in Figure 26 is the sensory device in the automated cannon—the radar screen, which transmits signals to the computer, which then computes them and, in turn, transmits signals to the cannon's servomechanisms. These signals are usually of very low electrical wattage, especially those in the computer itself, because they don't have to do anything except signal. This *Kleinstrommechanik*, low wattage circuitry, has been named "cybernetics" by the famous mathematician, Norbert Wiener, after the Greek, *kybernetes*, meaning "steersman," and it is the crucial ingredient in the automation process that senses what's happening, computes the necessary adjustments, and signals the rest of the mechanism what to do.

With its electronic data processing capabilities and its ability to automate processes, the computer has caused radical changes in the horizons of technology. Every field of science, from archeology to zoology, has taken advantage of new research opportunities made practicable by computer mechanization. It has also caused changes in how people earn their living. Agricultural and industrial processes, including everything from hog feeding to steelmaking, have been made more efficient and accurate with the help of the computer. The approximately fifty thousand computers now in use (there were less than two thousand in 1960), of course, replace the labor of many more thousands of workers, and automation has created unemployment among those workers who were not able to get retraining for other jobs. However, the computer is only one of the new production processes that have less and less use for unskilled labor and shouldn't be blamed for all the technological unemployment.

Only about 10 percent of all jobs in the United States can be filled by unskilled labor, and the proportion is decreasing every year. A high school education, which used to be a recommendation for a good job, is now a prerequisite for even the most menial task. The experience of the 1960s has shown that a healthy, growing economy can still absorb many of those considered structurally unemployed into the working labor force, but twentieth century production methods need progressively more quality labor than quantity labor. Education is improving worker quality, and the very fact that automation is primarily useful in those processes that are mechanical and repetitive and not very useful in those processes that involve interpersonal relationships and human sensitivity is a saving grace. The growth industries of an advanced economy, such as hospitals and tourism, stress the latter processes over the former, and this will be a source of new employment opportunities. Still, the fact that technological advance is a great boon to the economy—a source of new employment opportunities and a boost to our standard of living—is no solace to an unskilled worker out of a job.

The effect of the computer on managerial methods has been mainly to increase the capacity of centralized management to control ever larger organizations. Universities, large agencies of the government, and even large church organizations, as well as large businesses couldn't function without it. A vast international enterprise can perform the accounting for all its branches flung out all over the globe with telephone hookups and a computer in its home office, and the accounting can be done more accurately, faster, and more economically than if it were done according to traditional bookkeeping methods at every branch. Inventory management, payroll, personnel and customer records, quality control, market research, statistical analysis, and all management functions that involve the processing of large amounts of data have been computerized to good effect. Not only are old manual processes thus mechanized, but the computer enables management to tackle problems rationally that could only be guessed at before. Problem solving that involves so much data and so many computations that the problem itself would have changed by the time a manually computed answer was available now becomes feasible with the rapid electronic computer.

Among the most important new techniques of business management that rely on computers to make them tick are such esoterica as linear programming, optimal path and critical path, queue theory, and simulation. What they all have in common is the ability to handle masses of data within the framework of very complex interrelationships. These interrelationships, often consisting of hundreds of mathematical functions, are extracted from the problem by systems analysts and form the basis of the program that is "plugged in" to the computer to instruct it in what to do. All this has to be expressed in a "language" that the computer can be made capable of receiving, usually FOR-TRAN—which stands for "formula translator"—or COBOL—"common business-oriented language." The program instructions are compiled in a "program deck" of I.B.M. cards, magnetic tape, magnetic disks, or some other medium to communicate the input signal to the computer. The data, also accumulated on the cards or on some other medium, can then be fed into the computer, which, following its programmed instructions with a blind, idiotic fidelity, processes the data and produces an answer. This process may seem like a needlessly roundabout way to improve the firm's efficiency and profitability just another notch. But the beauty of the technique is that once it is set up, it can be used over and over again. The computer can be fed fresh data as often as necessary and can supply instant answers to problems or keep them in a kind of constant state of solution. Even if the basic interrelationships should change somewhat, as will always happen sooner or later in the dynamic business environment, the program itself can be altered by replacing the particular I.B.M. cards in the program deck that contain the obsolete instructions with new instructions.

SOME MATHEMATICAL ECONOMICS

One of the most effective early applications of computer technology to economics was in input-output analysis, first developed by Harvard University's Wassily W. Leontief in the 1940s and 1950s. This analysis is a sophisticated modern version of the physiocrats' economic table illustrated in Table 2. But instead of distinguishing three sectors of the economy—the farmers, the landowners, and the sterile classes—as the physiocrats did, modern input-output analysis may distinguish as many as 370 separate sectors, including such specific industrial groups as engines and turbines, tobacco manufactures, tires and inner tubes, apparel, and insurance. All the sectors are set up on a table like the physiocrats' economic table, and the best possible estimates of the sales from each sector to each other sector are made for a given year.

Given these estimates, it is then assumed that even though the economy may grow or shrink over the next few years, the general proportionality of the sales between the sectors won't change because it is fixed by the state of economic development, the market and resource patterns, and the level of technology in the economy, all of which change relatively slowly. Therefore, these estimates may be expressed as ratios instead of absolute dollar amounts. Then, when new consumption levels for the whole economy or for specific sectors wish to be hypothesized, by using sophisticated algebraic techniques and then feeding the data to the computer, one may calculate the resulting changes throughout all the sectors of the economy.

Thus, unlike the physiocrats' economic table (Table 2) or the circular flow diagram (Figure 11), which served only as descriptive analyses of the economy, the input-output analysis, with the help of computer technology, can be used as a predictive tool. For example, in times of war, it is very helpful to know in advance if a planned expansion in armaments production would be threatened by another sector's inability to expand proportionately unless some changes were made in that sector too. Perhaps, before more tanks can be produced, more railroad cars will have to be manufactured in order to transport them. In peacetime, input-output analysis can be used to predict, for example, how much the textile industry will have to expand in order to accommodate an increase in automobile production (textiles are used in automobile upholstery, head liners, etc.).

Another econometric (the name often given to mathematical economics) analysis that is simple enough to describe here but will still give a good indication of how complex the mathematical models can be is the Theil and Boot version of the Lawrence Klein econometric model of the United States between the two world wars. It is a Keynesian type of model in which $Y = C + I + G$, except that it is much larger, and, of course, the mathematical relationships between the variables are specified. The model consists of six equations. There are six unknowns, the dependent variables, which are: consumption, C; profits, P; investment, I; the stock of capital goods, K; production in the private sector of the economy, X; and wages paid in the private sector of the economy, W_1. And there are seven known independent variables; they are: last year's profits, P_{-1}; last year's capital stock, K_{-1}; last year's production in the private sector, X_{-1}; wages paid in the public sector, W_2; business taxes, T; government expenditures, G; and an annual adjustment for union activity, $t - 1931$.[3] Each of the six equations also has a constant term that serves as the floor on which the mathematical relationships are built. For simplicity, the equations are listed in Table 9, with the mathematical coefficients listed in the columns below their respective terms.

Table 9. An econometric model*

Dependent variable	Con-stant	INDEPENDENT VARIABLE						
		P_{-1}	K_{-1}	X_{-1}	W_2	T	G	$t-1931$
C $=$	41.8	$+0.74$	-0.10	$+0.19$	$+1.34$	-0.19	$+0.67$	$+0.16$
P $=$	38.1	$+0.86$	-0.16	-0.06	$+0.90$	-1.28	$+1.12$	-0.05
I $=$	26.6	$+0.75$	-0.18	-0.01	$+0.21$	-0.30	$+0.26$	-0.01
K $=$	26.6	$+0.75$	$+0.82$	-0.01	$+0.21$	-0.30	$+0.26$	-0.01
X $=$	68.4	$+1.49$	-0.28	$+0.17$	$+1.54$	-0.48	$+1.93$	$+0.14$
W_1 $=$	30.3	$+0.63$	-0.12	$+0.24$	$+0.65$	-0.20	$+0.81$	$+0.20$

Source: Adapted from Henri Theil, John C. G. Boot, and Teun Kloek, *Operations Research and Quantitative Economics* (McGraw-Hill, New York, 1965), p. 84; first appeared in Theil and Boot, "The Final Form of Econometric Equation Systems," *Review of the International Statistical Institute*, 30:136–152 (1962).

* For example, the first equation reads:

$$C = 41.8 + 0.74P_{-1} - 0.10K_{-1} + 0.19X_{-1} + 1.34W_2 - 0.19T + 0.67G + 0.16(t - 1931),$$

the second equation reads:

$$P = 38.1 + 0.86P_{-1} - 0.16K_{-1} - 0.06X_{-1} + 0.90W_2 - 1.28T + 1.12G - 0.05(t - 1931),$$

etc.

---

[3] This adjustment is the number derived by subtracting 1931 from the year being analyzed, say, 1937: $1937 - 1931 = 6$.

When the known values of the independent variables are plugged in, the values of the dependent variables will be obtained. That is the purpose of the whole exercise. To arrive at this point took an heroic amount of empirical and theoretical research over many years, reams of data, and some hard-nosed mathematical work. The model can be kept up to date by introducing new data, revising the coefficients, and, perhaps introducing new variables and eliminating old ones.

The reader may be interested in toying with the relationships. For example, a one billion dollar tax cut (T decreases by one billion) will increase consumption (C) by \$190,000,000 (see the first equation in Table 9) and will increase wages paid in the private sector (W_1) by \$200,000,000 (see the last equation in Table 9). In the same way, one can calculate the effect of a one billion dollar increase in government expenditures, G, on any of the dependent variables. And so on.

THE AFFLUENT CORPORATION ECONOMY

The compound effect of the technological progress and the rapidly growing markets, caused by the increasing population and the increasing standard of living in the United States, has been to favor large organizations. Of course, there is also a growing number of small firms, little shops, family-owned businesses and farms, and engineering companies with only a few dozen employees, but many of these are so closely tied to the giants in their industries that they behave more like divisions of large corporations than like independent businesses. The essence of American industrial structure is to be found in the giant corporation: General Motors, Standard Oil, Prudential, American Telephone and Telegraph, Sears, Lytton Industries, and other such huge firms. They are able to make use of the labor force to the highest degree of specialization that is possible with modern production and management technologies. And they have enough influence to control the forces that affect their business environment, their suppliers and their customers; no longer can they be buffeted about helplessly by whatever the markets dictate. The modern, large corporation has reached the point where it can actively steer its own course rather than be passively blown about by external winds.

In his book *The New Industrial State*,[4] John Kenneth Galbraith stresses this autonomy of the firm. According to his theory, autonomy is a natural outgrowth of modern technology, which requires long periods of planning and preparation because of its complexity, and which needs, therefore, a business environment where the quantities supplied and demanded and prices are as predictable as possible over a span of several years. Such security cannot be achieved in a free and open market; thus, the large firm makes every effort to control the market. It manages its sources of supply by using its bargaining power as a very large purchaser, by signing long-term contracts with its suppliers, and by becoming its own supplier—buying up the smaller supply firms or creating its own supply divisions, a tactic called vertical integration. The firm can use the same tactics to assure its steady demand if it sells to other firms. But if it sells to the consumer, the firm must seek to assure its demand by less direct, but not necessarily less effective, means such as advertising, building brand loyalties, making product design appealing, and controlling the retail outlets. With the supply of its materials and the demand for its products well secured, the large American corporation can shift into high gear, plan for years ahead, and begin to use the complex technology to the fullest extent, all of which will make it one of the most efficient producers in the world.

The inside group of managers, who run the whole show in the modern corporation, make up the "technostructure," a term coined by Galbraith. They are the specialists in electronics, industrial chemistry, product design, market research, labor relations, personnel, advertising media, production management, finance, cost analysis, computerized accounting, and the many other specialized fields of business administration to which the well-trained intelligence can apply its efforts. Because the de-

---

[4] John Kenneth Galbraith, *The New Industrial State* (Houghton Mifflin, Boston, 1969).

cisions made by these specialists cannot be evaluated by someone outside that specialty, they each have a very large amount of autonomy, and, taken as a group, the technostructure runs the firm unimpeded. Certainly, the owners of the firm, the capitalist stockholders whom Marx envisioned as the architects of exploitation, have hardly anything to say about the operation of the business. As long as the corporation meets its dividends and shows a healthy growth, the stockholders will not even bother to attend the annual meeting, which may be held in some obscure and inaccessible New Jersey auditorium, just to make sure that they don't attend. Corporate takeovers rarely happen to successful businesses.

Neither does the board of directors exert much managerial discretion. Unless members of the technostructure are themselves on the board, all the information this peak of the executive pyramid has to go on is fed to it from its specialists lower down, and the board functions as a particularly well-paid rubber stamp. Labor, which used to have some influence on management through the forces of the labor market and collective bargaining, has found its power waning. The advanced technology brings more and more of the labor force into the lower echelons of the technostructure itself, with which they identify themselves rather than with the labor movement. The remaining non-technostructure labor represents such a small proportion of the firm's total costs of production that it can either be given all its demands, or it can be ignored and eventually replaced by machines. Finally, the consumer, supposedly the sovereign in the marketplace, is manipulated into a predictable demand position by the effective forces of advertising and related techniques.

So, only the technostructure, of all the groups that are served by the corporation—the owners, the directors, labor, and the consumers—has any real influence on the way the firm is operated. Not even the economy's other institutions, the banking and financial communities, can break the technostructure's autonomy. The very large corporation is not as dependent on outside capital for its investments as smaller firms are. Most of its investment comes from its own undistributed profits, and when it does borrow, its needs are so gigantic that one bank or investment company can seldom handle it alone, and, as it has done with many of its suppliers, the corporation has gained the power of monopsony, the power of being the only buyer in the market.

Even the government cannot influence the technostructure's autonomy by the usual methods. For example, the monetary policy of the Federal Reserve Board, credit tightening or loosening, affects mostly small businesses, like housing construction contractors. The big firms, since they invest their own funds, remain largely unfazed by fluctuations in the Board's policies. But they do depend on the government to keep the general economic conditions stable and growing because nothing could be more disastrous to its best-laid plans than to have a serious depression or a runaway inflation. In fact, the big government intervention and Keynesian expansionist policies that accompanied the healthy economy of the 1960s were greeted with solid approval by the business community of large corporations because they realized how essential this economic well-being is to the success of their long-run planning. Only the smaller businessmen still mistrust the government and lend support to the laissez faire ideology.

Galbraith argues that since the government of an advanced, industrial, twentieth century nation is subject to the same technological advances as its large businesses, it too has developed a technostructure with substantial autonomy, and the business and government technostructures work together like the blood brothers that they are. In many undertakings where private capital and the government cooperate, such as aerospace and atomic energy, it is impossible to tell where the one technostructure begins and the other ends. In modern socialist and communist countries, the same kind of technostructure has developed and is working hard to win its autonomy, not from stockowners or the forces of a free market, but from the interferences of party officials and parliamentary controls. Until such autonomy is granted, long-run planning can always be upset by political considerations, and the technostructure won't be able to operate at full efficiency.

American corporations recognized this need for autonomy earlier than those in any other nation, and their astuteness goes far to explain why American businesses have grown so rapidly on foreign soil recently. To be sure, the large American firms have consistently spent more on research and development ("R and D") than their European cousins and are technologically superior to them. Also prodigious amounts of American investment capital have flowed overseas, often taking its own managements with it. But, as the Frenchman Jean-Jacques Servan-Schreiber writes in his book *Le défi Americain*,[5] Americans have superior methods of organization, by which he means the technostructure's autonomy.

The central motivating force in the affluent corporation economy, as long as it is not avowedly communist, is still the maximization of profits, but only indirectly. The technostructure does measure its success by the profits of its corporations, but the largest part of these profits remains with the firm and is invested in new corporate growth, because a technostructure's real measure of success is how rapidly the corporation is increasing its share of the market and how large it has become. Pointedly, the technostructure, itself, does not get to pocket the profits, but high salaries do exist and are a mark of distinction. Profiteering—in the spirit of an Astor, Vanderbilt, or John D. Rockefeller—has no place in the new scheme. Of course, budding tycoons still take great pride in earning their first million, but many more rising young executives take as great a pride in launching a new detergent on the market, being part of the team that built both the public image and the reality of a Mustang or Barracuda, opening up Mexico for Campbell's Soup, or pushing a cigarette to the top in sales. These are the goals and aspirations with which the members of the technostructure achieve their personal identity. Certainly they will become affluent in the process, but wealth prized for all the glories it can bring, à la King Farouk or Shah Jahan—who built the Taj Mahal—is somehow indecent and definitely un-American.

It is comforting, in this age when personal identity crises seem to be endemic, to find that the corporation serves as a rallying

---

[5] Jean-Jacques Servan-Schreiber, *The American Challenge*, English transl. (Atheneum, New York, 1968).

point around which intelligent, up-and-coming adults can identify themselves. It is, nevertheless, very much like putting the
cart before the horse, for we shouldn't forget the pride that
comes with creative accomplishment—a well-turned-out hand
ax, a neatly sewn dress, a fat herd of pigs, even an interesting
book on economics. But the goals with which the technostructure
identifies itself are on a different wavelength. For them, the
sense of accomplishment lies not in the actual creating of the
best detergent soap, or that glamorous sports car, or even that
best-selling cigarette, but in boosting those sales and increasing
the size of the corporation. What the technostructure wants to
accomplish is to hit the top of the sales charts and to make its
corporation number one.

And in order to accomplish these goals, the technostructure
has to reverse the economic sequence: the affluent corporation
economy doesn't produce in order to consume; it consumes in
order to produce. Goods must be sold, new products must be
developed, the competition must be met, the corporation's image
must be polished, advertising and public relations campaigns
must be invented, and whether or not all these achievements
are of any help to man's economic welfare is beside the point.
That, indeed, some advertising and some products may actually
cheapen and shorten life is inadmissible evidence. The possibility that the affluent corporation economy may be becoming
a perverse treadmill seems to elude those who are caught up in
the admittedly interesting and sometimes even exciting career
of accomplishing top billing for their corporation. No wonder
that many of the children of affluence, who see the picture with
fresh eyes, are disenchanted by what they see.

However, there seems to be little possibility of escape from
the affluent corporation economy; it seems to be a fait accompli
of modern industrialization. Although Americans are freer than
ever before in many ways, increasing numbers are chained to
the nine-to-five lockstep of their jobs, the color television, the
boat trailer, and the power lawnmower. Nonconformity to these
materialist ideals is difficult and costly. Very few people can
choose their own pace and their own hours of work. When most

Americans were farmers, they were free to be lazy farmers if they wanted to accept the decreased income. But what corporation office today would tolerate an employee who chose to work only on Wednesdays and Thursdays, even if he agreed to a proportional wage cut? And mass production means mass consumption so that there is very little room for individual consumer preferences. The vast majority of Americans, the rich and middle class alike, must all watch the same television, if they want to watch at all, drive along the same highways in essentially the same cars, eat the same breakfasts, and be clothed in the same wash-and-wear fabrics. For all their money, the rich are as imprisoned in standardized mold of industrial affluence as the rest of us. In such circumstances, individualism takes the form of the cultivation of very subtle differences. Styles that are "in" or "out" take on importance far out of proportion to their reality. And those who don't care to play this artificial game often appear to be society's "dropouts," strange souls who incur the fear and mistrust of the complacent majority.

The existence of such a dominant mainstream makes life very hard for those who are unable to get caught up in its affluent current. Poverty is an abnormality in such a society, and the physically or mentally handicapped, the geographically isolated, and especially the victims of prejudice and segregation live a life apart in ostracism. The poverty is not merely the age-old problem of living with a low income; it is more like being a foreigner in one's own country. The institutions of this almost universally affluent society are not designed to include nonconforming parts; the result is that these parts are consigned to living only among themselves. This is true of all social institutions, whether they are formally organized, like a school system, in which the poor are typically segregated de facto into inferior schools, or an informal structure, like the national diet. Poor Americans, whose family incomes are below 3000 dollars per year, though still richer than, let's say, the average Asian today, whose family income is not even half of that, still eat worse than those Asians because the mainstream American diet, which includes fresh milk, frozen foods, plenty of meat, fresh fruit in any season, and many processed foods, is out of their financial reach. There are few dietary alternatives in America for the poor because the supermarkets must serve the majority. A large proportion of the food bill of poor people goes to such readily available hunger palliatives as popsicles, soda, and chewing gum, and their physical health, if it ever existed, is gradually destroyed accordingly.

By contrast, the Asians, in spite of their relative poverty, eat the normal national diet: mainly rice, a little fish and meat, and fresh vegetables. This diet has evolved over thousands of years and is quite adequate, at times even ample. It is within the financial reach of the poor; in a sense, it was designed for them. Although they are relatively poorer than America's poorest class, they are better fed, and the telltale signs of diet poverty—poor health, misshapen children, a high frequency of obesity because of a heavy sugar and starch intake—are not nearly as common as in American slums.

The sin most often attributed to the affluent corporation economy is materialism. Of course, the main concern of any economy is the production of the material wherewithal to sustain life and provide comfort, and only the ascetic would quibble with that aim. That the Industrial Revolution culminated in the present deluge of consumer goods that are enjoyed in the advanced economies of the world is also a sign more of success than of sin. But there is in every age and in every society the tendency to emphasize that which can be done well and to deemphasize those things done less easily. The Industrial Revolution did usher in an age of materialism, both as a feature of everyday living and as a philosophic principle. This materialism has certainly contributed to the emptiness of life, especially now that it has spread to the broad masses in the advanced economies. But that it is a less worthy modus vivendi than the militarism of ancient Rome or the dogmatism of medieval Europe is questionable. Material ease, at least, provides the opportunity, if not the motive, to work toward higher achievements in the more exalted levels of culture.

But as a philosophy, it comes off poorly. Materialism's very attainability is its undoing. The tough-minded materialistic realism aspired to by hard-line communists loses its urgency when affluence is around the corner, as the Russians are beginning to find out. Supposedly God-fearing and God-serving Americans have always publicly disclaimed materialism as a philosophy, aspiring instead to "perfect virtue," an unattainable goal for ordinary mortals. As the rapidly diminishing returns of affluence set in, Americans can rejoice that the quest for virtue gives us an undiminished goal toward which to strive. And while all this may sound just a little facetious, it is probably what was behind the popularity of the Peace Corps and other similar undertakings. If there is a philosophical generation gap between the idealistic youth and the materialistic establishment in Western society, then this quest may well be the reason for it.

ECONOMICS AND THE UNIVERSE

Perhaps more peculiarly, the vice of the affluent corporation economy is not so much its materialism in consumption as its materialism in production. We have seen that the normal sequence has been reversed for many Americans. Corporate growth and increased sales have become the motives with which a large and important segment of society is identified, and these motives have already led to some strange behavior. How much of the arms race between the United States and the Soviet Union is really just two giant industrial societies doing what comes naturally, competing with each other in terms of the production of large quantities of highly sophisticated articles? When both nations already have an overkill capacity that exceeds their enemy's population by multiples of that population, can national security be the only reason for their continued expansion of war machines? Will "police actions" in underdeveloped nations, like the war in Vietnam, be seen by future historians as merely another exercise in the production of mountains of military hardware, simply because that's what American industry can do, even if this hardware is often inapplicable to that kind of bamboo-spear and dirt-tunnel warfare? Must we continue to foul our environment in the blind rush to produce more and more goods, many of them necessary only because of the fouled environment? Cars with which to escape the uninhabitable cities and to flee to the suburbs every evening? Air conditioners to cleanse and cool the filthy air and to shut out the din of traffic? And pills to soothe the nerves jangled by the frenetic pace? Surely it is legitimate to question the sanity of all this.

Pollution has grown to dire proportions in the advanced countries. The streams, rivers, and lakes are carrying so much sewage, industrial wastes, and trash, that the water's biota, mostly bacteria, cannot get enough dissolved oxygen to digest and degrade all these substances into their basic chemical components—nitrogen, phosphorus, and carbon. Instead, the substances are anaerobically transformed into an even more revolting fetid sludge. The waste from a single wood pulp mill equals the sewage of a large city. Even a major river, like the Ohio or the Hudson, is overwhelmed by the several mills, two or three thermal electric plants, and the several cities that disgorge their wastes into it. Furthermore, the abundant nitrogen and phosphorus from the wastes that can be successfully degraded are plant nutrients on which water algae feed. As the volume of these wastes increases, the nutrients increase, and the algae population increases, until our lakes and streams are filled to the top with thriving, green slime. All the while, heat from industrial cooling systems, especially electric power plants, threatens to turn these vile waters into uninhabitable tepid soup.

The atmosphere, too, is sorely burdened. The millions of years' worth of organic material, which was locked under the earth's surface during the carboniferous period and which trapped the carbon dioxide that had served as the earth's atmospheric greenhouse, is now being dug up. As the coal, oil, and gas are being burned, the carbon dioxide of 300,000,000 years ago is reintroduced to the air. The carbon dioxide level has increased rapidly during the recent centuries of industrialization, and it is less than whimsical to imagine dinosaurs wallowing in thick fern marshes once again at the North Pole.

In a much more sinister prediction, Rachel Carson writes in

Silent Spring[6] that some bright and sunny morning we will wake up to find the whole world around us dead. The burning of fossil fuels and the chemical processes of agriculture and industry are choking the atmosphere with uncountable tons of waste. When some of these substances, especially the hydrocarbons resulting from incompletely burned fuels, are oxidized and transformed by photochemical reactions in the air, they become particularly noxious and suffocating. Deadly chemicals are accumulating in the tissue of plants and animals, including humans, as the use of pesticides and herbicides is multiplying. Before World War II these were usually simple poisons, like copper sulfate and arsenate of lead, which are easily diluted or washed away. Since then, the chlorinated hydrocarbons, like DDT, lindane, and 2,4-D, and the organic phosphorus compounds, like parathion and malathion, have been widely used, and they tend to concentrate in the fatty tissues of living organisms. Traces of DDT have been found in plant and animal tissues everywhere in the world, from northern Greenland to Antarctica. The concentration has become deadly in species at the top of the food chain, like eagles (and man), who eat polluted animals that have eaten polluted vegetation growing in polluted soils and waters. Whether the pollution is throat-ticklingly and eye-smartingly obvious, like the smog that plagues every major and many minor cities in the modern world, or whether it is stealthily insidious, like the accumulation of DDT in our fatty tissues, its destructive effects are not yet completely understood and may be much worse than now expected.

The pollution dilemma revolves around the paradox that while everbody is against pollution on principle, those that cause it have important reasons to continue, and those common citizens that suffer from it are not in the position to pull the strings that will do something about it. Furthermore, it is usually the huge size of the population concentrations and the large scale of the agriculture and the industry, rather than the individual people, farms, or businesses, that overtax the environment and cause ordinary economic processes to become polluting.

---

[6] Rachel Carson, *Silent Spring* (Houghton Mifflin, Boston, 1962).

And, as always, it is difficult to impose on the mass of society restrictions that seem unusual and unnatural and that have never been imposed on the members of that society individually. Proposed antipollution laws are often resisted on the basis that they distribute the burden unfairly and that they restrict individual freedoms and the rights of property. Especially, local and regional laws are resisted on the basis that they will present an unequal burden to the local taxpayer and put the local industries at a competitive disadvantage. Until enough individuals across the country become articulate in their concern about pollution and create their own social weight of opinion, the dilemma will persist.

Until recently, economists have not been particularly carried away with concern over the environmental problems caused by industrial development. Just as in the other sciences, the few economists researching, writing, and teaching today who have always sounded an alarm over the issues of the environment are somewhat out of the mainstream. These humanist concerns seem to have gone out of style after the age of classical economics. Even the conventional analytical models of contemporary economics seem to prefer to exclude these concerns by ignoring them entirely or by shunting them off onto their own branch, called "economic externalities." These externalities include any "given" or windfall factor, such as the availability of transportation, technological know-how, a labor force, or resources, factors that are not themselves directly involved in the economic analysis of markets and businesses. For example, the regularly bright and sunny weather of Hollywood was considered an external economy of the movie industry there. The movie moguls, no matter how tyrannical, could neither turn on nor turn off the sun. But as the surrounding community grew and the smog thickened, the weather became an external *dis*economy.

In very recent years, concern over these economic externalities has grown. The environmentalists are beginning to be included in the mainstream. The literature is growing, and professional meetings include sessions on environmental economics. Attempts are even being made to extend the theoretical framework to include the changes in the environment caused by economic activity. Figure 27, the Materials Flow of the Economy, illustrates this approach, which sees the human race living on a "space ship earth" in which all inputs and outputs, all the original resources and all the final wastes, must be accounted for. In this perspective, "final consumption" isn't final at all. In fact, in terms of mass and energy, as much is returned to the earth as is taken from it. Furthermore, when the materials are returned in the form of smoke, sewage, garbage, junk, heat, noise, and a wide variety of noxious gases, the world becomes a very changed place—and the change is seldom for the better.

Implicit in this materials flow concept of the economy is that the less production that is needed to maintain an adequate level of affluence, the better. An efficient economy is one that gets big results with little effort. More industries, more mines, more businesses, more employment, and more consumer goods do not always mean more well-being for the people because all these also mean more destruction of our natural resources and despoilation of our surroundings. In some heavily polluted areas, such as Los Angeles, New York, the Ruhr Valley, and Tokyo, the people are beginning to worry that "more means less." Ultimately, all economists will have to face the problem of the environment head on because at the root of the problem is the economic activity of the human race.

Conservationists, of course, have been concerned about our environment and fighting for reforms for a long time. They seem to have two perspectives on the problem. Some, the nature lovers, argue that modern man must learn to walk the face of this earth more gently. Nature must be preserved, and the sweet forests and streams must be protected against the march of progress, which often leaves such blighting tracks. Humanity must leave nature to itself again and must obey its laws. Other conservationists consider it a management problem. They recognize that practically no blade of grass or gust of wind anywhere on this globe is completely immune to man's interference. Therefore, the total environment must be as carefully managed as that in an astronaut's space ship, which is precisely what the earth is, except on a very large scale. Perhaps, in their specific programs, these two perspectives will prove to have much in common.

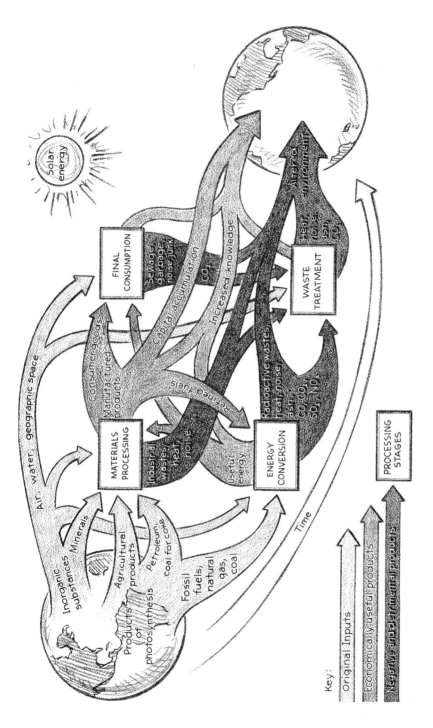

Figure 27. Materials flow of the economy.

The headlong rush to consumption for production's sake seems particularly destructive when we realize that our present pattern of natural resource availability is not inexhaustible. To be sure, the dire and recurring predictions that the earth will have given its last drop of oil within twenty years are drowned out by the frequent discovery of rich, new oil fields; the same is true with coal, iron, and most of our other natural resources. But a unique characteristic of the Industrial Revolution was its reliance on funded resources of fuels, metals, and minerals, on which our extraordinary twentieth century affluence is based. These funds, the concentrations of coal in the ground, the iron ore, the petroleum, the bauxite, and so on, all accumulated hundreds of millions of years ago and, obviously, without any help from mankind. They are accidents of history and are unreproducible. Of course, what is and what isn't a natural resource is subject to very rapid change. We have seen that just over a century ago petroleum was merely a curiosity and a nuisance. Perhaps some day steel will be made from beach pebbles and space ships will run on lawn clippings. But the tendency of our present age is to use up pre-concentrated funds of resources and to disperse the wastes to the four winds.

Every living species seeks pre-concentrated resources. The roots of grass search for moist and fertile soil, sheep seek the greenest grass, and we eat lamb chops and wear tweeds. Perhaps the level of concentration increases with the complexity of the species, but in the end, whether it's a blade of grass or one of us, we return again to the soil, "ashes to ashes, dust to dust." What distinguishes the Industrial Revolution is that because of it man has searched higher and lower than ever before for funded resources. Where, for aeons, he used only the top six inches or so of the earth's land for farming, he now uses the planet many thousands of feet down to the deepest pockets of oil and gas. And in doing so, these funds are destroyed, but their wastes become, again, mere dispersed ashes—mere dust. Unless we want to return to a pre-industrial standard of living, with an attendant decrease in population, we will have to learn how to avoid exhausting and polluting those naturally funded resources we already have; we will have to find new resources; and we will have to learn how to concentrate those potential resources, like solar energy, which presently exist only in relative dispersion.

So we have come full cycle. We are once again concerned with air, water, and land, just as we were when we began on page one. Although the main focus of economics tends today to be on the relationships between people as individuals and between people and their various organizations, we must remember that we are still earthlings. When the total human population has doubled, as it is supposed to do by the twenty-first century or so, man's economic relationships to the physical universe may be very different. And so will all his other economic relationships. The story of economics is, by no means, over. Who knows what the future will bring? The plot thickens!

CHAPTER 11

On Further Study

Every time a meteorologist steps out of his front door, he is on a field trip. The weather, be it good or bad, is the subject of his science. To almost the same degree, every time the economist observes any activity caused by man, he is also on a field trip.

Often the sight observed is very impressive. Looking at the New York City panorama from the New Jersey approach ramp to the Lincoln Tunnel or from the top of one of the city's own skyscrapers, who can fail to be thrilled at the sight of this great economic heart beating? Highways, railroads, ocean ships, airplanes, transmission lines, and radio towers are bringing in and sending out goods, energy, people, and information. Factories and offices staffed with millions of people are busy processing the energy, goods, and information. Thousands of restaurants, laundries, hotels, office supply shops, apartment houses, subways, hospitals, movie houses, and so on service the needs of the people and the industries that make the city go. All over the world, views like this of the major cities are popular with tourists, but the perceptive student of economics will be able to see much more than the ordinary traveler. At least in his mind's eye, he will be able to see how the city relates to the countryside and the rest of the world, how it affects the standard of living, how it is an indicator of the level of economic development, how it is the repository of much of the entire economy's wealth and knowledge.

Impressive economic field trips are not confined to city panoramas, of course. Large and small insights may be gained from noting the items the woman in front of you unloads out of her market basket at the supermarket check-out counter. Insights may be gained from working in a factory or on a farm—working anywhere for that matter—from reading advertisements and watching television, from visiting other people's homes, from driving through farm country and listening to the talk at a farmers' auction. Economic insights may even be gained from visiting untouched forests and open land where no commercial development has taken place at all. For some students, looking down on the green, gold, and brown checkerboard of the Midwestern farmlands from an airplane may have more meaning. For others, the relationships with their boss, their parents, or their children may give them even more economic understanding of how the world comes to grips with the basic economic problem, earning a living.

Some of the best "field trips" involve no travel. Most novels, movies, and plays can enrich our economic understanding in some way. D. H. Lawrence's descriptions of the industrializing of England in *Lady Chatterley's Lover* are among the best in all literature and should give that book enough "redeeming social value" to satisfy even the most blue-nosed puritan. Philip Roth's description of the standard of living achievable through a small, private proprietorship in an advanced economy in *Goodbye, Columbus* and Boris Pasternak's recounting of the economic breakdown caused by political revolution in *Doctor Zhivago* are, each in their own way, worthy economic case studies. Even Wagner's *Die Meistersinger von Nürnberg* and Arthur Miller's *Death of a Salesman* could be considered. They give two very different views of life in two very different urban economies at two very different periods of history. Indeed, some economic awareness may even be prerequisite to the full appreciation of these books, plays, and operas. Virginia Woolf's *Orlando* must be quite bewildering to the economically ignorant.

In short, economics is all around us, and we should cultivate the experience of it in many ways besides formal study. But, of course, formal study is the main avenue to economic understanding. Joseph A. Schumpeter is reputed to have made the purist claim that the best way to study economics is to study history and mathematics. Even the non-purist would have to agree that these two subjects contribute greatly to economic education, as would many other diverse subjects, such as sociology, psychology, geography, agriculture, urban studies, the law, engineering, public health, transportation, computer programming, and the closely related field of business and public administration. A great many different interests can find satisfaction in the study of economics. The American Economic Association officially catalogues its members according to thirty-six different areas of specialization, but among its nearly 20,000 members there must be thousands of different enthusiasms and points of view. And the best way to serve all of these is to study economics directly.

Some of the classic works of economics mentioned or described in this book would contribute much to the beginning student. Of course, they often seem old-fashioned now, but the classics do give the reader an idea of the development of the science. Besides, dealing with the original often has a far greater impact than dealing with a second- or third-hand interpretation. Among the suggested classics for the beginning student are:

Adam Smith, *An Inquiry into the Nature and Causes of the Wealth of Nations.*

David Ricardo, *Principles of Political Economy and Taxation.*

Thomas R. Malthus, *Essay on the Principle of Population.*
　　All of the above are conveniently available now in paperback through Irwin Paperback Classics in Economics, Richard D. Irwin, Homewood, Ill.

John Stuart Mill, *Principles of Political Economy*. In a great variety of editions.

Karl Marx, *Das Kapital*. Especially in the condensed version of Modern Library, New York, or in the full three volumes of International Publishers, New York, 1967, but rather hard-going in either edition.

Alfred Marshall, *Principles of Economics*, 9th ed. (Macmillan, New York, 1961).

Eugen Von Böhm-Bawerk, *Positive Theory of Capital*, William Smart transl. (G. E. Stechert, New York, 1891).

John Maynard Keynes, *The General Theory of Employment, Interest, and Money* (Harcourt, Brace, New York, 1936). Worth reading even though often somewhat opaque.

There are, of course, many more classics by almost anyone's definition, but many of them are better suited to more advanced studies. The beginner with a good mathematical background may want to dip into:

Antoine Augustin Cournot, *Researches into the Mathematical Principles of the Theory of Wealth* (Irwin Paperback Classics in Economics, Richard D. Irwin, Homewood, Ill., 1963).

Then there are the books that perhaps can't be called classics but that are, at least, landmarks in the science. Every economist has his own favorite list. A few of the many that are accessible to the beginner are:

Wesley C. Mitchell, *Types of Economic Theory: From Mercantilism to Institutionalism* (Augustus M. Kelley, New York, 1967), 2 vols.

R. H. Tawney, *Religion and the Rise of Capitalism* (New American Library, New York, 1947).

M. I. Rostovtzeff, *Social and Economic History of the Roman Empire* (Oxford University Press, New York, 1957), 2 vols.

Thorstein Veblen, *The Theory of the Leisure Class* (New American Library, New York, 1954). Quite relevant even today.

Joseph A. Schumpeter, *Capitalism, Socialism, and Democracy*, 3rd ed. (Harper & Brothers, New York, 1950).

———, *History of Economic Analysis* (Oxford University Press, New York, 1954).

A. C. Pigou, *Economics of Welfare*, 4th ed. (St. Martin's Press, New York, 1932).

Frank H. Knight, *Risk, Uncertainty, and Profit* (Harper & Row, New York, 1965).

Edward H. Chamberlin, *The Theory of Monopolistic Competition: A Re-Orientation of the Theory of Value*, 8th ed. (Harvard University Press, Cambridge, Mass., 1962).

Joan Robinson, *The Economics of Imperfect Competition* (St. Martin's Press, New York, 1933).

J. R. Hicks, *Value and Capital: An Inquity into Some Fundamental Principles of Economic Theory*, 2nd ed. (Clarendon Press, Oxford, 1946).

W. W. Rostow, *The Stages of Economic Growth, a Non-Communist Manifesto* (Cambridge University Press, Cambridge, 1960).

George Katona, *The Powerful Consumer* (McGraw-Hill, New York, 1960).

Paul A. Samuelson, *Foundations of Economic Analysis* (Harvard University Press, Cambridge, Mass., 1947). This one is recommended only for the mathematically astute.

Milton Friedman, *Essays in Positive Economics* (University of Chicago Press, Chicago, 1966).

John Kenneth Galbraith, *The New Industrial State* (Houghton Mifflin, Boston, 1969).

Of course, there are many good textbooks on all aspects of economics, and the student will find in them the most convenient source of information. Space will permit only a few to be listed here. The following, categorized by special subject, is a rather arbitrary selection of standard texts, which should be available in most academic libraries and book stores.

ECONOMIC HISTORY

Shepard B. Clough, *European Economic History: The Economic Development of Western Civilization*, 2nd ed. (McGraw-Hill, New York, 1968). One of the most readable and thorough books on the subject.

Edward C. Kirkland, *A History of American Economic Life*, 4th ed. (Appleton-Century-Crofts, New York, 1969).

HISTORY OF ECONOMIC THOUGHT

Jacob Oser, *The Evolution of Economic Thought*, 2nd ed. (Harcourt, Brace and World, New York, 1970). Particularly well written.

Eric Roll, *A History of Economic Thought*, 3rd ed. (Prentice-Hall, Englewood Cliffs, N.J., 1942).

Robert L. Heilbroner, *The Worldly Philosophers*, rev. ed. (Simon and Schuster, New York, 1967).

MONEY, BANKING, AND GOVERNMENT FINANCE

Peter L. Bernstein, *A Primer on Money, Banking, and Gold* (Random House, New York, 1968). Easy to read.

Harold M. Groves, *Financing Government*, 6th ed. (Holt, Rinehart & Winston, New York, 1964).

The Federal Reserve System (Board of Governors, Federal Reserve System, Washington, D.C.). See the latest edition.

LABOR ECONOMICS

Allan M. Cartter and F. Ray Marshall, *Labor Economics: Wages, Employment, and Trade Unionism* (Richard D. Irwin, Homewood, Ill., 1967).

Neil W. Chamberlain, *Labor* (McGraw-Hill, New York, 1958).

COMPARATIVE ECONOMIC SYSTEMS

Allan G. Gruchy, *Comparative Economic Systems* (Houghton Mifflin, Boston, 1966).

Jan S. Prybyla, *Comparative Economic Systems: Text and Readings* (Appleton-Century-Crofts, New York, 1969).

ECONOMIC THEORY

Kenneth E. Boulding, *Economic Analysis*, 4th ed. (Harper & Row, New York, 1966), 2 vols.

Richard H. Leftwich, *The Price System and Resource Allocation*, 3rd ed. (Holt, Rinehart & Winston, New York, 1966).

William J. Baumol, *Economic Theory and Operations Analysis*, 2nd ed. (Prentice-Hall, Englewood Cliffs, N.J., 1965).

Alpha C. Chiang, *Fundamental Methods of Mathematical Economics* (McGraw-Hill, New York, 1967).

Stefan Valavanis, *Econometrics* (McGraw-Hill, New York, 1959).

INTERNATIONAL ECONOMICS

J. B. Condliffe, *The Commerce of Nations* (Norton, New York, 1950).

P. T. Ellsworth, *The International Economy*, 4th ed. (Macmillan, New York, 1969).

ECONOMIC DEVELOPMENT

W. W. Rostow, *The Stages of Economic Growth, a Non-Communist Manifesto* (Cambridge University Press, Cambridge, 1960).

Robert L. Heilbroner, *The Great Ascent* (Harper & Row, New York, 1963). Easy to read.

Charles P. Kindleberger, *Economic Development*, 2nd ed. (McGraw-Hill, New York, 1965).

Jagdish Bhagwati, *The Economics of Underdeveloped Countries* (McGraw-Hill, New York, 1966).

CONSUMER ECONOMICS

David Hamilton, *The Consumer in Our Economy* (Houghton Mifflin, Boston, 1962)

M. C. Burk, *Consumption Economics* (Wiley, New York, 1968).

ENVIRONMENTAL AND RESOURCE ECONOMICS

Paul R. Ehrlich and Anne H. Ehrlich, *Population Resources Environment, Issues in Human Ecology* (W. H. Freeman and Company, San Francisco, 1970).

Orris C. Herfindahl and Allen V. Kneese, *Quality of the Environment: An Economic Approach to Some Problems in Using Land, Water, and Air* (Johns Hopkins Press, Baltimore, 1965).

Clarence F. Jones and Gordon G. Darkenwald, *Economic Geography*, 3rd ed. (Macmillan, New York, 1965).

Depending on his particular interests, the beginning student may also want to look at:

Herbert A. Simon, *The Shape of Automation for Men and Management* (Harper & Row, New York, 1963).

David C. McClelland, *The Achieving Society* (Van Nostrand, Princeton, N.J., 1961). Deals with the psychological motivation for entrepreneurship.

Kenneth E. Boulding, *Conflict and Defense* (Harper & Row, New York, 1961). Shows how economists might contribute toward a scientific understanding of peace and conflict.

In order to see what is happening currently in the science, students should examine the professional economic journals. Some of the main academically oriented ones are:

The American Economic Review (American Economic Association, Evanston, Ill.). A quarterly.

The Journal of Economic Literature (American Economic Association). A quarterly, which abstracts articles from other current journals.

Economic Journal (Royal Economic Society, London). A quarterly.

Quarterly Journal of Economics (Harvard University, Cambridge, Mass.).

The Journal of Political Economy (University of Chicago, Chicago). A quarterly.

Some of the nonacademic journals are:

The Federal Reserve Bulletin (Board of Governors, Federal Reserve System, Washington, D.C.). A monthly.

Monthly Labor Review (U.S. Department of Labor, Washington, D.C.).

Survey of Current Business (U.S. Department of Commerce, Washington, D.C.). A monthly.

International Financial Statistics (International Monetary Fund, New York). A monthly.

Monthly Bulletin of Agricultural Economics and Statistics (Food and Agricultural Organization of the United Nations, Washington, D.C.). About half of the space in each of the above five journals is given over to series of statistical data.

Publications that are almost entirely made up of statistical data are:

Economic Indicators (Council of Economic Advisors, United States Government Printing Office, Washington, D.C.). A monthly, which is a most convenient source of the latest statistical data on the state of the economy.

Statistical Abstract of the United States (U.S. Department of Commerce, Washington, D.C.). An annual.

Statistical Yearbook (United Nations, New York). An annual.

Demographic Yearbook (United Nations, New York). An annual.

Many other nonacademic organizations publish the work of economists. These organizations include major corporations and nonprofit organizations, special interest groups, private advisory groups, such as the Committee for Economic Development in New York, and research institutions, such as the Brookings Institution in Washington, D.C., the National Bureau of Economic Research in New York, and the Cowles Foundation in New Haven.

The Economic Report of the President (United States Government Printing Office, Washington, D.C.). An important annual document prepared by the President and his Council of Economic Advisors.

Ralph Andreano, Evan Farber, and Fabron Reynolds, *The Student Economist's Handbook* (Schenkman Publishing, Cambridge, Mass., 1967). Helpful in guiding the student to available sources of data.

The McGraw-Hill Dictionary of Modern Economics (McGraw-Hill, New York, 1965). Contains a good directory of economic organizations.

Economics is a very active science. It is alive with questions, issues, researches, study groups, publications, controversies, concerns, and even some answers. It is good to be in on the action.

Index

capitalists, 185, 312
captains of industry, 192
carboniferous period, 319
Caribbean Development Bank, 277
Carlyle, Thomas, 134–135
carriages, 85–87
carrying capacity, of the economy, defined, 77
Carson, Rachel, 319–320
cartels, 233
Cartwright, Edmund, 105
catallactics, 201
Catholic church, 43
    Reformation, 46–47, 83
Catholic Socialist Party, 152
Catholicism and the Protestant Ethic, 187
cattle breeding, 184
Cavendish, Henry, 114
Central America, 283
central banks, 96ff
    techniques of economic control, 101–102
central planning
    in communist countries, 170
    during World War I, 240–241
    during World War II, 271–274
Central Powers, 239
Chamberlin, Edward H., 227
Chang Kai-shek, 265
Chapelier Law, 150, 151
Chavez, Cesar, 155
checking accounts, 98
chemistry, in Industrial Revolution, 114
Chicago School of thought, 300
child labor, in Industrial Revolution, 146–148
childhood, anthropological role of, 9
China, 265, 266
    economic takeoff, 291
    "Great Leaps," 171
    People's Republic of, 169
Christian Socialist Party, 152
Christianity
    and end of slavery, 32
    dynamic life force in, 65
    effects of, in ancient Rome, 20–21
    in medieval Europe, 25
    reformation and revolution in, 45ff
cigarettes
    as currency, 271
    and supply and demand analysis, 207
CIO, 154–155
circular flow of money
    in market economy, 194–196

in physiocratic theory, 58–60
cities, early development of, 9
civil rights, 180, 299
Civilian Conservation Corps (CCC), 251
Clark, John Maurice, 253
class struggle
    in Marxist theory, 164–168
    vs. social reforms, 174
classless society
    in America, 173
    in Marxist theory, 168
closed-loop system, 303
clothing
    in Mesopotamia and Egypt, 8
    prehistoric, 5
    "ready to wear," 193
    underwear, 194
coal, 2
    use of, in iron smelting, 110–112
Coca-Cola, 279
coconut example, 132–133
Code of Hammurabi, 10–11, 16, 19
Colbert, Jean Baptiste, 54
Colbertism, 54
Cold War, 273
collective bargaining
    in corporation economy, 312
    history of, 149–155
collectives
    in communist countries, 170
    kibbutzim, 156–157
    see also communes
colonialism
    in late 1800s, 237
    in Marxist theory, 167
Combination Acts, 150, 151
command economies, 178–179
commercial revolution, 53, 55
Committee for Economic Development, 335
Common Market, 275–276, 279–281
Commonwealth vs. Hunt, 151
communes, 156–167
    in China, 171
    see also collectives
communications
    electric, 83, 244
    as a science, 84
    storage, 85
    in written form, 8
communism, 169, 174
Communist League, 161
Communist Manifesto, 161
communist parties
    in communist countries, 170, 249

Business administration an

Law

Securities

Banking

Education

Research

Military

Government service

International trade and aid

Communications media

The press

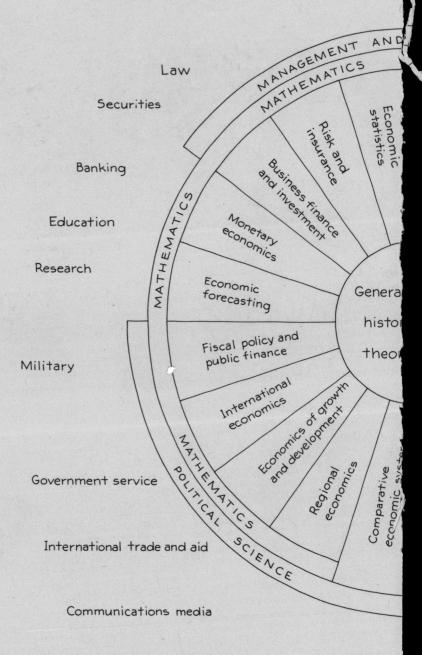

MANAGEMENT AND

MATHEMATICS

Economic
statistics

Risk and
insurance

Business finance
and investment

Monetary
economics

Economic
forecasting

Fiscal policy and
public finance

International
economics

Economics of growth
and development

Regional
economics

Comparative
economic syste

MATHEMATICS

MATHEMATICS
POLITICAL SCIENCE

Genera

histo

theo